Diversities in Early Childhood Education

Rethinking and Doing

Edited by

Celia Genishi and A. Lin Goodwin

Routledge
Taylor & Francis Group
New York   London

Routledge
Taylor & Francis Group
270 Madison Avenue
New York, NY 10016

Routledge
Taylor & Francis Group
2 Park Square
Milton Park, Abingdon
Oxon OX14 4RN

Printed in the United States of America on acid-free paper
10 9 8 7 6 5 4 3 2 1

International Standard Book Number-13: 978-0-415-95714-4 (Softcover) 978-0-415-95713-7 (Hardcover)

Library of Congress Cataloging-in-Publication Data

Diversities in early childhood education : rethinking and doing / edited by Celia
    Genishi and A. Lin Goodwin.
        p. cm. -- (Changing images of early childhood)
    Includes bibliographical references and index.
    ISBN 978-0-415-95713-7 (hb : alk. paper) -- ISBN 978-0-415-95714-4 (pb : alk.
    paper)
    1. Early childhood education. 2. Multicultural education. I. Genishi, Celia,
1944- II. Goodwin, A. Lin. III. Title. IV. Series.

LB1139.23.D58 2008
372.21--dc22   2007011498

Visit the Taylor & Francis Web site at
http://www.taylorandfrancis.com

and the Routledge Web site at
http://www.routledge.com

Dedication

To Ed and James, our touchstones for life

Contents

Series Editor's Introduction

Early childhood education has long been organized around and justified by the principles of developmentally appropriate practice (DAP) that were derived from developmental psychology early last century. The theories of learning and socialization inherent to this discipline were conceptualized in vastly different social, economic, and political contexts, and it has become increasingly evident that they cannot frame or explain the complex nature of the lives of the diverse groups of young children who attend our schools in the 21st century. Our education systems often seem to promote universal justifications for educational practices that are based on the view that children are a homogenous group that should aspire to the acquisition of a set of common attributes that are deemed to be necessary for all. The basis of this premise needs to be interrogated and challenged, with alternative viewpoints being canvassed and discussed in a collaborative forum. The books in this series are designed to assist students and professionals in early childhood education to engage in such dialogues from an informed base. They consider alternative theoretical perspectives and demonstrate their relevance to everyday practices. In doing so, they enable us to create learning environments that are underpinned by respect for all and adherence to the principles of equity and social justice.

In this volume, Celia Genishi and Lin Goodwin have assembled an excellent and wide-ranging group of authors who have an extensive array of experiences with young children, their families, and community groups. The content focuses on important issues associated with social justice and the diversity of lived experiences that early childhood educators encounter on a daily basis in their work with young children. They state that we need to move beyond a consideration of these issues that use a deficit, or culturally deprived, model grounded in comparisons of the ways in which such groups deviate from white, middle-class, social, cultural, and educational norms. Instead, the authors in this book provide ways in which we can use a cultural difference paradigm in order to understand how cultural differences can be a source of inspiration for early childhood educators who wish to understand the impact of the life worlds of students on their educational experiences. They achieve this via a consideration of diversities in the context of the design, delivery, curriculum, and control of early childhood programs.

The book is organized in three sections, with a focus on rethinking the ways in which we consider and enact education for all children in the early childhood years. These involve rethinking:

- Identities in transformed curriculum contexts
- Policies and programs for young children
- Teacher education programs and professional development opportunities for early childhood personnel

Kalantzis and Cope (2004) have suggested that we need to address the sociocultural aspects of learning in order to ensure that the basic conditions of learning are met. The first of these relates to whether the learner's identity is recognized and accommodated so that he or she is able to be engaged in the learning process. This process thus encapsulates the second condition of learning—transformation—which relates to increasing the knowledge bases and experiences of the learner. Kalantzis and Cope contend that the

> underlying attributes of lifeworld difference form the basis of identity and subjectivity … [and] are the fundamental bases of the learner's sense of belonging in an everyday or formal learning setting, and their levels of engagement. (p. 45)

The first section of the book explores transformed curriculum contexts. The authors challenge DAP and question the ways in which early childhood educators view diversity. They warn of superficial assessments of difference and provide us with rich scenarios of the ways in which they have created diverse contexts for learning that are respectful of the "funds of knowledge" (Moll, Amanti, Neff, & Gonzalez, 1992) that children bring to their educational experiences. They compel us to reconsider the ways in which we think of learning outcomes and how these are determined. This may require moving beyond what is mandated in "official" curriculum to a broader repertoire of authentic experiences in which children are able to utilize their life-world experiences in order to increase their knowledge and skills and broaden their experiences.

In shifting the conversation outward beyond the classrooms, the authors of the second section compel us to rethink policies and programs that are respectful of the roles that parents and the community have in the lives of young children. They warn of the dangers of adherence to the notion of "best practice," as if there were only one, and suggest that it might not always be a match with what families and communities want for their children. The sentiments of this section reflect that—in the United States, in particular—policies are often constructed with the best possible motives but that the ways in which they are enacted locally vary considerably, since they are usually broadly based and thus not able to reflect the diversity that exists across a wide variety of contexts.

In the final section, the authors reflect on the work of teachers, both in their preparation and in terms of their ongoing professional learning. The authors suggest that we should have culturally responsive and grounded programs for teachers to be able to gain greater insight into the diversities that are apparent in children's lives so that they are able to provide contexts in which individuals feel that their identity is honored and extended.

DAP privileged certain ways of being and knowing that did not recognize the diverse qualities of children and their families in a global context. In doing so, it had the effect of alienating the qualities of diversity that needed to be foregrounded and accommodated within a range of educational opportunities for children. Within the frame of DAP, it was suggested that there was a universal state that we should all be striving for that was based on Western ways of doing and knowing. It has become increasingly apparent that this view is not relevant to the lives of many children in our schools. This book enables us to share in the richness of diversities that characterize our world and shows us what is possible when we interrogate and "push back the curtains" to reveal what is on stage in early childhood education.

Nicola Yelland
Victoria University, Melbourne

References

Kalantzis, M., Cope, B. et al. (2005). *Learning by design*. Altona, Victoria: Commonground.

Moll, L. C., Amanti, C., Neff, D., & Gonzalez, W. (1992). Funds of knowledge for teaching: Using a qualitative approach to connect homes and classrooms. *Theory into Practice, 31*(2), 132–141.

Introduction

1

Responding to Multiple Diversities in Early Childhood Education

How Far Have We Come?

A. LIN GOODWIN, RANITA CHERUVU, AND CELIA GENISHI

How Far Have We Come? A Look at Early Childhood Education over Time

Since its inception in the United States, early childhood care and education has ostensibly been grounded in issues of social justice. With a focus on the welfare of young children, particularly those of the poor, two foundational assumptions have guided the field from the start: (1) home as the primary setting for the care and education of young children, which is to be carried out by parents, siblings, relatives, and other family caregivers; and (2) positive early experiences and environments as essential in laying the foundation for young children to become good citizens and participants in school and society. However, given pervasive conceptions of the poor as not just economically but also socially and culturally impoverished, these foundational assumptions have been undergirded by societal norms and beliefs about who is capable of providing "quality" care and education. These social assumptions led to the development of early childhood care and education outside of the home (Bloch, 1987). When families were perceived to have the inability or the inadequacy to care for their young, the responsibility for this care shifted to the middle-class, typically white, community, which was presumed to know best what young children required in terms of moral and educational development. Indeed, an examination of the evolution of the field in the United States reveals that "one of the original purposes of the nursery school was to serve as a forum for educating parents about the nature and nurture of young children," rather than leaving parenting to "trial and error" (Powell, 1991, p. 93).

Any analysis, therefore, of the social justice underpinnings of early childhood education or the field's attention to questions or issues of diversity must consider—and acknowledge—the three dominant paradigms that have defined social structures and interactions, as well as educational policies, in the United States. These are the inferiority paradigm, the deficit or culturally deprived paradigm, and the cultural difference paradigm (see Carter & Goodwin, 1994). The inferiority paradigm is grounded in assumptions of the genetic or biological inferiority of those who differ racially and culturally from whites; the culturally deprived paradigm compares racially, culturally, linguistically, and socioeconomically diverse peoples to a white, middle-class standard in order to illuminate the various ways in which they are deficient; the cultural difference paradigm shifts notably away from notions of inferiority or deprivation to an emphasis on the impact of cultural differences on the lives, experiences, and identities of diverse groups in ways that are not deviant but are unique and specific.

Each of the three paradigms offers insights into the design, delivery, curriculum, and control of early childhood programs. The inferiority paradigm is apparent in 18th- and early 19th-century Sunday schools, primary schools, and infant schools, established to work with the poor and unfortunate. The curriculum focused on "spiritual salvation" and moral development (Bloch, 1987; Nourot, 2005) in order to counteract children's inferior backgrounds and (lack of) upbringing. The same can be said of day nurseries, modeled after the French crèche and later associated with the settlement house movement. Founded on a missionary stance, they provided assistance to impoverished and migrant families (most of whom were African American) from the South in terms of hygiene, proper nutrition, and child care (Nourot, 2005). Further, at the end of the 19th century, during the first "great" immigration wave, schools aimed to civilize the newly arrived poor and culturally "different" by providing moral guidance and character development to their children in order to combat the poverty and crime associated with urban migration and immigration. Those in control of schools, white businessmen for the most part,

> held a common set of WASP [White, Anglo-Saxon Protestant] values, professed a common-core (that is, pan-Protestant) Christianity, were ethnocentric, and tended to glorify the sturdy values of a departed rural tradition. They took their values for granted as self-evidently true—not subject to legitimate debate. (Tyack, 1974, p. 109)

Although each type of school employed different approaches to developing children's character and morality, they were all based on the assumption that poor and immigrant children, as well as children of color, lacked the moral judgment, appropriate home environment, and teachers (primarily mothers) to develop the values and skills needed to become good American/productive citizens. Thus, the purpose of schooling was not to liberate but to sort and classify, not to intellectually expand but to standardize, not to transform but to conform.

The War on Poverty, mounted in the 1960s, is reflective of the culturally deprived paradigm. Sociologists forwarded the idea that children's home environments could negatively affect their intellectual development and cognitive ability, and "that educators should create experiences in schools that would counter the effects of deprivation" (Carter & Goodwin, 1994, p. 298). Researchers also contended that the early years were critical to children's development, so early intervention would ensure that poor children would not enter elementary school already "disadvantaged" by their poor and deficient home environments. Thus the passage of the Economic Opportunity Act of 1964 led to the creation of the Head Start program, which aimed to provide "disadvantaged" children some of the educational experiences and "advantages" they lacked. This kind of compensatory education was established to provide equal opportunity in later schooling and life. However, the compensatory definition of the programs labeled the culturally and linguistically diverse and poor as deficient or culturally deprived, and sought to "fix" them according to the standards of the dominant, white, middle-class culture. The Great Society reforms of this era, though wide sweeping and groundbreaking in many ways, fell short of their promise.

The cultural difference paradigm grew out of the work of social scientists in the early- to mid-20th century who argued that "different" was not synonymous with "deviant" and that the lives of people of color were grounded in and informed by values, beliefs, and norms that were culturally specific. Multicultural education and culturally responsive pedagogy are both examples of the cultural difference paradigm; both movements helped educators begin to see that children of color or difference have been marginalized and underserved by schools, and that the acknowledgment and integration of their cultural experiences in the curriculum can enhance learning and achievement. Guided by the cultural difference paradigm, there have been many changes made to curricula and services to children that demonstrate cultural sensitivity and multi- versus monoculturalism. Still, it can be argued that the cultural difference movement "is not entirely free of the assumptions of the deficit and inferiority approaches" (Carter & Goodwin, 1994, p. 303), and that while each paradigm might be associated more with one era over another, all three continue to operate simultaneously today, shaping our institutional structures, public policies, and educational systems in ways that both advance and retard equity and equal opportunity.

So it should not be surprising that as we move into the 21st century, the rhetoric regarding children and their care has—perhaps—changed (or become more child centered), but the concern and focus remain the same—the "disadvantaged" need programs and policies that are aimed to improve life chances. The creation of the No Child Left Behind Act (NCLB) and the debate on universal preschool are examples of the perpetuation of the discourse on improving educational and social conditions that exist for the poor and disadvantaged (Grieshaber & Ryan, 2006). Thus, while NCLB explicitly rejects any connection between academic failure and race or class, by singling out schools and educators as solely responsible for children's failure, it strongly forwards the idea "that the 'problem of schooling' is somehow unconnected to the larger social structures of inequality in which schools exist" (Kantor & Lowe, 2006, p. 485). Any progress towards social justice for all children is summarily blocked as long as the national emphasis is on placing blame on some particular entity instead of taking responsibility collectively.

Have We Come Far? Where Next Should We Go?

As the social, economic, and political landscape of the United States evolves, working towards social justice in early childhood care and education remains a continuous challenge in the field. At the heart of this challenge has been the ever-increasing diversity of our country. Our response to this diversity has been equally varied and has assumed many forms, from assimilation to acknowledgment to accommodation. These responses to diversity tell the story of how the United States has dealt with the expanding racial, ethnic, and cultural makeup of society. A running theme in this story has been the normalization of Western, Anglo-Protestant, middle-class values that have greatly influenced the response to diversity. The normalization of such a value system has created a tension between the democratic principles of unum and pluribus (Nieto, 2000) and the ideals of justice/fairness and diversity (Spring, 1997). What becomes apparent is that issues of social justice and diversity are inextricably linked, as patterns of social injustices fall along lines of race, ethnicity, culture, language, gender, class, ability, religion, and sexual orientation.

In early childhood care and education, this dominant value system has shaped society's notion of who is best suited to care for and educate young children (Robinson & Diaz, 2006) and what the curriculum should emphasize or exclude. It is the conceptualization of diversity within a dominant, normalized value system that roots present understandings and frameworks of diversity narrowly within notions of assimilation, acknowledgement, and accommodation, thereby perpetuating social injustices and inequities for people of diverse backgrounds. Indeed, the mainstream perspective has conceptualized diversity as a noun—a state of being or something that is seen. Such a perspective reflects modernist views and systems of thought upon which the field of early childhood care and education in the United States was created. This collection aims to rethink diversity in order to move more effectively and sincerely towards social justice for young children and their families. Toward this end, we offer a different perspective on diversity. In this view, diversity is reconceptualized as a verb—something to be enacted or expressed, something that is dynamic and agentic. This view of diversity is grounded in critical and postmodernist theories (Apple, 2004; Canella, 1997; Kessler & Swadener, 1992; Mac Naughton, 2004) and challenges the normativity of the Western, Anglo-Protestant, middle-class value system that has influenced the field. There is a great urgency for rethinking our understandings and practices of diversity in the current climate of standardization, test scores, and scientifically based research set against the backdrop of social inequities. The purpose of this collection is to offer illustrations of "doing"—illustrations of educators enacting equitable and inclusive practices that move us towards social justice in settings for young children, teacher education, and policy.

Organization of This Volume

This book is organized into three sections: Rethinking Identities of Children in Transformed Curricular Contexts, Rethinking Policies and Programs, and Rethinking Teacher Education and Professional Development. Each section offers diverse ways of rethinking and doing in the pursuit of social justice. Across the sections, each chapter describes research and practices that embody inclusiveness across a spectrum of ability, class, culture, ethnicity, gender, language, race, and sexual orientation. Each chapter also includes a theoretical or epistemological framework, a context for the practices and research, and a discussion that raises new questions and issues in "doing" diversity for social justice in early childhood education. The commonalities across the chapters support coherence and help each section to build upon the next. However, each section illuminates issues of seriousness and raises critical questions in relation to the care and education of children who represent multiple diversities and surely are our future. These issues and questions ground each section in the larger context, underscore the need for rethinking diversity, and offer specific insights into how far we have come and how far we have yet to go.

Rethinking Identities of Children in Transformed
Curricular Contexts: Issues and Questions

The authors in this section—Anne Haas Dyson; Marjorie Siegel and Stephanie Lukas; Susan Stires and Celia Genishi; Susan Recchia; Susan Grieshaber; and Leslie Williams and Nadjwa Norton—all take issue with commonplace definitions of growth, development, and learning. They challenge the field's reliance on developmentally appropriate practices (DAP) as the lens through which children's progress should be measured and assessed, because they understand the culturally grounded (and informed) nature of child development, in contrast to the (mono)cultural specificity of the DAP guidelines. Using the specific to assess the varied, diverse, and multiple can only result in too many children not meeting the "standard" and therefore being perceived as deficient, atypical, or abnormal. Each chapter also questions how educators typically interpret "diversity" and perceive children's identities. Authors problematize the "celebration" of superficial differences and argue that educators need to dig deep to discover children's "funds of knowledge" (Gonzalez, Moll, & Amanti, 2005) in order to authentically support children's learning. Similarly, they are critical of quick judgments made about children's capacities based also on surface characteristics and reinforce the need to listen closely and observe carefully in order to ascertain who children are, what they value, how they think, and all they can do, as well as what they need. Finally, all the chapters in this section critique the uniform curricular contexts supported by NCLB

8 • A. Lin Goodwin, Ranita Cheruvu, and Celia Genishi

that conceptualize knowledge and skills rigidly and narrowly, and focus on remediation and children's deficits rather than their abilities and capacities.

In raising these issues of seriousness, these chapters offer responses to several critical questions:

- What happens when educators put aside normative definitions of "achievement," "learning," and "progress," and look beyond assigned labels in order to really examine—and support—who children are and what they can do?
- How do expanded definitions of "culture" and "diversity" enable educators to see children with new eyes and rethink their pedagogy and curriculum?
- How can teachers work within—and against—the official or scripted curriculum in order to create spaces for all learners?

Rethinking Policies and Programs: Issues and Questions

In this section, each chapter moves the conversation beyond individual classrooms, teachers, and children to include those in the larger arena who also play key roles in the care and education of our youngest citizens. These include families and communities, policies and policymakers, and state and governmental mandates and agencies. In doing this, what issues do the authors— Althea Nixon and Kris Gutiérrez; Jennifer Adair and Joseph Tobin; Marci Sarsona, Sherlyn Goo, Alice Kawakami, and Kathryn Au; and Sharon Ryan and Carrie Lobman—identify? First, they challenge the common practice of positioning families and children's communities as less expert than educational professionals. This especially marginalizes families defined as "diverse" because they do not exemplify traditional family structures and child-caring practices or arrangements. Such positioning disempowers those who know children best, and blocks any possibility of partnerships between teachers and the many key adults present in a child's life. The authors also remind us that our ideas of "best" or "progressive" practice may not always match what families and communities want for their children. The issue is then, how do we either adapt our own notions of "best" and/or work with the communities to which our students belong to come to a shared definition of best? And finally, even while the early childhood field may profess to know what is best, there is internal conflict around definitions of best within the profession, as well as mandated ideas of best forwarded by states and policymakers. These conflicts raise issues for teacher preparation—what should teachers know and be able to do?—as well as implementation—how do teachers respond to different conceptions of good practice? What questions, then, do these chapters address in the context of these serious issues?

- What happens when early childhood educators invite families and communities into the educational enterprise as partners?

- How do alternative curriculum delivery systems enable educators to work within—and against—mandated policies so as to enrich children's educational experiences?
- What kinds of rethinking and doing does the profession need in order to ensure "quality" teachers for all children?

Rethinking Teacher Education and Professional Development: Issues and Questions

In the final section, the authors—Beatrice Fennimore; A. Lin Goodwin and Michèle Genor; Rachel Theilheimer; Rebekah Fassler and Dorothy Levin; and Susi Long, Clavis Anderson, Melanie Clark, and Becky McCraw—focus on teachers and on those who would be teachers. Collectively, their work examines teacher preparation and professional development through multicultural lenses in order to interrogate teachers' cultural knowledge and the potential impact of what teachers know—or don't—about their practice, instructional priorities, and pedagogical decision making. A key issue raised by these authors is how teacher education can or should be culturally responsive and culturally grounded, because teachers, like children, bring their entire selves into the classroom, and these multiple selves are complex, rich, and very influential in the identities teachers assume. A second issue involves notions of political correctness. Are all cultural understandings equal? Relative? Acceptable? Is there a cultural knowledge base that all teachers should possess? How can teacher education that is multicultural be authentic, not coercive? A third issue raised by these authors is the very idea of a teacher's identity and autonomy—what is possible in the current climate of more and more restrictions on teachers and teacher preparation programs, less and less professional leeway for teachers to make instructional choices or decisions, greater and greater standardization, and an emphasis on sanctions and punishments to ensure conformity?

The five chapters in this section pay attention to critical questions such as:

- What happens when teacher educators acknowledge the diverse lived experiences of their preservice students and incorporate these experiences into the curriculum?
- What do we mean by a professional mind-set that values learners' diversities and frames teaching as a social justice concern?
- How can teachers become conscious of their own assumptions, biases, and preconceptions, and what might this conscientization mean for their work with young children?

Separately, each chapter in this book offers possibilities as well as dilemmas; none pretends that what is being suggested is easy or simple. Rather than singular answers, the chapters as a whole exemplify all that diversity in early childhood education means (and should mean)—many different methods, ideas, suggestions, strategies, pedagogies, curricula, texts, contexts, definitions, tools, and questions—all intersecting with the countless diversities children and their families embody.

References

Apple, M. (2004). *Ideology and curriculum* (3rd ed.). New York: Routledge.

Bloch, M. N. (1987). Becoming scientific and professional: An historical perspective on the aims and effects of early education. In T. S. Popkewitz (Ed.), *The formation of school subjects: The struggle for creating an American institution* (pp. 25–62). London: Falmer Press.

Canella, G. S. (1997). *Deconstructing early childhood education: Social justice and revolution.* New York: Peter Lang.

Carter, R., & Goodwin, A. L. (1994). Racial identity and education. In L. Darling-Hammond (Ed.), *Review of research in education* (Vol. 20, pp. 291–336). Washington, DC: American Educational Research Association.

Gonzalez, N., Moll, L. C., & Amanti, C. (2005). *Funds of knowledge: Theorizing practices in households, communities, and classrooms.* Mahwah, NJ: Erlbaum.

Grieshaber, S., & Ryan, S. (2006). Beyond certainties: Postmodern perspectives, research, and the education of young children. In B. Spodek & O. N. Saracho (Eds.), *Handbook of research on the education of young children* (2nd ed., pp. 533–553). Mahwah, NJ: Lawrence Erlbaum.

Kantor, K., & Lowe, R. (2006). From New Deal to no deal: No Child Left Behind and the devolution of responsibility for equal opportunity. *Harvard Educational Review, 76*(4), 474–502.

Kessler, S. A., & Swadener, B. B. (Eds.). (1992). *Reconceptualizing the early childhood curriculum: Beginning the dialogue.* New York: Teachers College Press.

Mac Naughton, G. (2004). Exploring critical constructivist perspectives on children's learning. In A. Anning, J. Cullen, & M. Fleer (Eds.), *Early childhood education: Society and culture* (pp. 43–56). London: Sage.

Nourot, P. M. (2005). Historical perspectives on early childhood education. In J. L. Roopnarine & J. E. Johnson (Eds.), *Approaches to early childhood education* (4th ed., pp. 3–38). Columbus, OH: Merrill/Prentice Hall.

Nieto, S. (2000). Placing equity front and center: Some thoughts on transforming teacher education for a new century. *Journal of Teacher Education, 51*(3), 180–187.

Powell, D. R. (1991). Parents and programs: Early childhood as a pioneer in parent involvement and support. In S. L. Kagan (Ed.), *The care and education of America's young children: Obstacles and opportunities.* Ninetieth Yearbook of the National Society for the Study of Education (Part I, pp. 91–109). Chicago: University of Chicago Press, NSSE.

Robinson, K. H., & Diaz, C. J. (2006). *Diversity and difference in early childhood education: Issues for theory and practice.* New York: Open University Press.

Spring, J. (1997). *Deculturalization and the struggle for equality: A brief history of dominated cultures in the United States* (2nd ed.). New York: McGraw Hill.

Tyack, D. B. (1974). *The one best system.* Cambridge, MA: Harvard University Press.

Part I
Rethinking Identities of Children in Transformed Curricular Contexts

2

On Listening to Child Composers
Beyond *"Fix-Its"*

ANNE HAAS DYSON

When she started school, Maxine Hong Kingston did not speak to her teachers—but she did paint. She made houses and flowers in the sunlight, and then she covered them all with black paint. Her teachers saved her paintings, one black curling paper after another; they worried over them and then called her parents. The adults did not know that, for Maxine, those paintings were not signs of sadness or doom but of joyful possibilities. At home, she spread her pictures out and "pretended the [black stage] curtains were swinging open … sunlight underneath, mighty operas" (Kingston, 1975, p. 192).

In a related way, the surface structure of young children's brief written texts may obscure children's language resources, symbolic manipulations, and communicative intentions. The texts may have figured into grand adventures, or perhaps silly jokes or love letters, or even turns in collaborative play among tablemates. And, like Maxine's teachers, we as educators may find it hard to gain access to these textual operas, so to speak.

Our access may be especially constrained in these back-to-basics times, when accountability measures, like achievement tests, reinforce a tight focus on surface features of print (e.g., capitalization, punctuation, spelling, standardized usage or "grammar"). Even the instructional practice of "conferencing," a commonplace of teaching writing, can be so focused: A teacher and child sit together, read the child's written text, and then begin the main business of attending to "fix-its" (i.e., errors of convention).

The term "fix-its" was borrowed from the classroom I came to know in a recent study of child writing; the room was in a basics-focused city school serving a racially and culturally diverse community (Dyson, 2006). In this chapter, I draw on that study to illustrate the challenges of—and the resources to be found by—looking behind the paper curtain, as it were, of young children's composing.

In the sections ahead, I first introduce the project classroom, Mrs. Kay's first grade in a Midwest urban school, and also the theoretical lens that guided my efforts to understand young children's writing. Then I bring center stage one of Mrs. Kay's young opera composers, Tionna. Beginning with a teacher–student conference, I gradually consider the vernacular voices, the multimodal tools, and the communicative practices that reveal Tionna's opera.

Ultimately, like other authors in this collection, I aim to support reflection on how we as educators might transform our teaching practices so that we may better build on, and respond to, the diverse resources of our children. In teaching children to write, one way of doing this is to look and listen beyond the words on the page and thereby allow more of children's language, cultural, and textual knowledge and know-how to enter into and inform official efforts to help them compose.

Convention and Conversation: Learning to Write in Mrs. Kay's Class

"It's a basketball game!" came the shouts from Mrs. Kay's class as she drew a hoop on her large pad. Mrs. Kay turned to her children, bunched together on the classroom rug, and reported that she had gone to her son's basketball game the night before. "He scored 15 points … so we were very excited," she said.

The children responded with questions about the game itself: "What was the score?" "Were there any dunks?" Mrs. Kay responded in turn and then, on a large chart pad, began writing about watching her son play basketball.

In a similar way, Mrs. Kay (or her student teacher, Ms. Hache) began almost every writing period by modeling her own writing. "You know what?" she might say before telling them about an upcoming or experienced happening, and almost all children listened intently as her voice wrapped them up in her enthusiasm and, quite spontaneously, elicited their questions. She usually connected her own experiences with those of their families or of her projections of their future. "When you're a mom or dad," she told them, "you'll see when you go to a basketball game, … the kid that you watch the most is your own."

Mrs. Kay's writing, then, was situated within her experiences and also within her relationships with her students. She adopted a conversational stance, using all of the symbolic tools at her disposal to interest the children in what she had to say; and despite her frequent admonitions not to guess what she would write, guess they often did, slipping into the composer role with her.

As Mrs. Kay moved into her actual writing, the "basics" came into clearer view. Using Standard English, she called her children's attention to her periods and capital letters, to the spacing and arranging of letters and words. And every afternoon, when Mrs. Kay sat down with one child or another for a writing conference, she concentrated on "fix-its," that is, on violated conventions (e.g., errors of grammatical usage, capitalization, punctuation, and spelling). Mrs. Kay was an authority on the proper ways with words and, as her student Mandisa explained to me, she "help[ed]" the children know if their texts "sound right."

Mrs. Kay was aware of the listed basic skills for first grade, of the looming Iowa Test of Basic Skills, and of the expectations of the second-grade teachers (and her feeling that she would be blamed if the children were found lacking). The basics were particularly important in schools like Mrs. Kay's, which was applying (successfully) for federal support through a state Reading First grant. Like all schools so supported, the children in Mrs. Kay's school were primarily from low-income homes; they identified with diverse ethnic heritages, among them black, Mexican, white, and American Indian—all terms used by the children. Eighty-five percent of the school's children qualified for the federal school lunch program.

I observed the writing period and, indeed, the entire afternoon in Mrs. Kay's class on average twice a week over the course of an academic year (approximately 5 to 6 hours a week). I was interested in the nature of the enacted basics and, most importantly, in how the children responded to basic instruction.

During my time in Mrs. Kay's class, I came to know Tionna, 6 years old and of African American heritage. It is her production of "The Big Present" that is reconstructed in this chapter. I chose this production because it vividly and comprehensively illustrates the varied dimensions of children's composing highlighted herein: the children's repertoire of human voices, their multiple symbolic tools, and their guiding communicative practices. These dimensions were, in fact, basic (i.e., foundational) to children's entry into school writing.

Before the opera begins, I offer a little theoretical stage setting below.

Looking behind the Paper Curtain

The following is Tionna's "The Big Present" piece:

> This christmas I am geting a big big Preszint I got it from my mommy and is big.

As you, Tionna's (and my) readers, examine the above text, perhaps you notice Tionna's spelling, her lack of periods—and is that a missing word in that last line? What else is there to notice or to know in order to appreciate and instructionally respond to this text?

To answer this question—and to push beyond Tionna's paper curtain, I call attention below to how young children, like all speakers and writers, use texts to have a say in their world, and then to the repertoire of communicative media through which they find a place for writing.

The Social World: Writing as Conversational Turn   Any text—any configuration of signs, oral or written—takes shape within a social world. And one way of conceiving of that world is to imagine it filled with the human voices of everyday life. So a young child, like Tionna, grows up surrounded by voices, among them, those of family members, community institutions, media figures, teachers, and, of course, other children. As the language philosopher Bakhtin (1981, 1986) explained, these voices are infused with the intentions of typical communication practices, from joking and storytelling to advice giving and one-upmanship. When young children speak, they appropriate from the voices of other people to take their own communicative turn and thereby become an active participant in the social world that surrounds them.

In this dialogic and, more broadly, sociocultural view of composing words and worlds, language in use and situational context are inseparable. There is always the social world beyond what is articulated in spoken words or graphic symbols. Thus, just like Mrs. Kay, Tionna and her peers drew from and enacted voice-filled relationships as they gained control over writing. One way, then, in which to push back Tionna's textual curtain is to hear her text against the landscape of voices in the wider world of her family and community and also in the ongoing situation.

The Symbolic Repertoire: Writing as an Interweaving of Media   As young children find their way into the relatively new medium of writing, they lean on familiar symbolic tools (Vygotsky, 1978). Accompanying their "writing" may be drawing, talking, dramatic gestures, sound effects, and even singing (Dyson, 1989, 2003).

Young children's use of diverse media belies the instructional common sense, evident in Tionna's classroom, that "drawing" is merely a kind of planning (e.g., "Make your quick sketch first") and talking a displaced communicative tool ("Don't tell me; write it"). Mrs. Kay, in fact, demonstrated the limits of this stance. Her drawing was not so much a plan as a depiction of the spatial layout of the setting of interest (for example, the respective basketball hoops of the two playing teams, the bleachers for the fans). Moreover, Mrs. Kay exploited talk, not only *to represent* ideas (which might not be written) but also *to interact* about them with her children, *to monitor* or regulate her unfolding writing, and even *to perform* her writing for the class, as her spoken voice infused her written one.

Another way, then, to push back Tionna's textual curtain is to observe her unfolding composing, whatever the medium. One cannot appreciate the fullness of any child's text by plucking the writing from an accompanying multimedia production.

So now, against the backdrop of circulating voices, and given the orchestral possibilities of a rich symbolic repertoire, it is time to begin "The Big Present."

The Opera: "The Big Present"

During writing time one December day, Tionna wrote that text about her big present. The text is, in a sense, a paper curtain, presenting the linguistic remains of Tionna's communicative event. And it was this paper curtain that drew Mrs. Kay's attention and led to an impromptu conference.

The Conference: A Focus on the Textual Curtain   As the children were writing, Mrs. Kay had been making her rounds, asking this child or that one questions to extend the writing or guide the sounding out of spellings. Sometimes, though, she sat down for a more extended conference about a matter of concern. In the case of "The Big Present," Mrs. Kay's attention was particularly drawn by Tionna's last line, which seemed to have a grammatical problem: a missing word.

Mrs. Kay bent over, her hand resting on the table, and asked Tionna to reread her page. Tionna did so, and then Mrs. Kay responded:

Mrs. Kay: Does that make sense, "I got it from my mommy and is big"?

Tionna does not respond, and so Mrs. Kay returns to Tionna's text, pointing to the *and*.

Mrs. Kay: "a::nd" (hopeful pause)

Tionna still does not respond.

Mrs. Kay: What word could you be missing?
Tionna: "The."
Mrs. Kay: "It."
Tionna: (reading) "And it's."

Tionna then adds an editorial caret and writes *it*; the text now reads and *it is big*.

Mrs. Kay: Good for you!

Problem solved … or was it? In the section below, I begin to push back the paper curtain, allowing readers to hear more clearly the echoes of family and community voices reverberating in Tionna's.

"I's" or "Is" Big? Cultural Echoes and Vernacular Voices   Just as young children are urged to do, Tionna had "written" what she decided to "say" about her big present. And, just as Mrs. Kay had directed, she had listened to the sound of her own speech in order to write, as evident in the transcript below:

Tionna's Evolving Text	Tionna's Talk While Writing
	"and it" (to herself, planning)
and	"and, and"
is	"it's" (pronounced /i's/, not /iz/)
	"and it's" (rereading, again saying /i's/)
	"big" (planning)
big	"big"

As Tionna's spoken *it's* may suggest, she and Mrs. Kay did not speak the same vernacular: Mrs. Kay spoke a regional variety of Standard English; Tionna spoke African American language (Smitherman, 2006). This vernacular difference includes variations in how words are arranged (i.e., in syntactic rules) and in how they are pronounced (i.e., in phonological rules), as well as in word meanings and in rhetorical ways with words.

To illustrate, *it's* is pronounced *i's* in African American English due to phonological rules. To quote G. Smitherman (personal communication),

Generally, whenever you have a final consonant (or consonants) in AAL [African American Language], you are going to get deletion, simplification, or vocalization. In [spoken] "it's" the *t* may be deleted and the resulting pronunciation mirrors or retains the voicelessness [i.e., the lack of vocal chord vibration] of the *t*.

Hence, the pronunciation /is/ with its sisterly /s/, not /iz/ with its vibrating /z/ (see also Rickford & Rickford, 2000).

Tionna, then, using her speech as a major resource, presented a problem to Mrs. Kay; her teacher read not *it's*, but *is* and, thereby, identified the problem of the missing word ("Does that make sense, 'I got it … and is big'"?). If Tionna was having a problem, though, it was spelling a contraction, not missing a word. In fact, the very next day, Tionna again spelled the contraction *it's* as *i-s*.

Tionna had various such "problems." Some were clearly tied to her heritage language, among them the invariant *be*'s rather than *is*'s or *are*'s (e.g., "If you be bad" [Rickford & Rickford, 2000]) and tenses indicated by context rather than by inflectional ending (e.g., "He blow up his whole castle"). Other "problems" seemed developmental in nature (regularization of irregular patterns like "askted") or simply common features of casual conversation (e.g., "Me and so-and-so are going"). The mandated grammar objectives, however, made no mention of such matters. There was simply a "right" and a "wrong" way to have one's say (hence the power of schools as institutions to negate the diversity of society's ways with words).

To find her way into writing, Tionna, like young children generally, depended on the familiar and typified voices of her everyday life—the voices of those whose lives were most intimately interwoven with her own (see also Genishi, Stires, & Yung-Chan, 2001; Reyes & Halcon, 2001). These voices literally reverberated in hers as she orally articulated what she was going to say and monitored its encoding on the page. Thus, beyond the paper curtain of Tionna's text were the echoes of conversations and storytelling with family members, community acquaintances, and close friends.

Given current curricular conditions, we as educators might ask if all our children are able to draw on everyday voices to find their linguistic footing in the written medium. After all, young children differ in the languages and language varieties they speak and, thus, in what "sounds right." Extending children's repertoire to include the language of wider communication (i.e., edited American English) *is* a worthy goal for the elementary school years, but correction in and of itself is of limited effectiveness (Seymour & Roeper, 1999) and dubious in its intentions (i.e., to eliminate as opposed to expand children's ways with words).

Clearly, curricular acknowledgment and professional awareness of children's languages—including developmental, situational, and cultural variations—matter. They allow us to better attune pedagogically to children's authorial intentions and challenges and thus to help them make voices visible on paper. That is just the first step, though. To look further beyond Tionna's paper curtain, I turn the spotlight on Tionna's multiple media—her talk, her drawing, *and* her writing.

Translating Bigness: Writing and the Symbolic Repertoire   Tionna's written "Big Present" text was located underneath a picture of a decidedly big present (see Figure 2.1). Like Mrs. Kay, Tionna had begun composing by drawing and by talking. Indeed, as she drew her present, she remarked to her tablemates, "That's my present. My present was BI::G!"

In her talk, Tionna exploited the prosodic qualities of speech—its rhythm and, more particularly, its volume, tempo, and stress. In the project's transcript conventions, the two colons indicate that the sound of Tionna's *i* was elongated; the capital letters index her increased volume, and the underlining the emphatic stress she put on the word (conventions adapted from Ochs, 1979). There was no doubt, that present was "BI::G!"

Figure 2.1 The big present.

In drawing, Tionna used not rhythm, but space itself. As her picture indicates, the big present has a square shape and decorative details almost identical to the other two pictured gifts. But the big present occupies more space than both of those other two gifts combined.

In recontextualizing her message through writing, Tionna exploited an evaluative possibility of that medium: repetition to emphasize her point (see also Labov, 1972). The spoken "BI::G" present became, not just a written "big" one—a transcription without rhythm—but a "big big one," something more evocative of that space-devouring present.

Thus, behind the paper curtain of Tionna's text were the vivid images and rhythmic words that provided operatic resonance to "The Big Present" *and* displayed her own flexible use of a symbolic repertoire. Her drawing did not merely serve as planning but also provided spatial details and, combined with speech, lent evaluative gusto to her composition. Against the backdrop of her images and the echoes of her voice's rhythm, she made her authorial moves as writer. It was a "big big present," a repetition my word processing program is even now rejecting, since it has only conventions, not authorial intentions, governing its actions.

Relative to other observed children (e.g., Dyson, 1989, 2003), Tionna was strikingly adaptive in her translation across, and selective use of, symbolic media. Even when Mrs. Kay urged the children to stop drawing and to write, Tionna kept drawing as *if* spatial information mattered in her story (e.g., peer war play, in which the position of opposing teams' castles and warriors mattered; a vehicle accident, in which not only did the spatial positioning of her grandma's truck matter but so did the color of the traffic lights [this composition being the only time Tionna violated the rule against using crayons during writing time]).

More so than Tionna, many young schoolchildren's brief written texts are minimal accompaniments to elaborate, action-packed dramas played out in drawing and speech (a kind of composing particularly favored by boys [Dyson, 1989, 1993, 2003]). After a space battle, a car chase, or a football game may come a brief "I like …" or "I went …." Young writers' challenges include crossing symbolic borders and experiencing how ideas, like bigness, are translated and transformed across media and thereby learning both the potential and the constraints of those media. Such multimedia ease seems particularly important given the increasingly hybrid nature of texts (e.g., Web pages with audiovisual and written information [Cope & Kalantzis, 2000]).

Thus, when we as educators look and listen beyond the written text itself, we may gain better access to the fullness of children's productions, the expanse of their symbolic repertoire, *and also* to a more contemporary perspective on literacy. In this way, we join the children in the opera of our own becoming as more sophisticated communicators.

There is one last basic resource for Tionna's composing that needs to be brought center stage. That resource is represented by the kind of social dialogue—or communicative practice—in which Tionna is participating. It is that social engagement that energizes and organizes Tionna's opera, "The Big Present."

Claiming Bigness: The Operatic Repertoire   Tionna's "Big Present" production did not only allow her to express herself, but it also helped mediate her participation in the ongoing peer social scene, as evidenced by the vignette below.

> Tionna and her tablemates Manny, Brad, and Janette are all heavily into Christmas on this day. They critique each other's singing of Christmas songs (e.g., is it an open "sled" or an open "sleigh" that is such fun to ride?) and alternately claim to have the biggest tree and, at least in Tionna's case, the biggest present:
>
> *Tionna:*   (drawing) That's my present. My present was BI::G!
> *Manny:*   I make a present.
> *Tionna:*   Look it. I had a big present. It was this big.
> *Janette:*   No you don't. (dismissive)
> *Tionna:*   Yes I do! (raised pitch, definitive)
> *Janette:*   I got the biggest tree.
> *Tionna:*   [Our tree] almos' touch our ceilin'!
> *Janette:*   It almos' touch—
> *Tionna:*   'Cause soon as we put the angel on top of it, that angel's head bumped on the ceilin'.

Situating Tionna's composition in its communicative context brings her relationships with others onstage. Tionna's opera was a means of social engagement in both the unofficial world governed by the children and the official one governed by her teacher. She wrote the sort of personal experience piece modeled by Mrs. Kay (and favored by curricular guides) and, at the same time, she also joined in the enactment of a familiar social practice (peer one-upmanship), newly recontextualized as a writing-time activity.

In "The Big Present" event, Tionna responded to peers' claims and counterclaims about the specialness of their holiday celebration (and assumed the shared value of "bigness" for presents and trees). She was not just getting a present, but "I am getting a big big present." In another practice, writing-time wars (Dyson, 2007), Tionna was not a singular and special "I" but a member of the "we girls." She responded to her friend and tablemate Lyron's denial of girls' right to play war by forming a team of "tofe girls." In writing, those girls outdid the boys in number of castles and missiles: "No way the boys can beat the girls!"

In a dramatically different stance, in the peer practice of reporting who likes whom, so to speak, Tionna referred to physical attraction, not physical toughness. She willingly positioned herself as a focus for a boy, a "cute" boy who "was smileing at me at lunch." Tionna's decisions, then, about topic and "voice"—about the kind of situated "personality" she was using (Bakhtin, 1981, p. 434)—had to do with her social participation in her expanding operatic repertoire (i.e., her expanding communicative practices).

In fact, from early in the school year, Tionna, like young children generally, had shown a sensitivity to how voices sound in varied situations. During play, she used words, wording, and tone of voice to enact roles as diverse as mother, teacher, preacher, fast-food worker, love counselor, and hip-hop star. By the spring of the school year, Tionna was literally revoicing others' words within her writing.

For example, texts that appropriated what "Mrs. Kay said" were in a relatively Standard English, compared to those in which she replayed her talk with friends or cousins ("Mrs. Kay said" but her cousin "she say."). Noncontextualized and explicit correction did not result in Tionna's use of Standard English, but writing that seemed to build on the foundation of dramatic storytelling did. Tionna's sensitivity to, and flexibility with, human voices and, indeed, with all manner of symbolic material, allowed her to respond adaptively to her expanding world.

Tionna's "Big Present" production, placed against the repertoire of practices comprising her social world, suggests that supporting young children's writing means attending to the individual child in relation to others. It can be difficult to understand what and why a child is composing without situating that composition in any overheard talk during writing and, in addition, in the sometimes interlinked productions of child companions during writing.

Those companions matter because they may provide access to an involving give-and-take that provides a reason to write, not to mention potential ongoing assistance. A valuing of peers does not devalue the guiding role of the teacher or the critical anticipation and response generated by whole class sharing of writing (e.g., not all class members approved of war play), but it does acknowledge the intensity of most children's interest in other children and in ongoing activity (Dunn, 2004).

Moreover, given the fundamental role of communicative practices in energizing and guiding writing, it seems sensible to broaden official communicative situations in order to better tap into and stretch children's linguistic resources and symbolic tools. Tionna herself took relatively easily to the narrative planning and reporting Mrs. Kay modeled. But, like many of her peers, in the unofficial world, she made use of genres not included in the official one (e.g., making lists of invitees to desired parties, crafting greeting cards, writing notes, composing poems and raps). These familiar practices allowed Tionna and her peers common social ground for communication and furthered their making not only shared words but also a shared world in which writing mattered. Such involving practices may vary for children who live in different socioeconomic and sociocultural circumstances

(Barton & Hamilton, 2000); the valued purposes for writing (e.g., storytelling to impress or entertain, crafting child-valued "trading" cards for peer play), the kinds of relationships that writing entails (performing for an audience, collaborating with friends), the experiential material drawn on (e.g., storybooks, cartoons, Bible lessons), even the kind of writing script children use—all are linked to the material, cultural, and linguistic resources of varied families and communities (e.g., Dyson, 2003; Heath, 1983; Kenner, 2000; Vasquez, 2005).

By paying attention to children's, and to any one child's, repertoire of practices, we are enacting a view of writing pedagogy that allows for children with different linguistic and textual experiences and, moreover, we are working for a world in which the "educated" person does not have a single way of "sounding right." Rather, the educated person has a kind of linguistic and symbolic flexibility—an ease in adapting symbolic resources for varied social ends. Such flexibility is an outcome of engagement in complex social worlds in which one's writing figures into one's relationships with others who matter. In her own writing of "The Big Present," Tionna was entering into a certain kind of practice or social dialogue in which "bigness" and social one-upmanship organized her efforts. Given different practices with different ongoing relationships, different themes and topics, and different end goals, Tionna's writing varied. This emerging flexibility—hidden from view behind any one text—marked the opera of her own becoming as an author.

Toward Swinging Open the Curtains

"Sometimes it [my son's paper] doesn't look like anything. But then when I hear the story behind it, I can see a whole lot was going on." (first-grader Noah's father [Dyson, 2003, p. 194])

When Noah's father made the above remarks, I had just finished an evening meeting for parents of children in a research project. Noah's father had not been impressed at first with his son's work but, as the night progressed, he changed his mind. He heard the voices his son was appropriating—how attentive Noah was to speech; he saw the images that appealed to his son—the attempts to capture the quick pace of dinosaurs run amuck, of basketballs going through hoops, of water-gun bullets headed straight for their target; and, when Noah's dad situated his son's pieces in the context of classroom happenings—oh, he enjoyed how his son was right in there, having a say in the matters at hand.

For me, and I expect for others who are mesmerized by young children's classrooms, part of the appeal is the drama of it all—and symbols are mediators of those dramas. As a researcher, I have a front-row seat on children's productions and no professional role as director or critic. I am free to observe. Still, for researchers and teachers, there are ways of paying attention to, and talking with children about, writing that influences adult access to the "whole lot … going on" when children compose.

These ways of paying attention are influenced by conceptions of what's basic. The most obvious candidates for the basics are the visible aspects of written language use—spelling based on assumed sound/symbol connections, following rules of capitalization and punctuation, using the right grammar. These visible basics have dominated pedagogical thinking about children deemed at risk of school failure (particularly low-income children and children of color) from the very beginnings of intense interest in early literacy. In the 1960s and 1970s, researchers, studying their own or other relatively privileged children, were arguing that schools constrained young children's "emerging" literacy knowledge and know-how (e.g., Read, 1975); researchers concerned with low-income children assumed the lack of any such know-how and argued for "the basics" (e.g., Bereiter & Engelmann, 1966). The current guidelines informing federally supported Head Start programs and K–2 literacy programs maintain this focus (e.g., Moats, 2004). Isn't it a matter of fairness, of equity, to make sure children learn the basics?

In this chapter, by revealing the complexity of just one opera among many, I have tried to problematize narrow conceptions of what is basic—and of what is equitable. Fairness has to do, in part, with understanding how young children develop as users of written language. As Tionna illustrated, this development happens through participation in involving activities that entail attending to and manipulating symbols for communication and social connection. To create equitable classrooms for our children, we must understand and further the kinds of situations and activities—of practices—within which children write for and with each other. These practices, rich with potential voices and images, comprise the foundation upon which children learn to write.

Thus, "The Big Present" did not suggest that Tionna had mastered, at age 6, the conventional basics. Indeed, as with many young children, Tionna had a tenuous grasp of such basics as capitalization and punctuation (e.g., Cazden, Cordeiro, & Giacobbe, 1992), but her opera did suggest that she was on her way as a writer. She was learning to flexibly draw upon her expanding repertoires of graphic symbols (letters, words), images, and voices to join in on the communicative practices she shared with others, especially her peers. Given the socially complex times in which we live, Tionna seemed to be learning what might be deemed the contemporary basics—that is, how to adapt (fix up) her expanding resources (e.g., choices of textual features, content, and symbols) for the situation at hand.

In many ways, Mrs. Kay helped further a supportive context for young symbol makers and communicators like Tionna. She brought the children together through the engaging power of her own conversational and storytelling skill. And Tionna, in particular, seemed eager to have a hand at having a say through writing. But curricular documents offered Mrs. Kay only the discourse of basic skills, not of basic communication units like "practices." They took no account of children's cultural and linguistic complexities or of their interest in playful relationships with each other. An opera, it seems fair to say, is not a metaphor the composers of those documents had in mind.

But what if we do use the metaphor of an opera? It seems at least possible that more educators would collectively pay attention to children in new ways. Certainly they would still attend to children's written texts in writing conferences, but they might also view those texts as situated in children's experienced and enacted worlds. To return to the dimensions of child composing highlighted here, educators might hear *the diverse societal voices* echoing with children's very sound/symbol connections and with their choices of words and wording. Tionna then might gain the right to have *her own* conversational voice take shape on paper, just as Mrs. Kay assumed hers in writing a personal piece. Moreover, information on Tionna's language heritage would be part of the instructional support Mrs. Kay would be offered so that she might better "hear" and help Tionna and other children transform their voices on paper. At the same time, Tionna might be given opportunities to read, talk about, and enact a diversity of texts, including storybooks in varied vernaculars. In these ways, variations in ways of speaking, and of writing, would become part of the official curriculum; that is, heterogeneity, not homogeneity, would undergird language arts pedagogy, including writing.

In order to further uncover children's operas, educators of young children would need to pay attention to more than just the writing on a page; interwoven with that writing may be *other media that share the representational load.* Drawing in particular is a primary way that many young children, from varied cultures, represent, imagine, and extend their experiences (Arnheim, 2006; Fineberg, 2006). As such, drawing can be an impetus for writing and for talk, but it is much more than just "planning." It is a particular medium with possibilities and constraints, just as writing is. To become sophisticated participants in the multimedia texts of our times, children need to experience how meanings are transformed or revealed as they are differently articulated (e.g., in speaking, writing, or drawing). Given such a goal and a pedagogical interest in child operas, Tionna might gain opportunities to talk with her teacher about her representational decisions, made consciously or not, about ideas like "bigness." Projects might even be planned that build on particular children's interest in popular media, which so affects many children's visual representations (Thompson, 2006).

Examples of such familiar but usually untapped (in school) practices might include crafting a comic (allowing verbal dialogue to enter the spatial relations of a visual display), transforming it into a picture book or promoting it with an ad, or producing a radio show (furthering the infusion of prosody, and perhaps singing itself, into a written script). In such ways, we may more fully appreciate and extend the dramatic, if not strictly operatic, productions of the very young.

Finally, new pedagogical importance would be given to *the communicative practices* through which children participate in relationships that matter. Educators might gain insight into practices and valued relationships by attending to children's interactions with others as they write by considering how any one child's text is bound up with others, and by allowing children opportunities during conferences and whole-class forums for explaining, as well as for reading, what's happening in their products. Such forums allow teachers opportunities to provide children with a vocabulary for talking about their writing process and product (e.g., "collaborating" on a "fictional story," writing a "personal" love letter). And those forums also allow other children to respond as appreciative and critical companions (e.g., to voice an objection to "war play") (Dyson, 1993, 1997).

In such a forum, Tionna's seemingly personal text would no doubt elicit other children's stories (and perhaps even some one-upmanship). As her story finds a place among others' stories, Tionna might become more conscious of different perspectives on, experiences with, and even distance from, the gift-giving rituals of Christmas, not to mention the curiosity (and shaking and peeking) evoked by boxes, especially big boxes. And so oral discourse may feed children's composing in a community of others.

Classrooms are indeed full of the unfolding operas of children's making and also of their very being. By rethinking our curricula, we may find ways that allow children and their diverse resources greater visibility in our classrooms. In so doing, we may also gain a renewed appreciation of the privilege and the challenge of being a part of them all.

Note

The project in Mrs. Kay's school benefited from the much appreciated support of the Spencer Foundation. The findings and opinions expressed are, of course, my sole responsibility. I thank my terrific research assistants, Yanan Fan and Tambra Jackson.

References

Arnheim, R. (2006). Beginning with the child. In J. Fineberg (Ed.), *When we were young: New Perspectives on the art of the child* (pp. 19–30). Berkeley: University of California Press.

Bakhtin, M. (1981). Discourse in the novel. In C. Emerson & M. Holquist (Eds.), *The dialogic imagination: Four essays by M. Bakhtin* (pp. 254–434). Austin: University of Texas Press.

Bakhtin, M. (1986). *Speech genres and other late essays.* Austin: University of Texas Press.

Barton, D., & Hamilton, M. (2000). Literacy practices. In D. Barton, M. Hamilton, & R. Ivanic (Eds.), *Situated literacies: Reading and writing in context* (pp. 7–15). London: Routledge.

Bereiter, C., & Engelmann, S. (1966). *Teaching disadvantaged children in the preschool.* Englewood Cliffs, NJ: Prentice Hall.

Cazden, C., Cordeiro, P., & Giacobbe, M. E. (1992). Spontaneous and scientific concepts: Learning punctuation in the first grade. In C. Cazden (Ed.), *Whole language plus: Essays on literacy in the United States and New Zealand* (pp. 81–98). New York: Teachers College.

Cope, B., & Kalantzis, M. (Eds.). (2000). *Multiliteracies: Literacy learning and the design of social futures.* London: Routledge.

Dunn, J. (2004). *Children's friendships: The beginnings of intimacy.* London: Blackwell.

Dyson, A. H. (1989). *Multiple worlds of child writers: Friends learning to write.* New York: Teachers College Press.

Dyson, A. H. (1993). *Social worlds of children learning to write in an urban primary school.* New York: Teachers College Press.

Dyson, A. H. (1997). *Writing superheroes: Contemporary childhood, popular culture, and classroom literacy.* New York: Teachers College Press.

Dyson, A. H. (2003). *The brothers and sisters learn to write: Popular literacies in childhood and school cultures.* New York: Teachers College Press.

Dyson, A. H. (2006). On saying it right (write): "Fix-its" in the foundations of learning to write. *Research in the Teaching of English, 41,* 8–44.

Dyson, A. H. (2007). School literacy and the development of a child culture: Written remnants of the "gusto of life." In D. Thiessen & A. Cook-Sather (Eds.), *International handbook of student experience in elementary and secondary school* (pp. 115–142). Dordrecht, The Netherlands: Kluwer Academic.

Fineberg, J. (Ed.). (2006). *When we were young: New perspectives on the art of the child.* Berkeley: University of California Press.

Genishi, C., Stires, S., & Yung-Chan, D. (2001). Writing in an integrated curriculum: Prekindergarten English language learners as symbol-makers. *Elementary School Journal, 101*(4), 399–416.

Heath, S. B. (1983). *Ways with words: Language, life and work in communities and classrooms.* Cambridge, U.K.: Cambridge University Press.

Kenner, C. (2000). *Home pages: Literacy links for bilingual children.* Staffordshire, England: Trentham Books.

Kingston, M. H. (1975). *Woman warrior.* New York: Random House.

Labov, W. (1972). *Language in the inner city.* Philadelphia: University of Pennsylvania Press.

Moats, L. C. (2004). *Language essentials for teachers of reading and spelling.* Longmont, CO: Sopris West Educational Services.

Ochs, E. J. (1979). Transcription as theory. In E. Ochs & B. B. Schieffelin (Eds.), *Developmental pragmatics* (pp. 43–72). New York: Academic.

Read, C. (1975). *Children's categorization of speech sounds in English.* Urbana, IL: National Council of Teachers of English (NCTE).

Reyes, M. de la Luz, & Halcon, J. J. (Eds.). (2001). *The best for our children: Critical perspectives on literacy for Latino students.* New York: Teachers College Press.

Rickford, J. R., & Rickford, J. R. (2000). *Spoken soul: The story of black English.* New York: John Wiley.

Seymour, H., & Roeper, T. (1999). Grammatical acquisition of African American English. In O. Taylor & L. Leonard (Eds.), *Language acquisition across North America: Cross-cultural and cross-linguistic perspectives* (pp. 109–154). San Diego: Singular.

Smitherman, G. (2006). *Word from the mother: Language and African Americans.* New York: Routledge.

Thompson, C. M. (2006). The "ket aesthetic": Visual culture in childhood. In J. Fineberg (Ed.), *When we were young: New perspectives on the art of the child* (pp. 31–44). Berkeley: University of California Press.

Vasquez, V. (2005). Resistance, power-tricky, and colorless energy: What engagement with everyday popular culture texts can teach us about learning, and literacy. In J. Marsh (Ed.), *Popular culture, new media, and digital literacy in early childhood* (pp. 201–218). London: Routledge.

Vygotsky, L. S. (1978). *Mind in society.* Cambridge, MA: Harvard University Press.

3

Room to Move

How Kindergarteners Negotiate Literacies and Identities
in a Mandated Balanced Literacy Curriculum

MARJORIE SIEGEL AND STEPHANIE LUKAS

With the passage of No Child Left Behind legislation, U.S. policymakers have reshaped school literacy curricula, reducing it to a single standard that homogenizes the multiple languages and literacies children bring to school and ignores the rapid changes in the meaning and use of technologies in a postmodern world. In New York City, these two cultural storylines collide in Stephanie Lukas's kindergarten classroom, located in a public school serving a bilingual community where 92 percent of the students qualify for free lunch. In this chapter, we draw on a yearlong ethnographic study of the mandated balanced literacy curriculum in this classroom to explore the literacies and identities children were expected to take up as they participated in reading and writing workshops. What mattered most to Lukas was offering her students access to high-status knowledge—for example, science discourse and multimedia technologies—and finding spaces for the children's knowledge, questions, and interests to shine through the official curriculum. This was evident in a nonfiction unit of study in which children worked with partners to become experts on wild animals and to write a nonfiction book with a mouse as well as a pen. Our analysis of two pairs of partners shows when the workshop structures allowed for peer-directed interaction, children were able to negotiate with one another and make room for literacies and identities that were important to them. These children remind us that teaching for social justice means interrupting discourses about "at-risk" children by offering curricular challenges and "room to move" within the mandated curriculum. There is more than one way to be literate, and creating hybrid curricular spaces is urgently needed so young children can begin to find their way in, through, and around the "shrink-to-fit" school literacy being thrust upon teachers and children alike.

We begin with a story from Lukas, a New York City public school teacher who has taught kindergarten at P.S. 456 for the past 7 years.[1] The school, built in 1898, serves approximately 600 children in grades PreK–5, 92 percent of whom qualify for free lunch. In 2003–2004, the year Siegel spent several mornings a week studying the newly mandated balanced literacy curriculum in Lukas's classroom, there were 26 children in the class, representing nine languages and varieties of English. The neighborhood is home to a predominantly bilingual community of Puerto Rican and Dominican families, with a growing presence of South Asian families. In recent years, this neighborhood has begun to experience the gentrification that has spread throughout Manhattan, making it more difficult than ever for these families to survive economically.

Questions Asked of a New York City Teacher

I (Stephanie Lukas) teach in a neighborhood not far from where I grew up, but I did not have to face the same circumstances as the children I teach. I am continually amazed at the strength and power of their families, who are mostly Latino and poor. When I am out with friends or attending family gatherings, I often tell stories of how the families of my students work nights to try to make ends meet, figure out how to survive the shelter system, and escape abuse, and the response I commonly get is a question: "How many of your children do you think are going to jail?" Each time I hear this question I am ripped raw. I never know how to respond and usually don't try. To people who do not know or work with children who live in poverty, my students are just "kids from the ghetto." It is painful and shocking to me that some can only see my students as future prisoners.

I would not be a teacher if I did not "look at things as if they could be otherwise," to quote Maxine Greene (1988, p. 3). For me, each school year and each school day begins with excitement and the promise of great things to come. I learned to stop telling stories at the table and go about my work of securing the best for my children. In New York City, that means finding innovative sources of funding. Donors Choose—a foundation that invites teachers to post proposals so donors can select the projects they wish to support—is just one of those sources. When the $7 per child admission threatened to derail my plans for a field trip to the New York Aquarium, I wrote a grant to send the entire grade on this trip. It was funded (only days after I had posted it) by a couple in Northern California who are very active in the Monterey Bay Aquarium. After the trip, we sent them a letter thanking them, along with copies of our class book on fish. They were thrilled to hear about the children's wonderful experience at the aquarium and see how much they had learned. I knew I had found academic soul mates when they e-mailed their response to the book: "Do you think you might have any marine biologists in your class?" This is the kind of question that keeps me going, and guides my daily efforts to teach so that things might indeed be otherwise for my students.

Interrupting the Language of At Risk

As Lukas's story makes painfully clear, we teach in a time in which children acquire labels that are read as predictions for success in school and beyond.

Even before they arrive for their first day of school, the 5-year-olds in Lukas's kindergarten are deemed "at risk" by virtue of the fact that their family income is below the poverty line; identify as African American, Dominican, or Bangladeshi; are recent immigrants to the United States; live in a homeless shelter with a single mother; speak a language other than English; or have not attended preschool. This social calculus is taken for granted in the research reports (e.g., Snow, Burns, & Griffin, 1998) and federal legislation (i.e., No Child Left Behind, 2002) that have shaped the way literacy is taught in today's primary grades. In *Preventing Reading Difficulties* (Snow et al., 1998), for example, the authors distinguish group risk factors from individual risk factors, and conclude that

> early identification of children who will have reading difficulties might proceed better by considering target groups rather than by assessing individuals. Demographic data suggest that a majority of reading problems tend to occur in children from poor families with little education, although they may of course occur in families that are neither poor nor undereducated. (p. 119)

Following this logic, the next step is to select children from targeted groups for participation in early intervention programs designed to prevent future reading problems by providing children at risk with a pedagogical shot in the arm (hence the characterization of them as "inoculation-style" programs; Swadener, 1995, p. 18).

Yet this way of talking and thinking ignores what we know about literacy learning when examined in the context of children's lives. By attending to the social and cultural resources children bring to school literacy instruction, qualitative studies of young children's literacy learning have constructed a very different picture of children labeled at risk, documenting their "sociocultural intelligence" (Dyson, 1992, p. 434) and "funds of knowledge" (Moll, Amanti, Neff, & Gonzalez, 1992). These studies conclude that children are disadvantaged by the narrow definitions of school literacy and learning, which impose a linear order on the complex social and symbolic work children engage in when reading and writing (Ballenger, 1999; Dyson, 1993, 2003; Gallas, 1994; Harste, Woodward, & Burke, 1984; Heath, 1983; Hicks, 2002).

In this chapter, we intend to interrupt the language of "at risk" and show how Lukas works toward social justice by seeing her students as children "of promise" (Heath & Mangiola, 1991; Swadener & Lubeck, 1995), every one of whom has a potential future as a marine biologist. The remainder of this chapter is divided into two parts: (1) a description of the balanced literacy curriculum enacted in Lukas's kindergarten and how she expanded it to provide her students with access to high-status knowledge and changing forms of literacy; and (2) vignettes illustrating how children brought their own knowledge and literacy practices to the curriculum and the identities they took up in the course of school literacy lessons.

Creating Room for Children in a Mandated Balanced Literacy Curriculum

Mandating Balanced Literacy: The New York City Context

In New York City, a "balanced literacy" approach was mandated by the "Children First" reform initiated by the New York City Chancellor Joel Klein in fall 2003.[2] "Balanced literacy" has no single, unitary meaning (Freppon & Dahl, 1998) but in New York City, it came to signify a particular set of instructional routines and practices designed to teach children the "habits and strategies of effective reading and writing" (New York City DOE Web site, 2005). Teachers were expected to devote each morning to a "literacy block" consisting of a writer's workshop, a reader's workshop, read alouds, and word study, supplemented by shared reading, interactive writing, and guided reading groups in K–2 classrooms. The New York City Department of Education (DOE) handbook directed teachers to begin each workshop with a mini-lesson that explicitly taught a particular concept or strategy, followed by opportunities for children to apply what was taught to their own reading or writing. Each workshop concluded with a sharing time during which the teacher invited children to show how they had used the strategy. During the year, Writer's Workshop consisted of units of study of on required genres (personal narrative, how-to, nonfiction, poetry, fiction) whereas Reader's Workshop emphasized reading strategies (e.g., looking for chunks in words, using pictures to identify unknown words) and literary elements (e.g., character development) necessary for proficient reading.

The New York City literacy curriculum was an attempt to balance any number of dimensions of literacy curricula that have been debated in recent years, including process and product, skills and meaning making, and explicit instruction and responsive teaching. The decision to mandate a literacy curriculum that was not tightly scripted and offered teachers and children some curricular control was a bold move because the National Reading Panel report (2000) did not include research on reading and writing workshops. But the lack of a script does not mean a curriculum places no limits on teachers and children. In other words, New York City's mandated literacy curriculum was not simply a set of classroom routines and teaching methods but an authoritative way of talking about reading and writing. Teachers and students could not read whatever text they wanted in whatever way they chose because the balanced literacy curriculum treated some ways of reading and writing, and not others, as "natural" and "normal." Getting recognized as a successful student in a balanced literacy curriculum thus required that children show they could talk about and interact with texts in particular ways, using the symbol systems considered appropriate for learning to read and write. Five-year-old Jewel demonstrated her awareness of these restrictions when she announced, "If you don't put a Post-it in the book, you're not going to be a good reader" (field notes, March 10, 2004). Jewel's positioning of herself as someone who knew what it took to be a good reader stood in contrast to how she was positioned during Writer's Workshop earlier in the year. As Jewel worked on a drawing, Lukas stopped by to confer with her, acknowledging the picture Jewel had drawn but pointing out that Jewel needed to add her name and some words (Steps 1 and 3 in the writing procedure introduced in September and posted on a wall chart). After Lukas moved on to confer with another child, Daryl, one of her tablemates, looked over at Jewel's paper and told her she was doing "scribble scrabble" (field notes, October 28, 2003). Clearly, the children knew what it meant to be literate in the balanced literacy curriculum. Lukas negotiated the curriculum in ways that made room for children's diverse literacies and identities and thus expanded who could be counted as literate in the context of a mandated curriculum. In what follows, we describe how she tried to accomplish this by taking advantage of the "wiggle room" afforded by her school and by the balanced literacy curriculum.

Negotiating Curriculum Mandates: The Classroom Context

For the past 7 years, Lukas has had the opportunity to teach at a school that employs the workshop model for reading and writing. The literacy block lasts the entire morning, beginning when the students arrive at 8:30 A.M. until they go to lunch at 11:00 A.M. Morning meeting is the first event. The class gathers on the rug and goes through the same series of activities every day: working with the calendar, counting how many days they have been in school, charting the weather, reading the daily schedule, chanting the alphabet chart, and sharing the reading of a poem. Most of the block is devoted to the reading and writing workshops.

Each day follows the same schedule, guided by monthly curriculum calendars that outline the units of study for reading and writing. At Lukas's school, teachers are given a good deal of latitude by the school administrators because the school had used the workshop approach for many years before it was mandated, and there is little monitoring of daily practice by the administrators. Teachers must follow the curriculum calendar but need not stick to the suggested mini-lessons and can therefore negotiate the curriculum to fit the needs of their students. Lukas has had great success with this approach and has grown more confident with each passing year. She now relies on her students more than on any monthly curriculum calendar to tell her what lesson is needed next. Her goal is to bring the children fully into the work whenever possible. As part of the phonics program, for example, teachers are encouraged to do a "star name study" in which one child's name is studied each day at the beginning of the year. Lukas extends this practice to a weeklong study of the "star child"—not just her or his name—by having the class interview that child (which produces a text for shared reading), studying the child's name (cutting, arranging, and counting the letters), and, every Friday, drawing portraits of the star child and compiling them in a book for the child to take home. In this way, learning phonics becomes part of a broader study of the classroom community and contributes to building that community as well as building children's understanding of how texts work.

No lesson starts and ends with Lukas's voice. Before starting a unit about planting, for example, the class shares stories about plants in their homes (successful and unsuccessful!), discusses the plants and gardens from their home countries, and makes a list of the things they already know about what plants need to grow. Before they have even touched a seed, the children's stories about how worms and plants bend toward the sun launch their study of photosynthesis and soil nutrients. These are the spaces Lukas calls "wiggle room"—spaces where she includes the children's knowledge, questions, ideas, and experiences and links what *has* to be done with what *should* be done. Across the curriculum, there are mandates and then wiggle room. In math and science, teachers are handed workbooks, materials, and a teacher's guide. Lukas accepts these curricula as necessary and valid, and makes sure she covers all of the required lessons. Then she starts to wiggle. She finds things that interest the children and her, and they take off on explorations not connected to a box marked DOE. Over the past several years, Lukas has dedicated a good amount of classroom time to science. Her class has created a pond habitat using a tank and rocks, built a petite frog habitat and learned what types of frogs can cohabit, and dived deep to the bottom of the ocean and learned what lives there. The school administrators neither support nor discourage her from taking on these science projects. As long as she gets everything taken care of on her "required" curricular to-do list, she is free to go. One place she has been particularly successful in combining the mandated with the magical is in the nonfiction reading and writing unit.

Studying Nonfiction Texts: Access to High-Status Knowledge

The nonfiction unit introduces children to the features of nonfiction books (purpose, organization, design features, language) and engages them in reading nonfiction books on a particular topic as preparation for writing their own nonfiction book on that same topic. During the 2003–2004 school year, the nonfiction unit focused on wild animals, and each reading partnership chose an animal to study closely.[3] Lukas began the unit with a whole-class study of one animal (in this case, frogs), which served as a model for the work to follow. Once the children selected their animals, Lukas provided a plastic bag of books about the animal. Some books were written in simple language, and others were more complex with photos and detailed pictures. After each partnership had time to explore their books, they began searching for information. First, the tasks were general: "Can you find the same information in two different books?" Then the questions got more specific: "Can you figure out how your animal has babies and takes care of the babies?" As children found the answers to these questions, the partners began writing their own books.

From the beginning of each year, Lukas took her classes to the computer lab so by the time the nonfiction unit rolled around, they knew how to use KidPix to draw pictures, create diagrams and webs, and label their texts with words using both the letter stamp and the typewriter functions. The texts they produced with a pen and a mouse were made into books (complete with a color-coded table of contents), and celebrated at a publishing party for their families. Although reading, writing, and talking science formed the centerpiece of the nonfiction unit, Lukas incorporates several other ways for children to engage in science. Weekly science talks (Gallas, 1995) bring the children into the study by providing opportunities for them to engage in peer-led talk about a question or topic related to the nonfiction unit. Finally, Lukas's belief that science learning requires firsthand and real-world experiences meant that she found ways to bring her students in contact with the natural world by building animal habitats in the classroom and planning field trips to observe wild animals at the Bronx Zoo, learn about marine life at the New York Aquarium, and study pond life at the Harlem Meer in Central Park. Later, we will return to the question of how Lukas created the wiggle room needed to make room for children's interests and knowledge and to provide access to the high-status knowledge that is too often absent from the curriculum for children labeled at risk.

Who Can Be Literate? Children of Promise in Action

When children enter Lukas's kindergarten at the beginning of the year, they encounter a new and complex world that requires learning how to participate in a class shaped by the balanced literacy curriculum and access to science as well as multimedia technologies. Who can be counted as a literate student in this environment? Too often, only those children who bring school-sanctioned knowledge and literacy practices to school are regarded as ready and able to succeed with school literacy. But in Lukas's classroom, they enter as children of promise who bring knowledge, literacy practices, and identities from other spheres of their lives. The wiggle room Lukas cultivates gives the children room to move in, through, and around the curriculum and acknowledges the value of these resources in accomplishing the social and academic work of school (Dyson, 1993, 2003). In what follows, we present two vignettes, selected from our field notes and videotapes of children during independent work time in Reader's Workshop, the Writer's Workshop, or the computer lab that show what the children did in these hybrid spaces and how the definition of who could be literate was stretched as a result.

Vignette 1: Hector and Bianca

Hector and Bianca, two Dominican American children who were successful in taking up the practices and identities expected in a balanced literacy curriculum, had been assigned to work together as a "reading partnership." With his close-cropped hair and trademark overalls, Hector could have easily been mistaken for the main character in Crockett Johnson's classic picture book, *Harold and the Purple Crayon* (1955). Bianca, who sported two prominent pigtails, always knew what *was* happening in the room and what was *supposed* to happen. This vignette took place after the class had completed the whole-class frog study, and children were beginning to read nonfiction books about their animals. Hector and Bianca were studying dolphins. On this particular day, Lukas began with an announcement that Reader's Workshop would come first (Writer's Workshop usually came first). In a teasing voice that cued the children that she knew they weren't tricked by the change in schedule, she asked, "Is this crazy?!" Hector's explanation for this change was because "We loooove Reader's Workshop!"

Lukas's reason was a little different: they needed to have Reader's Workshop first so they could do research and gather information for their nonfiction books. She instructed the class to search the books in their plastic bags for information about where their animals lived and emphasized precision and detail in their reading and research since they would use the information to prepare drawings of their animals' habitats. "Look through your books to try and find where your animal lives. If you say in the water, where? In the ocean … ? You have to *really* look in your books and find exactly where [they live]." With a reminder that they would have to teach her about their animals, Lukas sent the partners off to their assigned reading spots with their bags of nonfiction books in hand.

Early in this event, we can see how Hector demonstrates his awareness that "loving to read" is highly valued in this classroom and positions himself as someone who "loves" Reader's Workshop. Ordinarily, this is the preferred way to be a student in Reader's Workshop, but in this particular writing unit, Lukas is oriented toward "talking science," which includes observing, describing, hypothesizing, questioning, reporting, and writing in and through the language of science (Lemke, 1990). Hence, she wants the children to view texts as repositories of knowledge and resources for their own research on wild animals. Her emphasis on precision in their answers about the animal's habitat and her choice of a drawing to represent what they had learned about where their animals lived is further evidence that Writer's Workshop had become a space for talking science.

Once Hector and Bianca go to their own spot and take two books from the bag, they take up identities beyond those of science learner and nonfiction writer as they read their books. After getting settled, each takes a book and starts looking through it. Hector talks quietly to himself as he pages through the book, describing the pictures as he goes. Suddenly, he turns to Bianca and they begin to talk.

Verbal Transcription	Nonverbal Transcription
Hector: Where do dolphins live?	
Bianca: In the ocean!	
Hector: How do you know?	
Bianca: I have the book. See, in the ocean.	Bianca points at one picture.
Hector: Hm, in the ocean. Yeah! The ocean. Did you know that Titanic crashed? The water had dolphins.	Hector looks through his own book. Hector talks about the Titanic for a while, while Bianca looks through her book and does not pay much attention.
Bianca: Look! A baby dolphin!	
Hector: That looks like a kid.	
Bianca: It looks like you, little Hector.	Bianca speaks to Hector in a sweet voice and approaches his face.
Hector: Oh! See the whale!	
Bianca: [unintelligible]	
Hector: Look at that whale.	Hector points at another picture.
Bianca: See, this is the mommy. See, you have one, too.	Bianca points in Hector's book.
Hector: Look at this ocean!	

In this excerpt, we notice that Hector and Bianca initially align themselves with Reader's Workshop by immediately looking in their books. Hector restates Lukas's question about where their animal lives and Bianca's response—"in the ocean"—echoes Lukas's exact words during the mini-lesson, which modeled the kind of language the children were expected to use. In the exchange that follows, Bianca demonstrates her understanding of the kind of knowledge valued in the nonfiction unit of study when she points to her book to justify her claim that dolphins live in the ocean. Although Hector views Bianca as knowledgeable about dolphins, he has knowledge too, and he makes his knowledge of the Titanic relevant to their reading by explaining that there were dolphins in the ocean where the *Titanic* crashed. Through talk, Hector and Bianca become people with knowledge that counts (Bianca's knowledge of school literacy practices, Hector's knowledge of popular culture) in learning science. This pattern continues in the next exchange when Hector notices a picture of a whale, and Bianca explains that it's the mommy and points out that his book has one, too. Using the word *mommy* to describe one of the dolphins invokes the language of home and family, and would not be a word the children would encounter in their nonfiction texts. Even though Bianca and Hector are expected to read like scientists, the hybrid space Lukas has created gives them room to stretch the meaning of literacy and weave together their own text from their positions as popular culture fans, members of families, and friends.

A little while later, Lukas calls the class to the rug to share what they've learned; after a few children have done so, she directs them to return to their reading spots to produce another page for their nonfiction books. Hector starts drawing a dolphin and indicates the dolphin is swimming under water by drawing a line over the dolphin. He sings and names his drawing as "a dolphin." He calls another child over and shows his picture. Then, he writes over the date Lukas has stamped on his paper and announces that today is "opposite day," a reference to an episode of one of his favorite TV shows, *SpongeBob SquarePants,* in which SpongeBob, a square yellow sea sponge who lives in the Pacific Ocean, is told to act the opposite of how he usually acts. Hector explains to Belinda and Bianca that "yes" means "no," since "yes" is the opposite of "no." He asks Belinda if she knows the opposite of "open" and immediately answers his own question, telling her that "closed" is the opposite of "open." When another child comes over and asks Hector if he has drawn a fish, Hector explains that he has drawn a "dolphin in the ocean." He starts writing these words under its drawing, stretching them out just as Lukas has demonstrated since the beginning of the school year.

While Hector is engaged in his writing, Lukas asks the class to stop writing for a moment and comments on how some students are copying words from the books instead of writing their own sentences. She explains that copying is like "stealing others' words" and that they do not need this, since they have their own words in their heads. Hector whispers that he wrote the words he had in his head and then rereads what he has written. He continues writing, adding the word "the," which he spells, then asks Bianca to look at his picture and starts saying what he will write, but then changes his mind and says that he will draw "extra dolphins." He says he is going to do 100 dolphins. He starts drawing more dolphins and asks Bianca if they look like dolphins. Bianca answers that they look like fish, but Hector does not pay much attention and continues drawing dolphins, simultaneously talking to himself (Figure 3.1).

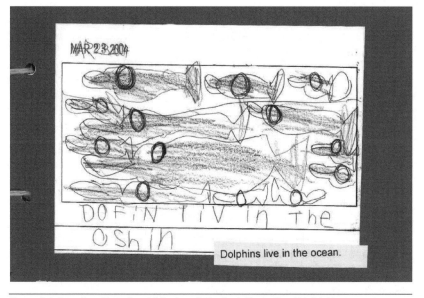

Dolphins live in the ocean.

Figure 3.1 Page from Hector's published nonfiction book illustrating 100 dolphins.

In this writing episode, Hector's actions and interactions again illustrate that his literacies and identities extend beyond those expected in the balanced literacy curriculum. He positions himself as a "good" writer who follows the 1-2-3s of writing workshop by first drawing a picture of a dolphin in the ocean and then labeling his picture with his own words, "stretching them out" as he has been taught. He also rereads, plans, draws, and seeks an audience for his writing, all of which are practices that Lukas has modeled during mini-lessons. But in between, Hector sings, tests Bianca's knowledge of opposites and shows off his own, engages in dramatic play, and kisses his picture! The precise and evidence-based science writing that he is expected to do has quickly morphed into a cartoonlike episode in which Hector imagines he is drawing 100 dolphins, a goal he evaluates as "good." In that split second, he has shifted back into the "good writer," one who has produced "so much" work and "finished" the task. The finished product leaves no trace of its multimodal production, so a teacher who had not listened in on this event would be unaware that it signified multiple literacies and identities.

We would argue that Hector and Bianca did complete the assignment but, in doing so, they took full advantage of the latitude Lukas made available to the children during independent writing time. The intersection of a writing workshop and talking science created a hybrid space that children could fill with literacies and identities that were important to them and that they seamlessly wove into the writing workshop. There is no doubt that Hector and

Verbal Transcription	Nonverbal Transcription
Hector: I'm doing more and more and more. More dolphins. This is the baby dolphin. I did three dolphins. Now I'm doing more and more and more. Now this baby dolphin is very little. I'm making more and more and more. I made more and more and more dolphins. I'm doing more of this. And one jumping out. I'm making one jumping out of the water. And this is the sun and this is another dolphin.	He goes to Elvin and tells him that dolphins live in the ocean. When he comes back, he continues drawing.
Hector: I'm almost getting a new paper. Now look at! I made 100 dolphins. No, this is 99. No, this is 93. This is 93 dolphins. Now, look at this! Oh! My beautiful work! I got 99. Now, I need one more dolphin and then … there! I have 100 dolphins. All these dolphins are gonna be gray in no time. Right? It's good to have so much. I finished all my dolphins!	Hector changes his voice at this point. He kisses his paper. He takes some crayons.

Bianca knew what "counted" as literacy during Writer's Workshop and were successful in displaying those practices and positioning themselves as "good writers." But they were equally adept at stretching the boundaries of this identity and making room for their childhood pleasures and literacy practices.

Vignette 2: Jewel and Terrance

Across the room, Jewel and Terrance demonstrated a different set of practices and identities than those we observed Hector and Bianca engage in during Writer's Workshop. Jewel, the youngest of five children in a family from Bangladesh, had learned to protect herself from her older and bigger brothers and was expected to adopt the modest, quiet demeanor of her older sister. Her parents did not speak fluent English, though her siblings do. Jewel, an English-language learner, would talk with Lukas and Siegel (she had many questions about the video camera) and with her peers during independent work time, but rarely spoke during whole-class lessons and activities. Terrance, an African American boy, is the youngest of three children his mother is raising on her own. Though eager to participate in whole-class activities and interact with his peers, Terrance often found it hard to accomplish this without violating norms of classroom participation. Both Jewel and Terrance struggled with Writer's Workshop, finding it difficult to take up the practices and produce the texts that were expected of kindergarteners.

Despite these challenges, Terrance and Jewel were placed together for several reasons. First, teachers were expected to form their students into "partnerships" by matching up children according to their abilities and engagement in workshop activities. Another reason for matching up Jewel and Terrance was that both had difficulty staying focused on reading or writing during independent work time so partnering them with other children created other tensions. This partnership arrangement did not always serve Jewel and Terrance well, but, unlike traditional approaches to ability grouping, being assigned as partners did not limit their access to high-status knowledge and literacies. When they did work together, they would often battle with their differences until one of them won out or a teacher came to settle the dispute. There were occasions, however, when they clearly showed that they had taken up the literacy practices and identities valued in the wild animal nonfiction unit and could display their understanding of science content, classroom practices, social order, and popular culture.

This vignette occurred shortly after the nonfiction unit had begun in early March. Lukas had initiated the unit through a whole-class study of frogs, and each strategy and practice she introduced in a mini-lesson was illustrated with frogs. Each partnership was then sent to their reading spots to apply the lesson to their own animals. To provide additional support and scaffolding, Terrance and Jewel were also conducting their own study of frogs. On this day, the class was working in the computer lab, and Lukas had demonstrated how to create a life-cycle diagram of a frog on a whiteboard. The children were then supposed to create a frog life cycle with their partners. In the past, the partners had been directed to draw a line down the middle of the screen so each child had her or his own space to work, but this time Lukas asked the children to collaborate on the design of the diagram.

This event begins with Jewel and Terrance each claiming that the other does not know the correct way to draw the life-cycle diagram, thus positioning each other as a student who was not literate in the practices needed to be successful in this hybrid curriculum space.

Verbal Transcription	Nonverbal Transcription
Jewel: You don't know how to write! All you do is line.	
Terrance: That's life cycle.	Turns to Nathan.
	Jewel holds the mouse and tries to draw something. After drawing one or two small circles, she stops and looks carefully at the screen. Terrance keeps calling Nathan, who does not respond. Jewel erases what she was drawing and starts making some more circles, which, as she explains, are the frog's eggs. She tries to keep her drawing only on her "part" of the page.
Terrance: Hey! These are my eggs! All you doing is [squiggles, squiggles].	
Jewel tells him that they need to divide ("cut") the page in the middle.	
Jewel: And then I'm gonna have my way and there's your way.	As she is talking she starts erasing Terrance's drawings. She starts drawing something.
Terrance: This is not a cycle. It's a line.	
Jewel: No! It's a cycle!	She starts erasing again.

However, their dispute over the "proper" representation of a life cycle and of frogs' eggs is revealing. Jewel repeatedly uses the term *cycle,* not *circle,* to display her knowledge of the language of science, and Terrance is equally insistent that his representation is a *life* cycle. In an earlier mini-lesson, Lukas had introduced several models of a life cycle in class including one that was round and did not use lines. The fact that both of them insist that the life cycle they've drawn is a *cycle,* not a *line,* indicates they see themselves as successful science learners who know what it means to represent the life cycle of an animal. Although Jewel tries to position herself as more knowledgeable and powerful than Terrance ("You don't know how to write! All you do is line."), he rejects this move, and she draws upon a familiar computer lab practice (dividing the screen down the middle) to propose a compromise and solve the problem.

Later, they demonstrate a level of sophistication in problem solving and cooperation.

Terrance: Jewel, how do you write … ?
Jewel: I can show you.
Terrance: That's a …
Jewel: No, it's like … skinny legs and big body. Wait! Wait! Let me type my name! Let me do my name first!

Instead of grabbing the mouse to type *for* Terrance, Jewel uses science language to describe what Terrance is supposed to draw. This "code" for describing the frog fits the classroom discourse for talking about letters—*g* is a circle with a long stick and a tail. So "skinny legs and a big body" functions similarly. In this brief exchange, Jewel does not give up her identity as a knower but shifts ever so slightly into the position of teacher and patient partner who can show

Verbal Transcription	Nonverbal Transcription
	Jewel spells her name, while Terrance looks around.
Jewel: Let's do "frogs" now. Let me! Let me spell frogs!	Terrance tries to type.
	She turns to the board, where the phrase "Frog Life Cycle" is written.
	Terrance asks the teacher to turn the board to their side so that they can read. After he returns to his seat, Jewel goes to the board and calls out the letters, one by one, and Terrance types them. After they finish, Terrance types his name and they count the number of the letters in each of the names.
Jewel: I got more letters in it. Now write the word … write the word … write! You didn't spell "frogs." I did it. You didn't spell the words.	Terrance does not look at her.

Terrance how to draw through the precise use of language. This continues as they collaborate on writing the label for their frog life cycle.

In collaborating to label their diagram of the frog life cycle, Jewel and Terrance have taken up the identities of "good writers" who are holding themselves to high expectations and demonstrating their familiarity with "word work" practices such as using printed text as a resource for spelling, identifying each letter in order, identifying and typing the same letter on the keyboard, and counting the number of letters in the words they have typed. What is impressive about their interaction is how fluidly they move across the multiple meanings of literacy in their classroom. They know what counts as literacy in the balanced literacy curriculum and what counts as talking and writing science in the nonfiction unit; more importantly, they know how to deploy this knowledge to achieve their purpose.

But that is not all they know. It would be easy to miss the way that Jewel and Terrance make use of multiple technologies (whiteboard, keyboard) to jointly produce a label for their diagram. It would also be easy to miss their sophisticated awareness of a hierarchy of literacy practices that elevates spelling above typing. Jewel tries to be recognized as the "speller" (perhaps because she believes that calling out the letters counts as "spelling," which she knows has higher status than typing in a balanced literacy curriculum), but Terrance refuses to be cast as a mere "typist" ("You didn't spell *frogs*. I did it."). In short, the very children who are often thought "not ready" for peer-led interactions, the precise vocabulary of science, and the demands of the screen again show us that we are the ones at risk if we do not "get over deficit" (Comber & Kamler, 2004) and look beyond compliant behavior for evidence of school success. For these children in particular, the hybrid workshop gave them the space to work things out for themselves and, in doing so, they showed just how much they had been paying attention.

Rethinking and Doing Literacy Lessons

We began this chapter with a story about the questions asked of a public school teacher whose students are constructed as "among the most difficult to teach" in the media as well as in current policy and research documents. It is not easy to enact socially just and equitable practices when deficit thinking takes on the aura of "common sense" and when a one-size-fits-all curriculum becomes the cure-all. But Lukas managed to find ways to create a hybrid, "permeable" curriculum (Dyson, 1993) while still achieving the literacy outcomes that were expected of the children by the New York City DOE. We want to conclude this chapter by commenting on the "rethinking" and "doing" that made it possible for Hector, Bianca, Jewel, Terrance, and the rest of Lukas's class to display their multiple literacies and identities on a daily basis.

As Lukas's opening narrative shows, she begins from the belief that each student has something to offer and not from a deficit model of difference.

Validating each child's experience and viewing her or him as knowledgeable is the most basic way she rethinks the category "at risk." This is why "science talks" (Gallas, 1995) are such a valuable addition to the classroom discourse. These peer-led discussions offer regular spaces for children to hear and discuss their own ideas about how the world works. Incorporating science into the nonfiction unit was also an attempt to interrupt the positioning of Latin Americans as low performing and underprepared for participation in a technologically advanced society (Bryce, 2003). When acquiring English is given priority over learning science, children get left behind by the curriculum. Lukas's decision to make the computer lab part of Writer's Workshop was based on the same belief. However enthusiastic she was about Writer's Workshop, Lukas wanted to ensure that her students, who had little access to multimedia technologies at home, would build a repertoire of literacy practices that included new technologies. Literacy researchers have begun to document the disconnect between the kinds of texts and literacy practices characteristic of new technologies and the texts children learn how to write in Writer's Workshop (Hammerberg, 2001). Lukas made room for both, despite the fact that the only writing she was held accountable for was the writing done in Writer's Workshop.

Lukas's desire to push past narrow ways of thinking and provide the most exciting classroom experience for each student led her to expand the amount of science learning as well as change the nature of that learning. Finding the wiggle room to do this was not difficult because she was able to cover the required lessons ("All About Me" and "The Five Senses") in a few weeks each semester. This gave her months to work in the science learning she and the children found exciting and engaging. Lukas also took advantage of the fact that many of the kindergarten science standards were not connected to any set curriculum, which meant she could pick something like life cycles and make that a unit of study. With the exception of the nonfiction unit, thematic teaching is not particularly encouraged in the balanced literacy curriculum, so Lukas used this unit as an anchor for the science talks, field trips, and classroom animal habitats she regarded as essential to kindergarten.

We think it's important to understand that Lukas's ability to turn her rethinking into doing was due to the school context in which she taught, and the reputation and relationships she had built during 7 years of teaching kindergarten. Yet some of her tactics may offer ideas and encouragement to other teachers who want some wiggle room in their schools and classrooms. First, Lukas got to do a lot of "wiggling" because she had proved that her students were ready for first grade at the end of the year. She also began teaching at a time when the administration was more flexible and there were no citywide curriculum mandates. Lukas began experimenting early on and was allowed to continue as long as no parents complained, her classroom had all the appropriate centers and displays, and her students could answer questions about what they did for each balanced literacy component when the superintendent came to her classroom.

Once Lukas had established herself as the teacher with all the animals and the one who planned all the trips, it was hard for a new administrator to change that image. She also made sure that each of these endeavors was funded without school money. By taking the initiative to secure her own funding, she did not have to prove the worth of her "extra" projects to the administration. Finding ways to have more adults in her classroom was another way she expanded the resources available to her students. She served as a cooperating teacher to preservice student teachers every semester, followed up on every volunteer program that came knocking, and enlisted her friends and family as curricular resources. Finally, Lukas created wiggle room through collaborations with teachers as well as researchers. She leapt at the chance to join a university-school collaboration aimed at improving science education through child inquiry and connections to their everyday lives. And, when her school was approached about participating in a reform-oriented technology grant, Lukas and her primary-grade peers became the school leaders, which not only gave them access to new technologies and pedagogies but also meant they could take their students to the computer lab twice a week instead of once. In short, Lukas created "room to move" for her students by constructing a particular identity for herself as a teacher-activist. Teaching for social justice in regressive times means collective rethinking and doing. Lukas sought out allies and collaborators, all with one aim: to make room for her students to show their promise.

Notes

1. With the exception of Stephanie Lukas, all names are pseudonyms.
2. The requirement that schools adopt "balanced literacy" was waived for 220 schools judged to be successful based on performance indicators, and allowed to continue using whatever curricula were in place at those schools. These waivers have recently become more widespread as the New York City public school chancellor has begun to promote school autonomy (coupled with accountability) as a reform policy.
3. It is routine practice for children to be paired up with another child for the reading workshop, and these partnerships are often maintained over several units of study.

References

Ballenger, C. (1999). *Teaching other people's children.* New York: Teachers College Press.

Bryce, N. (2003). *Socially situated activities and identities: Second-grade dual language students and the social construction of science.* Unpublished doctoral dissertation, Teachers College, Columbia University.

Comber, B., & Kamler, B. (2004). Getting out of deficit: Pedagogies of reconnection. *Teaching Education, 15*(3), 293–310.

Dyson, A. H. (1992). *Whistle for Willie,* lost puppies, and cartoon dogs: The sociocultural dimensions of young children's composing or toward unmelting pedagogical pots. *Journal of Literacy Research, 24*(4), 433–462.

Dyson, A. H. (1993). *The social world of young children learning to write in urban primary schools.* New York: Teachers College Press.

Dyson, A. H. (2003). *The brothers and sisters learn to write: Popular literacies in childhood and school culture.* New York: Teachers College Press.

Freppon, P., & Dahl, K. (1998). Balanced instruction: Insights and considerations. *Reading Research Quarterly, 33*(2), 240–251.

Gallas, K. (1994). *The languages of learning: How children talk, write, dance, draw, and sing their understanding of the world.* New York: Teachers College Press.

Gallas, K. (1995). *Talking their way into science.* New York: Teachers College Press.

Greene, M. (1988). *The dialectic of freedom.* New York: Teachers College Press.

Hammerberg, D. (2001). Reading and writing "hypertextually": Children's literature, technology, and early writing instruction. *Language Arts, 78*(3), 207–216.

Harste, J., Woodward, V., & Burke, C. (1984). *Language stories and literacy lessons.* Portsmouth, NH: Heinemann.

Heath, S. B. (1983). *Ways with words.* Cambridge: Cambridge University Press.

Heath, S. B., & Mangiola, L. (1991). *Children of promise: Literate activity in linguistically and culturally diverse classrooms.* Washington, DC: NEA Professional Library, National Education Association.

Hicks, D. (2002). *Reading lives: Working-class children and literacy learning.* New York: Teachers College Press.

Johnson, C. (1955). *Harold and the purple crayon.* New York: Harper and Row.

Lemke, J. (1990). *Talking science: Language, learning, and values.* Norwood, NJ: Ablex.

Moll, L., Amanti, C., Neff, D., & Gonzalez, N. (1992). Funds of knowledge for teaching: Using a qualitative approach to connect homes and classrooms. *Theory Into Practice, 31*(1), 132–141.

National Reading Panel. (2000). *Teaching children to read: An evidence-based assessment of the scientific research literature on reading and its implications for reading instruction: Reports of the subgroups.* Washington, DC: National Institute of Child Health and Development.

New York City Department of Education. (2005). *Balanced literary overview.* Retrieved October 24, 2005, from http://www.nycenet.edu/Offices/TeachLearn/Office CurriculumProfessionalDevelopment/DepartmentofLiteracy/default.htm.

No Child Left Behind Act of 2001 (Pub. L. 107–110), 115 Stat. 1425 (2002).

Snow, C. E., Burns, M. S., & Griffin, P. (1998). *Preventing reading difficulties in young children.* Washington, DC: National Academy Press.

Swadener, B. B. (1995). Children and families "at promise": Deconstructing the discourse of risk. In B. B. Swadener & S. Lubeck (Eds.), *Children and families "at promise": Deconstructing the discourse of risk* (pp. 17–49). Albany: State University of New York Press.

Swadener, B. B., & Lubeck, S. (Eds.). (1995). *Children and families "at promise": Deconstructing the discourse of risk.* Albany: State University of New York Press.

4
Learning English in School
Rethinking Curriculum, Relationships, and Time

SUSAN STIRES AND CELIA GENISHI

In this chapter we focus on one English language learner named Alice, whose learning Susan Stires documented from prekindergarten (preK) through her fifth-grade year at the same school in New York City. In her preK year, the two of us, with Donna Yung-Chan, Alice's teacher, were able to see Alice as a newcomer to school (Genishi, Yung-Chan, & Stires, 2000). Although the classroom was not designated as "bilingual" or "English as a Second Language" (ESL), Donna was bilingual in English and Cantonese, the Chinese language that most of her children spoke and heard at home. On any day during the school year, a visitor could hear both languages used, by children and their teacher, although as the year went by, more English was used by all. Donna had the advantage of speaking Cantonese and of being able to create a curriculum that blended much social interaction with rich content: social studies, science, literacy, math, and art.

The preK curriculum for the school was HighScope (Hohmann, Banet, & Weikart, 1979), which follows a plan-do-review format. In Donna's room, children planned at the end of group time by choosing an activity for their "work time." The choices are displayed on a board to which the child attaches his or her name. So that you have a sense of Alice as an English learner in the spring of her preK year, we offer this exchange:

Example (Genishi et al., 2000, p. 68):

Alice:	Want to go to water table.
Donna:	You want to go to the water table? Okay, what do you need to do first before you go to water?
Alice:	I do water.
Donna:	Okay, you go to the water table, but what do you need to do first? What do you need to put on?
Alice:	Bubbles.
Donna:	You're going to the water table and you're going to play with bubbles, but what do you need to wear? (Gently pulls Alice back as she starts to walk away.)
Tommy:	Smock!

Donna:	We don't want to get this beautiful dress wet. What do we need to wear? Do you need to wear something?
Tommy:	Smock!
Alice:	Jacket.
Donna:	Okay, we call that a smock. Can you say smock?
Alice:	Smock.
Donna:	Okay, you need to sign your name, right? (Alice nods.)

Donna patiently and persistently takes advantage of this planning moment to teach a new word—one that classmate Tommy clearly knows—to Alice, at a time when Alice is just beginning to express herself in English, her second language.

If we look back and characterize the kind of preK learner Alice was, we might think first of her large eyes that seemed to attend to whatever was happening and the short ponytail that occasionally stuck straight up from the top of her head. We remember her as a watchful, quiet participant in child-initiated events like dramatic play and in teacher-initiated events like morning meeting. If we created a list of talkers versus quiet children, she would have been on the "quiet children" list. As years went by, Alice and her family stayed in the neighborhood known as Chinatown, and Alice attended the same school until she was ready for middle school.

In the rest of this chapter we consider Alice in the first grade (and beyond) as she learns not only English but content that is compatible with that of Donna's classroom, content that is often rooted in science. We present the experiences of a fortunate learner, in a school where the students perform well enough on mandated tests that the administrators can allow teachers to create curricula that weave the basics of literacy and math into content that is not often associated with children from economically underresourced neighborhoods. Like Stephanie Lukas in chapter 3, Alice's teachers have been able to rethink what is possible in their classrooms with children who are labeled as "disadvantaged" linguistically or economically. And with Anne Haas Dyson, we are pushed to rethink what the meanings of "basic" might be in a curriculum for social justice. Many children attend schools where learning is highly restricted due to reading programs that emphasize the so-called basics, including the smallest elements of language, and deemphasize the relationship between the teacher and his or her students. It is as if they are being asked to put together 5,000 indistinguishable pieces of a puzzle with a stranger, instead of one with 25 pieces, many visible clues, and a friend by their side. The source of many decisions to place young children in such programs is the federal legislation known as No Child Left Behind (2002). If these programs and associated mandates restrict typically developing children from English-speaking backgrounds, they place a stranglehold on linguistically, culturally, and economically diverse groups of children.

In addition to rethinking aspects of the early childhood curriculum, we ask readers to rethink two other concepts, which we elaborate on in our final section: first, the "model minority myth." This well-known essentializing of identity asserts in part, for example, that Asian-heritage children always turn out to be good students, as if simply being Asian guarantees their success in school. We acknowledge that the child we are focusing on would be called a successful learner, but we provide documentation that Asian children do not magically acquire knowledge—such as knowledge of words like *smock*—and of their potential identities, their classrooms, and the world. They need and benefit from thoughtful teaching, embedded in relationships that engender further complicated learning. Second, we ask for a rethinking of time as a key element in the success of children like Alice who become English speakers, readers, and writers over a period of years, an accomplishment that Stires's story about Alice reveals next.

Alice as Budding Scientist

One afternoon, after reading aloud a section in *Egg to Chick*, an early reader non-fiction book by Millicent Selsam (1970), Rosie, a first-grade teacher, conducts a discussion. She is trying to help her class make a connection between fertilization and pollination, the latter being a concept and word they understand from an earlier study of plants. She opens the discussion by wondering aloud what is created in the fertilization process. One of Rosie's many students from Chinese immigrant families is Alice, whose hand shoots up and stays up while she listens intently to Rosie. Using the illustrations in the text, Rosie retells the major points of the fertilization process that she recently read aloud. Finally, just as Rosie pauses before answering her own wondering, Alice calls out, "The egg!"

When Rosie then asks the class about what in plants is similar to this process, Alice replies, "Plants need sunlight," thus demonstrating some of her general knowledge about plants. To bring the students back to the question, Rosie asks them to think about pollen and what happens to it. Several children offer some thoughts, including Alice.

As Rosie and the class listen, Alice works her way to her answer, "Hum, the, the, the plants, the plants hum have…nectar is under the ovule?" She pauses and refers to a chart in the classroom. "I mean that [ovule] there's on the bottom. And the bee can't get to it. [pause] The bee helps to put seeds, uh pollen, on the other flowers [pause] and to turn to a seed in the ovule."

Next, Rosie restates Alice's last point and talks about the making of something new through both pollination and fertilization. Alice is so excited that she speaks at the same time as Rosie and only the word "plant" is audible. She repeats her statement, but still at the same time as Rosie is speaking. When the students discuss what develops new from a plant, Alice again shoots up her hand. This time she shouts, "Seed!" Her classmates all clap.

As is obvious from this anecdote, Alice, a first-grader from a Chinese-speaking family, is in the process of learning about important scientific content. It is also obvious that Alice is highly engaged in the process and is closely following her teacher's thinking, talking in tandem and even at the same time Rosie is talking about the subject. What may not be as obvious is that this conversation took place in an urban public school, although that may be concluded from the fact that many—in fact, most—of the children are from Chinese immigrant families. What is not obvious is that the teacher herself highly values content-area learning and integrates it into her teaching of literacy. It is also not obvious that Rosie is also a Chinese American who values her students' home languages (including Spanish) and cultures and uses them as a resource in her teaching and her students' learning. The anecdote focuses on Alice, whose learning in Rosie's classroom will be discussed in depth below; however, it is important to note that there was a similarly high level of social and academic engagement for Alice's classmates as well.

The Language "Explorer" View: A Theory of Practice

As we said, we plan later to theorize the overarching concepts of the "model minority myth" and time. Within that large frame, though, I next discuss a theory that is closer to the site of everyday classroom events. In David and Yvonne Freeman's transactional ESL theory (2001), also referred to as the language "explorer" theory, there is a triangular emphasis on *social interaction, content learning,* and *cultural sensitivity.* In my intense study of three first-grade English-language learners (ELLs), including Alice (Stires, 2002), the case-study students and their peers clearly benefited from all three elements. Although the classroom was not a designated ESL classroom and the teacher was not specifically aware of the Freemans' theory, her curriculum and instruction contained the elements that the Freemans identify.

The high level of social interaction present in the classroom was the result of the teacher's belief in the values of exploration and talk for young children. Social interaction was also embedded in the balanced literacy and hands-on math curricula that had been adopted by the district and the supplementary writing curriculum adopted by the school. In all areas of the formal curriculum and the informal give-and-take of the classroom, there was a constant amount of talk that was generated by the students. The talk was not only in relation to the teacher's questions but also consisted of ideas initiated by the students. They asked their own questions and sought answers to those questions. They thought out loud and they evaluated their own and others' conclusions, suggestions, and comments. In short, talk was the glue of the classroom and it underlay much of the curriculum. The children's behavior contrasts sharply with stereotypical images of quiet Asian American children who might not be comfortable with the majority language yet perform well only in math.

There had been recent focus on content-area learning in the professional development in the school. However, content-area studies were particularly important to Rosie herself because of her experiences with them during student teaching. Content was also important to her because of her own interest in the world around her and her strong desire to expose her students to that multidimensional world. According to the Freemans (2001), when the focus is off language and on content, language is more easily learned. The excitement generated in the students and the teacher by content-area studies certainly gave rise to a flow of language in English, primarily because it was the language of instruction, but also in Chinese and some Spanish, the first languages spoken by 95 percent, or all but one, of the students in the class.

Finally, Rosie, although only in her second year of teaching at this school (where 80 percent of the students came from Chinese-speaking homes and 15 percent from Spanish-speaking homes), clearly demonstrated cultural sensitivity. She is a Chinese American who also did not speak English before she went to school. She is now a Chinese American who, although she can communicate in Cantonese, regrets not keeping up with her native language learning. Hoping for a different story line for her students, she urged them to value and maintain their own cultural and linguistic resources.

Taken individually, these elements can be described, but the significance for ELLs is in the flow among the three: social interaction, content learning, and cultural sensitivity. That significance is highly complex and is orchestrated by the teacher in his or her relationships with students and their relationships with each other. In her classroom, Rosie provided opportunities and support for the children, trying to link their personal meanings to the instructional materials, activities, and discussions. There was content as well as skills and strategies to be learned, and it was content that Rosie cared about for her students. While she taught them in English, she also made it very clear to them that they had a rich heritage to value and draw from. Frequently, she referred to traditions and Chinese words or asked the children about them, particularly of the children from Spanish-speaking backgrounds. Throughout, Rosie was personally, as well as professionally, interested in her students and their learning.

The Classroom Community, Content, and the Learning of English

Teaching ELLs is one of the central concerns of today's teachers since over 3.5 million students come from non–English-speaking families. In my case study of three first-grade students (Stires, 2002), I provided a detailed description of their learning to speak, read, and write in English. Because our earlier study (Genishi, Stires, & Yung-Chan, 2001; Genishi et al., 2000) included the same three children, I was aware of their backgrounds as students and as ELLs. They came to preK speaking a dialect of Cantonese, which was also spoken by their teacher, Donna Yung-Chan. By the end of that year, one of the three, Kenneth, who often sought out the two English-dominant speakers in the class, had gained much in terms of his expressive capacities in English. The other two, Alice and James, used basic English words (like *bathroom*) and phrases only occasionally, but their receptive capacities in English were developing well. Overall, one of our most important findings was how scientific topics—the weather or the life cycle of a butterfly, for example—significantly influenced all the students' learning of English.

The first-grade study in Rosie's class began in the spring when the class was studying the genre of nonfiction in reading and writing workshop. It continued until the end of the year while the class engaged in two content-area topic studies on plants and birds. Although the teacher used some fiction and mixed genres, which the students called "half-and-half" books, the majority of the books used were nonfiction. At the same time as the class studied these topics, the students were to apply what they had learned about nonfiction and to engage in individual inquiry studies in which they became "experts."

Over the 6 years that I studied the children's learning, they developed expertise in multiple topics, a probable outcome of their early content-related apprenticeships with their first-grade teacher. In the third grade, they related what they had learned about trees to their first-grade study of plants. They also added information to their knowledge about such specific topics as bark as protection, age and growth according to tree rings, and the making of paper. By the fifth grade, they joined an after-school science club, and they all acknowledged that science was their favorite subject.

All of the classes had well-developed classroom libraries, and in first grade Rosie borrowed books from other teachers and the school library to provide her students with the materials that they needed. The students had real reasons to read, talk, and write about engaging content, and they did so intently. In addition, Rosie read aloud nonfiction in order for her students to increase their learning and for her to demonstrate how nonfiction works. She herself was engaged in learning with her students—something the Freemans (2005) advocate as part of their explorer model of language learning. Rosie conducted demonstrations and experiments for them, such as hatching chicks, and took them to botanical gardens and other places, like a vacant lot with members of the park service in order to set out plants. Further, she set up the classroom environment for the students to learn content. During the morning reading workshop, while Rosie read with guided reading groups, the students either worked at hands-on learning centers or read. At the centers they made observations, like measuring the growth of their red-bean plants or recording one of the newly hatched chick's movements. Their reading was done individually or in pairs about their expert topics, such as bears, insects, or snakes. During writing workshop, they read or wrote about their topics. Even after they began a poetry study, the students often continued to write about these topics.

The entire object of the science studies was to make meaning and learn about the world in and out of the classroom. Although all of the families were concerned about their children's education, many family members did not speak English, worked long hours for relatively little money, and lived in an urban environment. The kinds of experiences that they could provide were limited to walks in nearby neighborhoods and an occasional meal in a restaurant. However, the children's excitement about what they were learning led to some joint educational experiences. For example, James had his mother save all the seeds from her food preparations; Alice grew a scallion on her windowsill at home; and late one evening, Kenneth asked his mother if she could provide him with an egg carton so that he could make a model of a caterpillar. (She went out to the grocery store just to honor that request.) In addition, all three brought home nonfiction books, as well as their guided reading books, to share with their families what they had been learning in school. So, in addition to hands-on experiences in the classroom, the special science class, and the field, much of the information—sometimes shared at home—came to students vicariously through books in school.

Many of the students' families had limited financial resources, but this in no way meant that they were deprived of rich cultural experiences. Indeed, they continued to draw upon the funds of knowledge embedded in their families' cultures, as in the following example from third grade when once again Rosie was their teacher. The focus was again on content, but this time it was on social studies rather than science. The class and Rosie were planning a study about Egypt since more than half of the students had requested to study that country on their own. Rosie suggested that they do what the class in the popular Amber Brown series by Paula Danziger did: make passports and pretend that they were traveling to the country by plane. After explaining the use of the passport, she then referred to me because I happened to have my passport with me since I was getting a visa later that day. I talked briefly about a visa and showed the passport to the students by moving around to small clusters of them on the rug while Rosie made more plans for the country study.

Kenneth: I want to see the country the stamp's from.
Alice: I have a China stamp.

(The students talk about how the passport from China looks different from one from the United States.)

Alice: Those are different, those are different. United States passport [inaudible]. I have that too.

(Rosie calls the group together and clarifies the use of different passports.)

Alice: (Helping out with the clarification) The blue passports are, the blue passports are for when you are born in the United States.

Although there were many individual differences among the students, similar learning, attitudes, and values existed in the class, which truly was a community of learners (McNaughton, 2002). In order to examine the importance of the relationship between the teacher and her students, in this next section I focus specifically on Alice, who identified most strongly with her teacher.

Alice's Learning and Her Relationship with Her Teacher and What She Is Taught

Dyson (1990) concludes her article "Talking Up a Writing Community" by suggesting that our most important teaching tool may not be a strategy or a material but a stance of appreciation of children as interesting people with interesting things to share. She states, "Text, like talk, may thus further the child's sense of belonging, that feeling of community that makes our school lives together both personally satisfying and socially meaningful" (p. 113). One half of a relationship between a student and teacher is automatically ensured if the teacher adopts this stance. The other half of the relationship grows from the beginning of the school year as the child responds to such appreciation. Trust grows between the teacher and students and spills over into the developing relationships among the students themselves. Socialization that surrounds academics makes possible the particularity of information about the learning of English in classrooms like Rosie's. Language is used to communicate, to express, and to make sense of the world (Lindfors, 1990). And it all takes time.

When Rosie read over the transcriptions of the videotapes of Alice that I shared, she was impressed with Alice's ability to make connections, her commitment to ideas, and her willingness to learn. This high level of involvement had much to do with the social interaction that Rosie encouraged, as well as with the interesting science material that she explored with the students. It also had to do with how Alice saw herself in relation to Rosie, including the fact that both of them were Chinese American females. The following summary of Alice's learning shows where Alice's ability to make connections, to commit to ideas, and to be a willing learner took her as a first grader.

Alice read both for pleasure and to learn, and she socialized around her reading. Although most of her independent reading was for her expert projects (one was on bears and the other on chickens), she usually worked with a partner, her friend Matthew, also Chinese American and learning English. They discussed what they were learning and took turns reading and taking notes. In guided reading groups, where Rosie was always present, Alice enjoyed making observations and discussing them. Frequently, her comments were predictions and connections with the text, but she also made inferences and empathized with the characters. One day in a reading discussion of one of the differences between Arnold Lobel's characters, Frog and Toad, Alice made an announcement (/ represents a pause):

Alice: I'm like Frog.
Rosie: You don't like to stay in bed [like Toad]?
Alice: I don't, I don't, I don't. I love to get up. In the morning I'm hungry. And when I finish my breakfast / and then I tell my dad to wake up and go to work. And then he always be late for work // faster.

In addition, Alice both answered Rosie's questions about what took place in the stories that she read in the guided reading group and stated her wonderings and asked questions. For example, one day after reading about how birds that nest on the ground stay hidden, she asked, "Or the enemy gonna get them [the eggs]?"

Although by the end of the year Alice was reading with fluency (including attending to punctuation) and expression, her hesitancy to attack unknown words still persisted. For example, she often knew part of a word like "eat" in "treat" or "owl" in "growl" but was unable to blend it with the onset. (She did manage to read "embarrassed" because she knew the word "embryo"!) In writing, however, Alice was much less inhibited. She had developed a core of words that she could spell conventionally, and she used invented spelling liberally. In her writing self-evaluation interview, Alice stated that she had learned to spell "a lot of words" as well as learned a number of strategies for spelling unknown words.

Unlike reading, writing appeared to be more like play for Alice, and she became a prolific first-grade writer. She wrote in many different genres and often mixed genres as she produced texts (McNaughton, 2002). Although she attended to the lessons that Rosie taught about writing, such as the use of repetition in poetry writing (Figure 4.1), she clearly had her own agenda and often wrote letters, stories, or lists that were unrelated to lessons.

Writing became a habit for Alice by the end of first grade. She also did quite a bit of writing at home and used writing when she played school. At the parent interview, her mother described (through a translator) how Alice took the pages of a used calendar and made charts like the ones that her teacher made and hung on the walls of her classroom at school. In the classroom Alice often attempted to be Rosie's assistant. At home, she was Rosie.

Alice listened so closely to her teacher's directions, explanations, information, and questions that she often anticipated what Rosie would be saying. One day during interactive writing when Rosie brought out a large cutout of a talking bubble for an announcement to be posted by the cage of the class lovebird, Alice asked if it was a thinking bubble. Then she corrected herself, "A talking bubble—'cause before I notice talking and thinking bubble are the same, but

My Bookbag

My bookbag my bookbag

where is my bookbag?

Bookbag bookbag

where are you hiding?

Come out come out

where ever you are?

By A_____

Figure 4.1 Alice's poem.

I know what you're thinking so I change my mind." During guided reading sessions when Rosie introduced a new text, Alice kept up a conversation as she listened and responded to each point that Rosie made. Similarly, she followed Rosie's reading aloud so closely that she was always ready to raise her hand and respond to questions or make comments. This pattern continued into third grade when Alice once again was Rosie's student, and also into fifth when she had a new teacher who was in her first year of teaching.

Speaking was highly encouraged and there were various parts of the day devoted exclusively to time for the students to express their observations and feelings, try out their ideas, and connect with others. Alice used this time to great advantage, both during "Morning Meeting" and "Good News" time (a meeting time after lunch and recess for the students to share a kindness displayed to them by a classmate). During one Good News session, Alice had the following to report:

> Last time Matthew told me that the fly was eating my lunch and he helped me to shoo the fly away. Today in the lunch room Janie had a zip-up bag, and I didn't have a zip-up bag and I said, "Can I put my book in your zip-up bag?" and she let me and I say, "Thank you."

Talk surrounded all of the academics as well, and the students engaged in reading and writing workshops (which were integrated with their content studies) for relatively long periods. They were encouraged to use oral language, in which they were more proficient than in their written language. Sometimes they used it to make observations or speculations, sometimes to compare ideas, and sometimes to ask questions, as is evident in these examples. In the first, Alice is candling the incubating eggs (examining them using a strong light) with Rosie and a few classmates.

Alice: Can't see anything yet. // Maybe it's a chick. // We don't see any chick. We don't see any chick.

(Rosie repositions the egg.)

Alice: We can't see any chick. Maybe the chick died in there.

(Alice repeats her statement directly to Rosie.)

Rosie: I don't think so.
Alice: (Looking more closely) Oh, I saw something, I saw something, I saw something. That the chick. That's the chick.
Rosie: I think that that dark spot is the eye or maybe an air bubble.
Alice: (Backing up from the candling station, where the eggs were examined) In the first place [first time candling] when I saw egg number two, I saw a eye and a body.

In the second example, after James shared what he had learned about plants (the bee drinks the nectar, and the pollen sticks to the bee's legs), Alice asked him a question:

Alice: Why do, hum, hum / is it that hum / why why do pollen stick sticks on bees' feet? Why pollen sticks / who do pollen sticks on bees' feet? Please.

James: 'Cause pollen is sticky.

Alice: Nope. Oh, I know sticky, I know what's the sticky one. The pistil.

Brandon: It's 'cause the bee's legs are fuzzy.

Finally, Alice used language, specifically her English, to reason. After a shared reading of a journal about chicks, there was a discussion about how to tell the sex of the chicks, with several children offering their theories. At its conclusion, Alice, who had been quiet and listening to the discussion, added the most conclusive evidence, "Miss Young—I have something else. Hum, then when the chick come out, and when the chicks are big, and then the one chick have eggs, then you know a girl or boy."

Alice's strong identification with Rosie was evident in how she adopted both her role as a teacher and sometimes the very words that she used, such as remarking, "Someone said something smart," in recognition of another student's good idea, just as Rosie would have. Alice was not only aware of Rosie as her teacher, she was also aware of her as a person. One day when Rosie was upset over something, Alice reached out, patted her, and said, "Cool down," in a caring, but offhanded manner that one of her teenaged sisters may have used with her. She made things and gave them to Rosie, such as the colored eggs that she dyed during spring break, and after first grade ended she wrote to Rosie. She later had the good fortune to have Rosie as her teacher again in third grade and is still in contact with her today.

Cultural Sensitivity, Critical Perspectives, and Social Justice

Since the term *cultural sensitivity* focuses on the teaching rather than the learning in the classroom, it is important to examine what Rosie did that made it possible to claim that her teaching was culturally sensitive. In addition to communicating with the parents, Rosie showed her cultural sensitivity in three major ways. First of all, she bridged for them by restating things in Cantonese (Fu, 1995) when she determined that they did not understand her in English. Conversely, when she thought that there was something that they could teach her in Cantonese or Spanish, she asked them to do so. Second, she made references to knowledge, traditions, and customs that she knew were present in their homes (Brock 2001; Moll, 1999). Finally, she encouraged the children to use and to study their home language and appreciate their culture when they were under pressure to drop it in favor of American culture and English (Fillmore, 2000; Tse, 2001).

Along with the other students, Alice, in turn, enjoyed bridging for Rosie when she asked the students what an English word, such as *veins* or *tweezers,* was in Chinese. By doing so, Rosie was not only learning more Chinese, but she was also validating her students and empowering them to display their knowledge. Too, Alice and the other students appeared to enjoy sharing their home traditions, such as telling about how tea eggs are made. Although Rosie shared many of these traditions, here she was sharing power by having the children describe in their voices what those traditions and customs were. She provided the necessary support, the time, and the opportunity.

The encouragement that Rosie gave to the students to use and study their home language and appreciate their culture was of great significance but less easily threaded into the language of the classroom. She spent at least one Morning Meeting time talking seriously to the students about her own experience of losing her first language, how she came to regret it, and her efforts to regain the language. Alice's response was silence. She had openly expressed a dislike of Chinese with a preference for English, and she had resisted her mother's efforts to enroll her in Chinese school. Rosie was introducing her to an entirely new perspective. Following that meeting, Rosie made occasional references to the topic, and each time Alice, uncharacteristically, had nothing to say. She just listened, apparently trying to incorporate these ideas into her life.

Alice, like the majority of the students, lived in an insulated community of Chinese immigrants. She identified with her immigrant family and their customs and traditions. She used her home language with them unself-consciously. In contradiction, her favoring of English and resistance to Chinese came from her admiration of her three teenaged sisters, who spoke English, and from television, which was popular in most of the children's homes. However, it also came from her positive classroom community where she was learning in English, with which she and her classmates strongly identified. The complexity of ideas that Rosie offered about maintaining her home language and culture appeared to be something that Alice did not understand as readily as other ideas Rosie presented, but she did not pursue her original position of favoring English after Rosie's talk.

Summing Up and Stepping Back: Theorizing to Rethink a Myth, Time, and No Child Left Behind

Looking back to the Freemans's (2001) three-part theory about language learning, we saw a number of elements underlying Rosie's demonstrations of cultural sensitivity and, by extension, her vision of social justice—including her ways of leaving no child behind. We saw opportunities for meaningful *social interaction* and verbal and material support available to all students. Power was shared within the classroom, and there was caring (Noddings, 1992) between the teacher and students. We also observed science in the foreground, a *content area* that is seldom taught to students who are "at risk" in underresourced communities (as Siegel and Lukas pointed out in chapter 3 of this volume; Kozol, 2005). Rosie's approach to not leaving children behind was intimately linked to expanding the content of her curriculum, to invite students to learn the ideas of science while simultaneously learning how to read and write. In addition, she used varied and differentiated instruction for all the students in the form of demonstrations, presentation, conferences, and practice. Finally, Rosie showed *cultural sensitivity*: she explicitly acknowledged and valued diversity within the classroom and told students about the potential for enriched lives by maintaining one's home language and culture.

Alice received a quality, socially just education in America, the country to which her parents had chosen to immigrate, to work, and to prosper. She learned to speak and listen in English as well as read and write, also a choice her parents made. Her learning of English was deeply embedded in the overall learning experience so that she did not run the risk of not learning about important content while learning another language. It is socially just in that her linguistic and cultural resources were honored so that she would value and maintain them, although there will continue to be outside pressures to assimilate into the English-dominated world. Having a teacher whom she cared for and who cared for her as a student and as a person, one who appreciated her and in whom she placed her trust, ensured that her educational experience was socially just. However, not all English learners are as fortunate as Alice and her classmates. Many are subjected to the choice of programs over people, driven by legislation or marketing claims of "best practice."

The in-depth look at Alice in Rosie's room was framed by an explorer theory of language learning (Freeman & Freeman, 2001), a theory of practice that well matched significant aspects of Rosie's teaching and her students' learning. We next step out of Rosie's room and look through broader frames to consider the model minority myth and the elusive construct of time as they relate to Alice and her friends.

The model minority myth (Lee, 1996), like all myths, contains some facts and some fiction—rather like the "half-and-half" books that Rosie's children named. Asian-heritage students do sometimes excel in school; they sometimes assimilate into white middle-class culture; they sometimes speak nothing but Standard English. But some Asian-heritage students never finish high school; some join gangs and actively resist the middle class; and some become adults who are uncomfortable speaking English (Chae, 2004; Zhou & Lee, 2004). The details just presented about the learning in Rosie's room suggest that real-life students like Alice are not easily mythologized. Even if they turn out to be model students, their identities as Asian-heritage students or Asian Americans are neither instantly formed nor reducible to straightforward types.

To appreciate the fluid and complex quality of Alice's identity as a "model student," we can view her briefly through the lens of postcolonial theory. Postcolonial theorists address ways in which colonized and, more generally, minority cultures are oppressed and represented as the "other" (Bhabha, 1994; Said, 1994), as racialized, exotic, and ultimately inferior. This kind of representation seems to be at odds with the model minority myth, which many would claim is full of compliments about Asians. Yet the myth operates as a myth to define Asians in essentializing ways, such as "studious," "conforming," and paradoxically "not of color," or "invisible," as they blend into majority culture without a distinctive cultural or political identity. Postcolonialists work to counter such essences when they argue that the colonized or "othered" can create their own in-between spaces between cultures, areas of hybridity so well illuminated in memoir (Mura, 1992) and fiction (Jen, 1999; Smith, 2000). In those spaces, even young children can resist being defined by others; as the postcolonialists say, they can "return the gaze" of the majority/dominant group. Thus Alice's favoring of English and resistance to Chinese school may be subtle forms of her acceptance of "othering." She further did not announce, "I am Chinese," as her friend Kenneth did, or state, "I'm a Chinese guy," like James. That is, she did not appear to return the gaze. Instead she embraced her new classroom community and chose to use English there. At the same time, she was happy to share her knowledge of the Chinese language and customs in Rosie's room. She identified with her family and used her home language with her parents and grandparents, as well as in the neighborhood. Thus she willingly participated in an in-between space where she displayed her own hybridity, a hybridity that was nuanced enough to include speaking English in school and speaking Cantonese and enacting Chinese customs with family members outside the classroom. She appeared to return the gaze outside of Rosie's field of vision. And who can say whether in the future Alice will more intently return it by remembering Rosie's first-grade talks about retaining or reviving the Chinese aspects of one's identity?

Nuance is reflected throughout Alice's story, a story that like all others unfolds over time. Recall how we would have placed her on the "quiet children" list at the end of her preK year. Whereas some of her classmates were fluent English—and Cantonese—speakers by then, Alice was just beginning to say some things in English. In kindergarten she used English in the public arena of the classroom but Cantonese with her friends and tablemates. At the end of the year when writing what she learned in kindergarten, she wrote that she learned "the English." In the first grade, Alice's English was fluent but still developing, as we would expect, further evidence that Asian-heritage children, like others, learn language over time and, even after several years of schooling, may be working through the grammar of English. For example, note the structure of the following sentences, presented earlier about knowing whether a chick is male or female:

> *Alice* (to Rosie and the class): I have something else. Hum, then when the chick come out [of the egg], and when the chicks are big, and then the one chick have eggs, then you know a girl or boy.

The grammar is not elegant or standard, but the idea that only a female chicken can lay eggs is accurate and understandable.

Time would pass before Alice's English became "native-like." Eventually she, like her peers, incorporated many "Americanisms" in her speech and was interested in many aspects of American youth culture. In general, teachers did not make a point of correcting her errors in speaking because of a focus on communication, but they did give her information about a few salient grammar issues in writing, as Peregoy and Boyle (2005) recommend. Much of what happened in that in-between, hybridized space over a number of years is invisible to us; yet we know that this young "model" student needed the time to learn about school, speak Cantonese there, begin to speak English, and improve her English. In other words, she built up social capital, enabling her to make her own sociolinguistic choice as to what language she preferred and what kind of student she would be. She chose along the way—to be quiet, to be watchful, to be Rosie's helper, to be a speaker of English in the classroom. And she was well supported along the way by teachers whose curriculum was expansive, not restricted to narrowly defined literacy or math, and by her family, including older, English-speaking sisters. Alice's progress, and that of her classmates, was impressive but not mythic. She relied and thrived on Rosie's teaching and the social support Rosie and Alice's peers offered.

Alice also had the good fortune of being in a school where teachers and administrators framed time in ways that we would call learner or child friendly. As a consequence, ELLs like Alice had a period of years to become competent speakers, readers, and writers of "Englishes." To appreciate the kind of time that Alice and her peers enjoyed, we look through another theoretical lens, that of "panoptical time" (Lesko, 2001, p. 35; see Foucault, 1979, for a connection to the "panoptical gaze"), which "emphasizes the endings toward which youth are to progress and places individual adolescents [or children] into a sociocultural narrative that demands 'mastery' without movement or effect." We suggest that in the current educational moment, we live in panoptical time, which captures learning and experience in a highly compressed way, defined by adults who focus on test scores that show mastery of a narrow set of skills. In fact, we could call it "No Child Left Behind time" or "NCLB time." With its emphasis on Adequate Yearly Progress measured by standardized test scores, NCLB time can be seen on a simple chart, showing test scores over a period of years, for Alice from preK through grade 5. The scores demonstrate a particular kind of "mastery" of reading or math skills and constitute the "effect" of specific curricula, none of which would envelop knowledge of science or other broad curricular content that Rosie taught. Of course, there is nothing in the chart of scores that captures the caring, relational aspects of Rosie's curriculum that Alice responded to and wove into her own life narrative in and out of school, nor would it show Alice's or her friends' growing knowledge of science and social studies. And it would certainly not capture their pleasure and verbal excitement, their words tripping over Rosie's, as they try to articulate their learning.

We have offered this story as one way to counter mythologizing children like Alice. Like many other children who live in underresourced neighborhoods with a high proportion of immigrant families, she is neither at risk of academic failure nor simply a model student because she is Asian American. Instead, she has demonstrated hybridity and complexity as a learner in a school where teachers were able to teach in richly detailed and challenging ways. Alice, Rosie, and company wove together a broad curriculum with feeling, talk, and funds of academic and local knowledge. As we conclude, we hope to act on behalf of social justice by continuing to focus on broad curricular content for English learners; on the real time in which curriculum, relationships, and children's learning unfold; and on the need to counteract the imposition of NCLB and its panoptical time.

Note

There are countless activist groups that rethink and redo educational policies and practices, many in our local areas. Here are three, with a national/U.S. reach, that are accessible online and increasingly relevant to the education of young children:

- *The Educator Roundtable*—educatorroundtable.org: This extensive online organization mobilized around inequities in No Child Left Behind legislation, with the aim of improving future legislation.
- *The National Center for Fair and Open Testing (FairTest)*—fairtest.org: Its purpose has been to end the misuse of standardized testing through advocacy and focused publications.
- *Rethinking Schools*—rethinkingschools.org: This is a nonprofit publisher that focuses on issues of equity/inequity as they relate to the continual reform of elementary and secondary education.

References

Bhabha, H. K. (1994). *The location of culture*. New York: Routledge.

Brock, C. (2001). Serving English language learners: Placing learners learning on center stage. *Language Arts, 78*(5), 467–475.

Chae, H. S. (2004). Talking back to the Asian model minority discourse: Korean-origin youth experiences in high school. *Journal of Intercultural Studies, 25*(1), 59–73.

Dyson, A. H. (1990). Talking up a writing community: The role of talk in learning to write. In D. Rubin & S. Hynds (Eds.), *Perspectives on talking and learning* (pp. 99–114). Urbana, IL: National Council of Teachers of English.

Fillmore, L. W. (2000). Loss of family languages; Should educators be concerned? *Theory Into Practice, 39*(4), 203–210.

Foucault, M. (1979). *Discipline and punish: The birth of the prison* (Trans. A. Sheridan). New York: Vintage.

Freeman, D., & Freeman, Y. (2001). *Between worlds: Access to second language* acquisition. Portsmouth, NH: Heinemann Educational Books.

Fu, D. (1995). *"My trouble is my English": Asian students and the American dream.* Portsmouth, NH: Heinemann Educational Books.

Genishi, C., Stires, S., & Yung-chan, D. (2001). Writing in an integrated curriculum: Prekindergarten English language learners as symbol makers [Special issue]. In A. H. Dyson (Ed.), *Elementary School Journal, 101*(4), 399–416.

Genishi, C., Yung-Chan, D., & Stires, S. (2000). Talking their way into print: English language learners in a prekindergarten classroom. In D. S. Strickland & L. M. Morrow (Eds.), *Beginning reading and writing* (pp. 66–80). New York: Teachers College Press.

Hohmann, M, Banet, B., & Weikart, D. (1979). *Young children in action.* Ypsilanti, MI: High/Scope Press.

Jen, G. (1999). *Who's Irish? Stories.* New York: Vintage.

Kozol, J. (2005). *The shame of the nation.* New York: Crown.

Lee, S. J. (1996). *Unraveling the "model minority" stereotype: Listening to Asian American youth.* New York: Teachers College Press.

Lesko, N. (2001). Time matters in adolescence. In K. Hultqvist & G. Dahlberg (Eds.), *Governing the child in the new millennium* (pp. 35–67). New York: RoutledgeFalmer.

Lindfors, J. W. (1990). Speaking creatures in the classroom. In D. Rubin & S. Hynds (Eds.), *Perspectives on talking and learning* (pp. 21–39). Urbana, IL: National Council of Teachers of English.

McNaughton, S. (2002). *Meeting of minds.* Wellington, New Zealand: Learning Media.

Moll, L. (1999, June). *Funds of knowledge: Rethinking culture and schooling.* Paper presented at the Beyond Tomorrow: From Sociopolitical Awareness to Practice, and Back Again conference, New York.

Mura, D. (1992). *Turning Japanese: Memoirs of a sansei.* New York: Anchor/Doubleday.

No Child Left Behind Act of 2001 (Pub. L. 107–110), 115 Stat. 1425 (2002). Retrieved from www.ed.gov/nclb/landing.jhtml May 24, 2007.

Noddings, N. (1992). *The challenge to care in schools: An alternative approach to education.* New York: Teachers College Press.

Peregoy, S. F., & Boyle, O. F. (2005). *Reading, writing, and learning in ESL: A resource book for K–12 teachers.* New York: Pearson Education.

Said, E. (1994). From Orientalism. In P. Williams & L. Chrisman (Eds.), *Colonial discourse and post-colonial theory: A reader* (pp. 132–149). New York: Columbia University Press.

Selsam, M. E. (1970). *Egg to chick.* New York: Harper Trophy.

Smith, Z. (2000). *White teeth: A novel.* New York: Vintage.

Stires, S. (2002). Building another world: Three first graders' learning of English language and literacy in school. *Dissertation Abstracts International.* (UMI No. 072699)

Tse, L. (2001). *"Why don't they learn English? Separating fact from fallacy in the U.S. language debate.* New York: Teachers College Press.

Zhou, M., & Lee, J. (2004). Introduction: The making of culture, identity, and ethnicity among Asian American youth. In J. Lee & M. Zhou (Eds.), *Asian American youth: Culture, identity and ethnicity* (pp. 1–30). New York: Routledge.

5

Teaching Caring

Supporting Social and Emotional Learning in an Inclusive Early Childhood Classroom

SUSAN L. RECCHIA

What does it mean to be part of an early childhood classroom community where all of the children feel included and cared for? How do children's ways of being with their peers and their teachers reflect these feelings? What do teachers do within their everyday classroom practices to build and facilitate an inclusive social community for children with diverse learning needs? Theoretically at the heart of the early childhood curriculum and of great concern to early childhood teachers, these issues are often left unaddressed in the most widely used methods of differentiated instruction for young children with disabilities in early childhood special education (Safford, Sargent, & Cook, 1994).

Special education curricula, which emerge out of a long tradition of deficit-oriented assessment practices, discrete skills-based teaching strategies, and behavior modification techniques, have created a separate and unequal set of classroom experiences for children with disabilities. Young children who process information and respond to others in ways that require curricular adaptations are all too often viewed as unable to access the general education curriculum. Thus, children with learning differences frequently spend their classroom hours engaged in a different set of activities than those of their nonlabeled peers. Their assessed need for "special education," which until recently was likely to be delivered within a segregated, self-contained, early childhood classroom, has left them marginalized from the broader social context of classroom-based experience deemed so important for early learning and development.

Even within inclusive settings, children with disabilities frequently experience a different curriculum from their "typical" peers (Odom et al., 2004). Recommended teaching strategies for early childhood special education assume that children with developmental disabilities respond best to clear behavioral approaches to social learning (Guralnick, Hammond, Connor, & Neville, 2006). Unlike many early childhood general educators who work to create classrooms that allow children to explore the social environment freely, early childhood special educators are more likely to assume that they must teach particular children with disabilities how to engage socially apart from their peers, through direct, often one-on-one, instruction. As a consequence, children receiving special education services are less likely to experience opportunities to take part in a play-based curriculum, to express their own ideas and have them honored, or to feel they are a part of a larger social peer group in the classroom (Erwin & Guintini, 2000; Recchia & Lee, 2004).

Recent changes in special education laws and policies have created mandates for inclusive education beginning in early childhood. As more young children with disabilities and diverse learning needs are being included in general early childhood classrooms, both early childhood general and early childhood special educators are being challenged to rethink their ideas about creating environments that will foster equitable social learning opportunities and an inclusive sense of community for all of the children in their classrooms. New models of practice are needed that go beyond creating Individualized Education Plans for children with disabilities that encourage separate learning experiences and segregate them from their peers, even within inclusive classrooms.

In this chapter, I describe the ways that one preschool teacher, whom I call Kathy, approached teaching and learning in her integrated early childhood classroom. I will draw primarily on data from observations of two children in Kathy's room, Joey and Maria. The classroom was first observed as part of a larger study (Recchia, 1998; 1999; Recchia & Soucacou, 2002; Recchia & Soucacou, 2006) that looked at nine preschool special education classrooms to explore: (1) the emergent social experiences of young children with special needs in the context of daily classroom activities, (2) what teachers do to facilitate social experiences and build community in their early childhood special education classrooms, and (3) how the experiences of these children and teachers help us better understand the process of building socially supportive classroom environments for young children with special needs. For this chapter, I look more closely at the ways in which social experiences unfold for the adults and children within the day-to-day activities of Kathy's integrated preschool classroom. My intent is to raise questions about issues that challenge teachers and young children as they co-construct the social environments of their classrooms. Through careful analysis of the interactive social experiences that unfold in Kathy's classroom, I hope to offer insight, new ideas, and expanded possibilities for imagining inclusive, caring early childhood classroom communities that nurture social and emotional understanding for all children.

Background and Theoretical Framework

Studies of young children with disabilities have focused on particular social skills deficits as isolated events without investigating the complex ways that behaviors take on meaning within a dynamic classroom environment. Teachers' ways of responding to children within a larger group context as facilitators of social experience are rarely explored (File, 1994; Mahoney &

Wheeden, 1999; Taylor, Peterson, McMurray-Schwartz, & Guillou, 2002), and recommendations for practice tend to focus on direct instruction to decrease deficits for individual children. These findings counter what research tells us about many early childhood general education settings, where teachers have been found to spend much less time than their special education colleagues directly instructing young children in social skills (File, 1994). Rather, what has been shown to influence children's interactions with peers and their general sense of well-being in the classroom is the overall quality of teachers' relationships with their young students (Arnett, 1989; Howes, Matheson, & Hamilton, 1994; Kontos & Wilcox-Herzog, 1997; Pianta, 1997; Sroufe, 1983). These findings have been slow to translate into the field of early childhood special education, where there has been a more limited focus on the affective components of teacher-child interaction in both research and personnel preparation (Rimm-Kaufman, Voorhees, Snell, & La Paro, 2003).

The teacher's role in supporting young children's social experiences is unique because it is the teacher, as opposed to a parent, who is more often present to help when children are facing social challenges in large groups (Webster-Stratton, 1999). Greenspan (2003) has emphasized the importance of sensitive, nurturing, and individually tailored child-caregiver interactions as the basis for high-quality early care and education for all children. These interactions include affective engagements to help children solve problems and regulate behavior, reciprocal verbal interactions with responsive and sensitive adults, and ongoing adult support for the development of peer interactions. Taking a more global perspective on young children's social experiences in their early childhood classrooms might also include how teachers build communities in which children regard each other with respect, interest, and trust.

Recommended practices in early childhood special education, with their strong emphasis on skills-based interventions as the basis for teaching and learning, have provided little encouragement or guidance for teachers to help them consider more holistic ways of approaching social and emotional learning with the young children in their classrooms. In fact, my own field observations over many years have revealed very few early childhood classrooms serving children with disabilities that operate in this way. Despite a growing body of literature that ideologically supports more naturalistic approaches to working with children with disabilities in inclusive settings, teachers often inadvertently discourage spontaneous social engagements in their efforts to redirect inappropriate social behaviors, taking away the very opportunities they hope to create for young children with disabilities (Kliewer et al., 2004).

What was different in Kathy's room was the way that the teachers accepted children's differences as part of their unique ways of being and were able to embrace individual characteristics in ways that support the importance of human relationships in learning (Noddings, 1994). Noddings describes a "caring curriculum" as one that is relational in nature, where caring teachers not only respond to individual children in ways that make them feel cared for, but also in so doing, they model what it means to care for others for the whole group (Noddings, 2002). By creating and nurturing a classroom environment where children were encouraged to be aware of each other's needs, Kathy was able to promote relationships that led to mutual caring. As Kathy modeled positive language and attitudes toward difference, the diverse children in her classroom were affirmed in their peer relationships. By creating a classroom discourse that dialogically and pedagogically explored and embraced differences, Kathy was able to nurture relationships within the classroom, which helped lead her students toward a broader appreciation of difference (Baglieri & Knopf, 2004). In Kathy's room, true inclusion came about as she created a social environment where individuality and diversity could coincide within a caring community.

Description of the Program, Participants, and Procedures

Setting and Participants

Kathy's classroom was housed in a large, urban, early childhood special education preschool that served children from 2 through 5 years of age. Altogether there were 12 classrooms in the program, and Kathy's was one of two prekindergarten integrated classrooms that served children with and without special needs inclusively, with approximately one-half of the children having diagnosed disabilities. There were 12 children in Kathy's room at the time the study took place. Kathy was a fairly new teacher with one year of previous experience. She had a master's degree in early childhood special education. Kathy worked with an assistant teacher, Doris, who had a bachelor's degree.

Originally, four children were closely observed in Kathy's classroom, but this chapter will highlight the experiences of two, Maria and Joey. These children were selected because of their particular characteristics and the ways in which their individual needs seemed to call on Kathy to be especially creative in her social responses to them. Characteristics of the teachers, children, and classroom are further articulated in Table 5.1.

Data Collection Procedures

This study was conceptualized as a vehicle for looking at child and teacher social behavior in context. Data collected through naturalistic classroom observations were coded and analyzed for emergent themes within a qualitative framework. Qualitative methodology was selected for its ability to support a more in-depth look into the complexities of classroom interactions (Merriam, 2001).

Observations took place during the morning hours when young children were most actively engaged. Observers began by conducting two 2-hour visits to each classroom, observing the context and making themselves familiar to the teachers and children. Following these initial visits, each study child was observed for two 1-hour sessions on two separate occasions during daily classroom activities.

Table 5.1 Kathy's Classroom

Classroom Context	Adults	One head teacher and one regular classroom assistant. Other adults are occasionally present in the classroom, such as therapists or other observers.	
	Children	Attendance ranges from 10 to 12 children on any given day. Integrated classroom in which half of the children have diagnosed disabilities. Children's disabilities primarily include speech and language delays. All children are mobile and have some functional oral language. Children demonstrate a range of competencies across cognitive, social, and language domains.	
	Classroom Activity	Organized, semistructured free-play periods throughout the day. Many developmentally appropriate activities; some more academically oriented planned activities. Most work done in small groups, but some whole-group activities such as "circle time" each day.	
Children's Characteristics	Name	Joey	Maria
	Age	4 years, 2 months	4 years, 9 months
	Diagnosis	Pervasive developmental disorder (PPD-NOS)	Typically developing English-language learner
	Profile	Happy, playful male child who experiences difficulties in relating and communicating with peers and adults in the classroom.	Verbal and social female child who enjoys classroom activities and social interaction with peers and adults.
Teacher's Characteristics	Age	(not provided)	
	Experience	1 year's experience	
	Curricular Priorities	Rates ability to meet children's social needs at 4 on a Scale of 1 (low) to 5 (high).	
		Ranks importance of social development as two out of six areas of development.	
		Feels least effective strategy is "Sticking to rote learning."	
		Feels an important thing to be added to her curriculum to enhance students' progress is "More books to stimulate new ideas and pictures for the children to learn from and share with each other."	

Continuous running records of children's social behaviors, including initiations and responses from teachers and peers, were recorded for each child. Because several children were observed within each classroom during the original study, our observation process entailed about 12 hours in Kathy's room over the course of 6 different days. This process allowed us to see the overall classroom dynamics and interactions between teachers and all of the children in the classroom. Two observers were involved in this process, which provided an opportunity for comparing notes and sharing reflections on what we saw. As soon as possible after each observation, observers expanded their notes into a detailed transcript for later coding.

Once all classroom observations were completed, teachers were asked to respond to a brief questionnaire, which included requests for demographic information and several questions about their curricular priorities (see Kathy's responses in Table 5.1). Responses were later reviewed alongside the classroom observations to find points of agreement and disagreement.

Coding Procedures

Transcripts were first reviewed by two researchers independently to establish a sense of children's and teachers' overall social experiences. Each researcher created a summary of experience for each child, focusing on social behavior with peers and adults. The researchers then compared and discussed their findings and developed a descriptive profile for each child. These preliminary steps allowed the researchers to immerse themselves in the data and to gain an overview of the children's classroom social experience, guiding the emergent themes analysis.

Five themes were ultimately agreed upon within which anecdotes from the running records could be categorized. These included: (1) adaptations made by teachers that helped support individual children's positive social experiences, (2) positive emotional connections made between teachers and students, (3) sustained negative interactions between teachers and students, (4) ways that teachers promote positive social engagements and interactions with peers, and (5) ways in which teachers help their students with conflict resolution. Kathy's room stood out in part because so few negative interactions were observed between the teachers and the children.

Social and Emotional Life in Kathy's Classroom

On my first visit to Kathy's classroom I was surprised by many things. Having spent the year observing the ways that early childhood special education teachers help children build relationships in nine different classrooms (Recchia, 1998, 1999; Recchia & Soucacou, 2002), I thought I had a good sense of the challenges that teachers face and how difficult they were to overcome. In every classroom I had spent time in, both integrated and self-contained, there were children who could challenge even the calmest of teachers into losing control and responding in less than supportive ways. More often than not, within a short time of observing, something would happen that would remind me of my own worst moments as a preschool special education teacher, and I would find myself torn between taking the teacher's and the child's perspectives. Often the issues were related to classroom management and what seemed to be the teacher's concern about maintaining order and harmony, and focused particularly on those children who were less responsive or compliant. But Kathy's room was different.

> Kathy has a very warm demeanor and does lots of explaining with the children. They have just returned from the park and are having a hard time sitting still and waiting for their turns—several are calling out. But Kathy seems very comfortable with this. She manages the group easily and seems very relaxed. All of the children participate in singing the "Days of the Week" song. Kathy comments spontaneously about their performance. She helps those who need help getting their chairs to the table for lunch, and gently reminds the children who need reminding of the "rules." For example, today it is Bobby's turn to be the helper. When Stefan tries to take over, Kathy lets him know simply and clearly that Bobby is the helper. The children ask her openly for what they want and accept her gentle reminders without much resistance. She freely dispenses appropriate praise for children's accomplishments (for one child, this is following Grandma's request to take two bites of a sandwich before eating a treat) and enthusiastic interest in their food from home (such as Stefan's ravioli). Her positive affect seems to be reflected in the children. (Observation notes, first visit, May 28, 1997)

It was common practice for Kathy to join the children at the lunch table and engage them in conversation, defining this time as social in nature. Although the other teachers I observed often sat with the children during lunch, their responses were seldom as playful. Kathy asked questions and, if the children gave silly responses, she played along. She very naturally used a lot of humor to engage the children, something that I had not seen many teachers do in other classrooms. In her interactions with the children, Kathy provided support for their ideas and initiations, even when they might be considered "inappropriate." For example, when Brad talked with his mouth full, Kathy made light of this, playfully reinforcing his language.

At the same time, she seemed to make great efforts to call children's attention to the things that she wanted them to notice, anticipating how they might respond to certain situations later. For example, she was sure to let Joey know that she was placing his lollypop into his lunchbox by calling his attention to her action, and waiting for his responsive nod. After observing for awhile, it became clear to me that Kathy was systematically pairing nonverbal actions with verbal responses for the children with language delays. She did this in such a natural way for all the children that it took a while to see it as a specific strategy.

Another way that Kathy naturally accommodated children's differences was by allowing children to move at their own pace. Unlike the constant hurrying along that happens in so many preschool special education classrooms (Goodman, 1992), Kathy seemed comfortable having the children start and end activities at different times. When they did assemble for full-group activities, they often worked in small groups, and some would finish their work before others. She was careful to have alternative activities ready for the children to engage in. Sometimes children just watched the others for a while before joining in. The atmosphere in the classroom was loose and easy.

As in most preschool classrooms, situations arose that could have easily led to conflict or hurt feelings. Kathy had a way of explaining things to children in anticipation of this, such as when Anton watched as several friends ate pieces of a cookie that Jason brought in his lunch. When Anton asked if he could have some, Kathy gently explained that "Jason gave a little piece to Stefan and a little piece to Donny and now there is no more." When she talked to the children she made sure to make eye contact and to be on their level, personalizing the interactions. Children in this classroom spoke openly about their happiness at being in school. I heard one child spontaneously say, "I'd like to be in Kathy's school for ever and ever!"

A number of children in Kathy's room were English-language learners. Most spoke Spanish at home, and Kathy used Spanish with several of them in the classroom. She switched easily between English and Spanish, especially at times when it seemed the children needed help with contextual understanding. There were many signs that Kathy had made connections with the children's families, as she often commented in ways that bridged home and school experiences. One child, Maria, had arrived that year from Poland. Although neither Kathy nor her assistant spoke or understood Polish, they honored Maria's desire to share words or songs in her native language from time to time.

> Kathy asks Maria, "Are you going to speak Polish today?" She responds, "I think so," and proceeds to speak to the other children in Polish. She obviously has done this before, but they all watch her with interest. Doris (the assistant teacher) appears to have understood Maria, and asks her, "Did you tell us about your friends Luca, Patrick, and Olivia?" Maria answers, "Yes." (Observation notes, June 3, 1997)

In Kathy's room, children's unique contributions were honored in simple but important ways. When Bobby brought in a book that he had made at home with his family the night before, Kathy made a point to have him share it with the class at circle time. The pages had letters on them but no real words.

Bobby shared his complicated story about children getting hurt and going to the hospital and the police coming. Kathy said, "That's a great story, Bobby," and told the children that "He wrote it all by himself at home last night."

Kathy and her assistant teacher, Doris, had a careful way of communicating. They often touched base with each other briefly to stay in synch in a friendly and supportive way. They worked easily together, with each of them frequently following a small group of children through particular activities. Doris had a quieter, more serious demeanor than Kathy, but was able to be playful with the children in her own way. The children demonstrated a similar comfort level with Doris, approaching her easily when they needed help.

Responding to Individual Differences While Supporting Group Experiences

Kathy often used physical ways of making connections with her students. She became involved in the children's playful activity in ways that the other classroom teachers rarely did. She seemed to make special accommodations for Joey, a child with a pervasive developmental disorder who often had trouble making connections with others, and she seemed to be able to do this in a very inclusive way that did not single Joey out. During one classroom observation, Kathy demonstrated this talent as follows:

> Joey calls out to Kathy, and says, "I can't reach!" Kathy reaches over to him across the table and responds, "Yes, I can reach you, see?" She then reaches over to touch all of the children sitting at the table; this appears to calm and focus them. (Observation notes, June 3, 1997)

Kathy appeared to know Joey well and to understand and anticipate those things that would make his day go more smoothly. She was often observed to interpret his words and help give meaning to his actions for the other children. She did this by collaborating with him rather than by overtly directing his behavior. In the example described below, Kathy had introduced a battery-operated toy microphone to the group for "Chat Time." She passed it around the circle so each child could have a chance to speak or sing into it, sharing something of their own choosing with the group.

> Joey now has the microphone and says something into it about how he likes to play with Power Rangers, but his words are quiet and mumbled. Kathy tells him, "I can't hear," and gets up to assist and show Joey how to hold the microphone. He repeats what he says, and Kathy repeats his words again for all the children. (Observation notes, June 3, 1997)

Kathy knew that Joey enjoyed sitting in a "big chair," one of the classroom chairs that was somewhat larger than a typical child-sized chair, and she allowed him this pleasure. In fact, she engaged the other children in supporting Joey's use of the special chair, creating an atmosphere of collaboration rather than one of competition. She also made a special effort at times to provide the extra physical stimulation that Joey needed in playful ways, an intervention that helped him with his sensory regulation challenges, as evidenced in the following observation:

> Kathy gets close to Joey, and says, "I'm going to eat someone's nose, I'm going to eat someone's knees, … I'm going to eat Joey!" She picks him up, holding him by the knees as she hangs him upside down, and tickles him as he laughs, giggles, and squirms. (Observation notes, June 3, 1997)

Kathy seemed to make a special effort for all of the children in her classroom to create an environment where individual differences were honored and respected. Maria, the young Polish speaker who was still learning English, sometimes struggled to express herself clearly. When Maria seemed unable to express herself appropriately to a peer, Kathy helped to fill in the words for her and encouraged her playmate Stefan to stand up for himself. Kathy provided gentle explanations for why Maria's sometimes boisterous activity might be inappropriate in the example below.

> Maria turns back around to look at Stefan, and says, "Look what I'm going to do. Watch." Smiling and laughing, she begins to lightly bop her forehead with the Duplo block, saying "Ooowww." Stefan joins in and they are soon both amusing themselves in this activity. Kathy notices the children's activities, and interrupts her reading to look towards the children. "Stefan," she says in a comfortable tone, "what happened to your head?" She next addresses Maria with, "Maria, that's not such a good idea." Trying to further explain she says, "That's not such a good idea, it creates a boo-boo." Maria looks at her and retorts, "But it doesn't hurt me so much, Kathy." (Observation notes, June 5, 1997)

Creating a Playful Atmosphere That Promotes Social Interactions and Builds Community

Kathy was frequently observed to be an active participant in the children's play. She had a knack for stepping in at just the right time and successfully drawing the more reluctant children into play with others, as demonstrated in this pretend play sequence:

> Kathy takes out a toy telephone, and calls out in a very musical tone, "Hello, Maria, someone's calling your name, I think, I think. I think that I hear it again. If it isn't Joey on the phone!" She hands a second toy telephone to Jeremy, and the children simulate talking. The play continues from Jeremy and Maria, to Joey and Jessie, then on to the other children until everyone has had a chance. Joey participates fully, simulating talking to Jessie. Even when it's not his turn, he is obviously enjoying

this activity, clapping his hands to the musical beat and bobbing his head up and down. (Observation notes, June 5, 1997)

Kathy, like several other study teachers, rated her classroom's ability to meet the children's social needs as 4 on a 5-point scale, and it was clear from our observations that she took on this responsibility with a high level of action and awareness. Although she rarely imposed social rules on the children, she did not miss many opportunities to encourage the children to be kind to their friends, as demonstrated in the observation below.

Kathy says, "I think everybody's friends." Dominic says, "Nobody is Clara's friend." Kathy replies, "You know what, I'm Clara's friend, and I'm going to sit right next to her." (She pulls up a chair and does this). Soon Maria stands up and says loudly across the table, "Clara, I'm your friend." Kathy tells her thank you, and Nellie also adds that she too is Clara's friend. (Observation notes, June 5, 1997)

Through her active, participatory style, Kathy frequently demonstrated for the children what they needed to do to show their peers that they were their friends, rather than simply relying on verbal descriptions of behavior as many other teachers often did. Her supportive presence and contagious enthusiasm seemed to catch on quickly for the children in her classroom, leading to a more overall positive classroom climate than observed in other classrooms.

Responding to Conflict in Ways That Nourish Peer Support

Kathy typically addressed conflicts between children by suggesting an alternative that brought them together, such as sharing, as described below. Although these children did not exactly follow her suggestion, they were able to resolve the conflict in their own way with her supportive input.

Joey is called to Kathy's table, but he and Stefan squabble lightly over sitting in the same chair. Joey then gets up and looks around. He says, "Hey, where's my big chair?" Kathy says, "I don't know, maybe Stefan can share with you." She then turns to Stefan, and says, "Stefan, can you share your chair with Joey?" Stefan doesn't answer, but decides to move to a different chair next to Kathy, freeing up the controversial chair for Joey. Joey is now seated directly opposite Kathy. (Observation notes, June 3, 1997)

Suggesting that the least effective strategy is "sticking to rote learning," Kathy wanted to enhance her curriculum with "more books to stimulate new ideas and pictures for the children to learn from and share with each other." She continually created opportunities in her classroom that encouraged peer interactions and cooperative play. She was frequently observed to be an active participant in the children's play, and a facilitator of their social interaction and problem solving. She responded to Joey, who was not always easily understood by his peers, in ways that not only seemed to optimize his ability to express himself socially but also encouraged others to respond to him in more socially positive ways. With Maria, an English-language learner who sometimes needed extra help expressing herself, Kathy was careful to explain the classroom rules in ways that she could understand. Through her ongoing and active involvement in the children's play and her attention to social opportunities, Kathy was able to support and scaffold social interactions and help children resolve conflicts with peers in a very natural and authentic way.

Discussion and Reflections

Historically, before the passage of laws that mandated providing education for young children with special needs in natural community settings, most preschoolers with disabilities were educated in segregated, self-contained learning environments where teachers focused primarily on addressing children's cognitive deficits through direct instruction (Safford et al., 1994). These changes in the law called for more inclusive approaches to early care and education, and the creation of environments that serve diverse groups of children. Learning alongside their typically developing peers, young children with disabilities are increasingly participating in more child-centered classrooms, where less emphasis is placed on direct instruction aimed toward teaching discrete skills and more time is spent teaching the "whole child" through a play-based and emergent curriculum (Mallory, 1994).

Simply bringing children with and without disabilities together in more developmentally appropriate early childhood classrooms, however, does not guarantee that all children have access to the curriculum or that all feel included and cared for within the classroom community. As the field of early childhood special education begins to slowly transform toward more child-centered pedagogy, the social and emotional learning needs of young children with disabilities has come into focus in a new way, challenging teachers to rethink their ideas about adapting classroom curriculum to accommodate all children.

The role of the teacher as a mediator and supporter of children's social relationships, particularly as applied to young children with special needs, has received little attention in the literature, and there are few models for how to put these early childhood principles into practice. Kathy's complex and important role as it played out in the daily rituals of her early childhood practice within an inclusive preschool classroom provides insight for early childhood teachers. This exploration of one early childhood teacher's ways of nurturing social experiences in her inclusive classroom inspires new ways to consider building a caring classroom community that go beyond the usual models for direct instruction of social skills so often found in the early childhood special education literature.

What did Kathy do that made her practice special? It was in her doing and being that Kathy enacted a caring curriculum. Her choices for when and how to intervene reflected a constant consciousness about creating harmony and respect in the group. She honored individual differences in ways that conveyed this message:

> Children don't have to "give up" their idiosyncratic interests or desires; what is important to them can be incorporated in ways that embrace the needs and welfare of the group as a whole.

Kathy's decisions fostered caring for others without sacrificing children's self-esteem. She made those decisions based on context rather that rules alone, and conveyed this deeper meaning to the children through her social connections with and among them.

In her own rethinking and doing, Kathy demonstrated a way of enacting social justice for all of the children in her classroom. We saw it in her awareness that equal is not always equitable as she negotiated how to balance meeting the needs of the group with honoring individual differences. Kathy approached classroom dilemmas in ways that upheld respect for children's sense of who they were and what they needed. Sometimes what is fair may need to be reconsidered. Unlike in many so-called inclusive classrooms, individual children were not singled out as having special needs in ways that marginalized them, undermining equity in experience and opportunity. Rather, Kathy created a curriculum that embraced all the learners in her classroom and brought them together in socially inclusive ways.

As Kathy embellished words with animated actions and gestures, she helped make classroom messages clearer for both Joey, a child who struggled to make social connections, and Maria, an English-language learner who benefited greatly from the linguistic scaffolding Kathy provided. Kathy's ways of adapting curricula offered a value-added component for these two different kinds of learners in a very inclusive way.

How did Kathy help build a sense of community in her classroom? First, she planned activities that were of high interest, fostered social interaction, and created a playful atmosphere for all of the children. Despite the busy nature of the ongoing activity in her classroom, Kathy was aware of the different ways that individual children were engaging in the curriculum. She was flexible enough to end an activity that was not interesting to the children. Second, she was comfortable having conflicts occur in her classroom and capitalized on them as opportunities for learning. She allowed children to work out conflicts among themselves, scaffolding the process when necessary. She gave clear messages to the children, setting limits as needed, but always seemed to begin with the expectation and the presumption that they were capable of finding their way to a workable solution. Third, Kathy made a point to create special one-on-one moments to nurture her relationships with the children. She acknowledged and validated children's feelings, engaged in children's play, and involved children in tasks to help each other solve problems.

In this inclusive preschool classroom, Kathy enacted a curriculum that made room for many kinds of learners. She invited children to share their unique experiences by engaging in activities in small and large groups. She knew the children as individuals, and she consciously and consistently made adaptations to accommodate their diverse learning needs. When conflicts arose, Kathy expressed her expectations for the children clearly and simply, establishing her authority as the teacher and making ground rules that helped all of the children feel safe and respected. Kathy and her assistant, Doris, demonstrated ongoing collaboration in the ways that they negotiated their work with the children. Their playful ways of participating and engaging the children in activities engendered a spirit of cooperation and fun in the classroom, further enhancing positive peer relationships.

Inclusion seemed easy in Kathy's room, where it was often hard to tell at first which children were diagnosed with disabilities. Most of these children's disabilities were considered mild, and none of the children appeared to have serious behavior problems. In part, however, the ease with which this inclusive group worked so well together was due to Kathy's strong emphasis on building community, which seemed to be at the heart of all that she did with the children. Kathy's ways of teaching and caring contributed to a classroom culture that nurtured young children's own sense of caring for others.

As inclusive education increasingly becomes the norm in countries around the globe, there is a need to reenvision teachers' roles and responsibilities as advocates for young children with special needs for whom learning about the world of social opportunities often takes place within their early childhood classrooms. Early childhood teachers are ideally situated to start at the beginning with young learners to create classroom environments that will contribute to improved educational equity and access, and redefine the parameters of social inclusion.

As issues of community and diversity gain increasing importance and influence in our constructions of teaching and learning, teachers and teacher educators must continue to find new ways to envision possibilities for children's futures that promote educational equity and social inclusion. This study addresses a topic that is at the heart of educational equity and access for all learners, and provides a forum for thinking imaginatively about possibilities for greater effectiveness in building inclusive classroom communities, beginning with our youngest learners.

Note

I wish to thank the teachers and children involved in this project for their participation and inspiration. The writing of this chapter was made possible in part by a grant from the Spencer Foundation. The views expressed are solely the responsibility of the author.

References

Arnett, J. (1989). Caregivers in daycare centers: Does training matter? *Journal of Applied Developmental Psychology, 10,* 541–552.

Baglieri, S., & Knopf, J. H. (2004). Normalizing difference in inclusive teaching. *Journal of Learning Disabilities, 37*(6), 525–529.

Erwin, E. J., & Guintini, M. (2000). Inclusion and classroom membership in early childhood. *International Journal of Disability, Development and Education, 47*(3), 237–257.

File, N. (1994). Children's play, teacher-child interactions, and teacher beliefs in integrated early childhood programs. *Early Childhood Research Quarterly, 9,* 223–240.

Goodman, J. F. (1992). *When slow is fast enough.* New York: Guilford Press.

Greenspan, S. I. (2003). Child care research: A clinical perspective. *Child Development, 7*(4), 1064–1068.

Guralnick, M. J., Hammond, M. A., Connor, R. T., & Neville, B. (2006). Stability, change, and correlates of the peer relationships of young children with mild developmental delays. *Child Development, 77*(2), 312–324.

Howes, C., Matheson, C. C., & Hamilton, C. E. (1994). Maternal, teacher, and child-care history correlates of children's relationships with peers. *Child Development, 65,* 264–273.

Kliewer, C., Fitzgerald, L. M., Meyer-Mork, J., Hartman, P., English-Sand, P., & Raschke, D. (2004). Citizenship for all in the literate community: An ethnography of young children with significant disabilities in inclusive early childhood settings. *Harvard Educational Review, 74*(4), 373–402.

Kontos, S., & Wilcox-Herzog, A. (1997). Influences on children's competence in early childhood classrooms. *Early Childhood Research Quarterly, 12,* 247–262.

Mahoney, G., & Wheeden, A. (1999). The effect of teacher style on interactive engagement of preschool-aged children with special learning needs. *Early Childhood Research Quarterly, 14*(1), 51–68.

Mallory, B. (1994). Inclusive policy, practice, and theory for young children with developmental differences. In B. L. Mallory and R. S. New (Eds.), *Diversity and developmentally appropriate practices: Challenges for early childhood education.* New York: Teachers College Press.

Merriam, S. B. (2001). *Qualitative research and case study applications in education.* San Francisco, CA: Jossey-Bass.

Noddings, N. (1994). An ethic of caring and its implications for instructional arrangements. In L. Stone (Ed.), *The education feminism reader* (pp. 171–183). New York: Routledge.

Noddings, N. (2002). *Educating moral people: A caring alternative to character education.* New York: Teachers College Press.

Odom, S. L., Vitztum, J., Wolery, R., Lieber, J., Sandall, S., Hanson, M. J., et al. (2004). Preschool inclusion in the United States: A review of research from an ecological systems perspective. *Journal of Research in Special Educational Needs, 4*(1), 17–49.

Pianta, R. C. (1997). Adult-child relationship processes and early schooling. *Early Education and Development, 8*(1), 11–26.

Recchia, S. L. (1998, April). *Teacher-child relationships and peer interactions in preschoolers with disabilities.* Roundtable presented at the annual meeting of the American Educational Research Association, San Diego, CA.

Recchia, S. L. (1999, April). *Social experiences of preschoolers with disabilities in diverse classroom settings.* Poster presented at the 1999 biennial meeting of the Society for Research in Child Development, Albuquerque, New Mexico.

Recchia, S. L., & Lee, Y. J. (2004). At the crossroads: Overcoming concerns to envision possibilities for toddlers in inclusive childcare. *Journal of Research in Childhood Education, 19*(2), 175–188.

Recchia, S. L., & Soucacou, E. (2002, December). *Observing social relationships in context: Preschoolers with disabilities, teachers, and peers.* Poster presented at the 18th annual DEC Conference on Young Children with Special Needs and Their Families, San Diego, CA.

Recchia, S. L., & Soucacou, E. (2006). Nurturing social experience in three early childhood special education classrooms. *Early childhood research and practice, 8*(2). Retrieved on July 17, 2007, from http://ecrp.uiuc.edu/v8n/recchia.html.

Rimm-Kaufman, S. E., Voorhees, M. D., Snell, M. E., & La Paro, K. M. (2003). Improving the sensitivity and responsivity of preservice teachers toward young children with disabilities. *Topics in Early Childhood Special Education, 23*(3), 151–163.

Safford, P. L., Sargent, M., & Cook. C. (1994). Instructional models in early childhood special education: Origins, issues, and trends. In P. L. Safford, B. Spodek, & O. N. Saracho (Eds.), *Early childhood special education.* New York: Teachers College Press.

Sroufe, L. A. (1983). Infant-caregiver attachment and patterns of adaptation in preschool: The roots of maladaptation and competence. In M. Perlmutter (Ed.), *The Minnesota symposium on child psychology* (Vol. 16). Hillsdale, NJ: Erlbaum.

Taylor, A. S., Peterson, C. A., McMurray-Schwarz, P., & Guillou, T. S. (2002). Social skills interventions: Not just for children with special needs. *Young Exceptional Children, 5*(4), 19–26.

Webster-Stratton, C. (1999). *How to promote children's social and emotional competence.* London: Paul Chapman.

6
Marginalization, Making Meaning, and Mazes

SUSAN GRIESHABER

Nate, a boy from the Pacific Islands in year 3 (equivalent to second grade in the United States), was described by his teacher as performing at a lower level of competency in class and "struggling with literacy and numeracy." Despite this, as part of a classroom computer activity of maze making, Nate completed the set task at a more sophisticated level than many others. While working on the maze, Nate engaged in an unsanctioned literacy and numeracy practice on another computer window, which drew a small audience of boys who watched in awe as he created a complex digital artifact. In this chapter, I provide the classroom context for the maze-making episode and then track the progress of Nate as he worked on the maze, comparing Nate's finished product to mazes completed by other boys in the class. I speculate about the ways in which this achievement might have an impact on his identity as a class member and consider the necessity of including nontraditional literacy and numeracy practices as part of meaningful learning, especially for those who might be constructed as low achievers by their teachers in basic literacy and numeracy.

Literacy, Numeracy, and Early Childhood Education

The lengthy presence of indigenous people as well as many years of immigration to Australia have resulted in a population that is culturally diverse. Migrants are a major source of cultural, linguistic, racial, and religious diversity; overlooking the rich cultural, social, and cognitive resources that come with migrants is counterproductive to all facets of society (Cummins, 2004, p. xv). Florida (2003) detailed the conditions under which migrants in the United States contribute critically and creatively to the vibrancy of society; significantly, feeling safe and valued were paramount and correlated with areas of greatest growth and vitality. Feeling safe and valued may also be associated with success factors for young children in the first years of school.

The Queensland Preparing for School Trial (Thorpe et al., 2004) involved over 1,800 children in 39 sites throughout the state and showed that children from culturally diverse backgrounds were "at educational risk" (p. 181) because they made much less progress in social and communication development when compared with other children. In this study, those from culturally diverse backgrounds were defined as Aboriginal, Torres Strait Islander, Asian (notably Vietnamese), and Pacific Islander children. Children from these groups had higher levels of behavioral difficulties and poorer adjustment to school. For example, indigenous and Pacific Islander children had significantly higher rates of peer problems and unhappiness at school and lower scores on adjustment. The research showed that within classrooms, high levels of interaction had the effect of reducing behavioral problems and increasing academic attainment, particularly in literacy. The key message from these findings is that school management and classroom pedagogical practice make a difference. The strongest effect was on behavior, which, in turn, opens opportunities for literacy and numeracy learning for children from culturally diverse backgrounds.

Literacy achievement of young children is affected in significant ways by the intersection of social class, race, and gender (Gilbert & Gilbert, 1998). Although Thorpe et al. (2004) found that better performance in children's early literacy at entry to Queensland prep/preschool was associated with higher income and that girls performed better than boys, children whose mothers had less education (year 10 [ninth grade] or below) scored lower. Moreover, despite the assumption that boys and girls are homogeneous populations with standardized achievements (Titus, 2004), there are groups of girls who experience difficulty with literacy learning (Alloway, 2000; Gorard, Rees, & Salisbury, 1999). In relation to numeracy, early childhood teachers remain reluctant to take a more active role in supporting students' learning, mainly because they have low levels of confidence in regard to mathematics, as well as poor content and pedagogical knowledge (Copley, 2004; Perry & Dockett, 2004). These factors limit the ability of early childhood educators to teach mathematics effectively and to respond to changes in mathematics education.

Literacy has become a highly contested term, especially in the context of the new media age (Kress, 2003). Although *literacies* is a more accurate description of the range of literacy practices that are undertaken in everyday life (New London Group, 1996), Kress (2003) maintains that *literacy* refers to "lettered representation" and that descriptions need to be created for talking about media other than those associated with lettered representation. Of interest in this chapter are literacy and numeracy practices that are related to using the digital technology of computers in classrooms. In regard to numeracy, the term *mathematical literacy* is used widely in international contexts, but in Australia, *numeracy* is more common. To be numerate is to "use mathematics effectively to meet the general demands of life at home, in paid work, and for participation in community and civic life" (Australian Association of Mathematics Teachers [AAMT], 1997, p. 15). Literacy and numeracy, then, are integral to the social and cultural practices of everyday life, as well as the everyday life of classrooms.

Children's Identities

To date, in early childhood education there has been little engagement with ideas about the construction of children's identities and how these are mediated through power relations associated with race, ethnicity, culture, class, sexuality, and gender. Here, I draw on subjectivity to refer to the identity and identities of individuals. Subjectivity is different from the "subject" of psychology, which conceives of individuals as rational, unified, and coherent. Subjectivity refers to "the conscious and unconscious thoughts and emotions of the individual, her sense of herself and her ways of understanding her relation to the world" (Weedon, 1997, p. 32). It is about who we are and how we see ourselves, and introduces the idea of complexity, the possibility of aspects of everyday lives being fragmentary, and the shifting nature of subjectivity/identities of individuals. It cannot be reduced to essential ideas about an individual that make her what she is. But it does propose an understanding of subjectivity that positions the individual as the ongoing site of conflicting forms of subjectivity (Weedon, 1997). For Nate, it explains how he can be seen by his teachers as struggling with literacy and numeracy and on another occasion, such as the one reported here, complete a set task at the computer at a highly sophisticated level. In conjunction with his out-of-school experiences, it goes some way towards explaining his seemingly contradictory abilities in the classroom, abilities that are seen by the teachers as lacking and by the small group of boys as particularly impressive.

Research about children's subjectivity in relation to mathematics or numeracy is scarce, but Marsh (2005) has identified the complexity of relationships among self, others, literacy, and identity. Marsh (2005) argues that there is a "dynamic synergy" (p. 33) among these four aspects of children's lives and that they provide some insight into how multifaceted and contested the process of becoming literate can be. She says that not only do young children's literacy practices shape who they are, but that who they are already also limits

> to some extent the kinds of literacy practices which they take up and the intense dialectic between self and others—in this case—family members—which impacts on literacy practices and identities. (p. 33)

In talking about the importance of self in shaping literacy practices, Marsh (2005) used Moje's (2000) ethnography of gangs as an example of the deliberate adoption of particular literacy practices to symbolize choice (of literacy practices), gang membership, and how the selection of specific literacy practices indicates particular subjectivities. Likewise, ways in which classroom peers influence the choice of literacy practices and how these choices affect subjectivity and identity construction are revealed in Dyson's (1997, 2002) work in elementary classrooms.

Children who are struggling with school literacy and numeracy can become invisible in the classroom; it can also be common classroom knowledge that these children are experiencing difficulties. More to the point are those whose out-of-school practices are invisible in the classroom because they are not recognized and legitimated. I suggest that things could be otherwise: New media texts are instrumental in the construction of young children's social identities, with information and communication technologies, popular culture, and media offering opportunities for exciting pedagogical work and deep intellectual engagement for even very young children (see Marsh, 2000). Well before they get to school, popular culture and media are "deeply inscribed in the ritualized play and materiality of childhood" (Marsh, 2005, p. 5).

There has been little emphasis in early childhood education on race, ethnicity, class, or gender in conjunction with literacy, numeracy, and tools and artifacts (e.g., computers) that are located in specific cultural spaces such as young children's classrooms. This chapter attempts to understand the construction of literate and numerate identities in combination with factors such as culture, ethnicity, and gender in the context of a school and classroom where computers are part of the raison d'être.

Although in year 3 at school, the literacy practices of "gangsta" adolescents as described by Moje (2000) are instructive in the case of Nate. The gangstas in Moje's study were placed outside the possibility of school success because of their "physical characteristics and social affiliations" (p. 651). They also engaged in literacy practices that were not sanctioned by schools but were highly articulate in their use of a variety of written and oral literacy practices. For instance, written discourses of poetry, parody, rap, tagging, and graffiti were significant in identity construction of gang members. Proficient taggers could "win admiration" and "gain power and respect" (p. 665), and written notes signaled metalinguistic awareness as well as "a merging of conventional and gang literacies" (p. 668). Thus, for the five gang members that Moje studied closely, literacy practices were ways to "claim a space, construct an identity, and take a social position in their world" (p. 651). Having been constituted as a "struggler" by his teachers, the positions available for Nate as a class member have been limited. The excerpt from the transcript below examines one instance of how Nate claimed a space, his attempts at constructing a different identity from that ascribed by his teachers, and his way of taking a social position in the classroom.

What does it mean to construct a child as struggling with literacy and numeracy? What else does it mean when that child is from the Pacific Islands and a boy? Of interest in this chapter are the unintended effects of the teachers' inscription of Nate as struggling with literacy and numeracy and the way this constitutes a truth about him, thereby making particular identities available to him and restricting others. Of greater interest is the way in which Nate moves in, around, and beyond this inscription as depicted in an episode of maze making, reinscribing himself momentarily by obliterating the cultural baggage associated with performing literacy and numeracy in problematic ways to another potentially awkward display (even in this school) of digital literacy sophistication. Who Nate is and who he is allowed to be is governed (to an unknown extent) by his proficiency with literacy (Gee, 1996) and numeracy. Here, I investigate the way in which Nate created a space to construct his own social identity, bringing into question his inscription as student at risk in literacy and numeracy.

Naming Nate as struggling with literacy and numeracy functions to identify him as experiencing problems or as at risk in his endeavors with literacy and numeracy. This can also have the powerful effect of marginalizing him by marking him as different from those who are competent in these areas. Once the categorization of Nate has occurred, there is little likelihood that he will be able to transform his struggling status to one of competence and success, simply because such labels are constitutive (Foucault, 1972). That is, the label constructs Nate's classroom identity for him and makes it difficult for those in the classroom to see and understand him in other ways. Campbell (2005) related an incident in a child-care center in Melbourne, Australia, where Mick, age 5 and a migrant from the Pacific Islands who spoke English as an additional language, was prevented from playing with construction materials by two middle-class Anglo Australian boys. The boys managed to stop Mick from playing on the basis of a developmental or normalized construction that he did not know how to play appropriately: "'Cos he doesn't know how to do it [play collaboratively]" (p. 147). The teacher's response of "Well, you could show him how" (p. 147) positioned the Anglo boys as "'teachers' of Mick, and designated [them] as the gatekeepers of when and how he could be included as a boy when using the construction materials" (p. 147). So Mick was doubly compromised, firstly because the boys refused to let him play with the materials, and secondly, because according to the teacher, the way that he could learn to play with the materials is from the very boys who were refusing to let him play. Mick's skin color, ethnicity, social class, and position as an English-language learner are all factors that were instrumental in how the boys and the teacher prevented Mick from playing in the short term (Campbell, 2005) and had a constitutive influence on the (im)possibility of his inclusion in the future.

The School and Classroom

Tremain College (a pseudonym) is a public school located approximately 15 miles southwest of the capital city of Brisbane, in the state of Queensland, Australia, and is in one of the rapidly developing residential areas of southeast Queensland. The school began operation in 1998 with support from the state Department of Education and the real estate company that designed and developed the suburb. Technology was an integral part of the development plans for this residential area, as all those who bought house-and-land packages "were given the option of having an Apple computer connected to a networked server that was maintained by the developer" (Cooper, McRobbie, & Baturo, n.d., pp. 49–50). Thus, the school Web site indicates that it is the first computerized community of its type in the world. Tremain College was also an Apple Classrooms of Tomorrow school and the eighth of its kind in the world. Initially, each classroom was provided with six Apple computers, a printer, and a large monitor that could display a computer screen. Wiring for the computers was located in the ceiling so that electrical cords drop from the ceiling rather than emerge from the walls or the floor.

Tremain College is a multiage school and since 1998 has adopted an integrated approach to curriculum, and valued child-centered constructivist approaches to teaching and learning. Technology is an integral part of the classroom:

> The computers are deliberately placed in the centre of the room so that students may access them at any time under their teacher's direction and as an integral part of their daily program. (Cooper et al., n.d., p. 50)

The aims of the school included showcasing Apple computers, providing professional development to assist teachers in the use of computers in classroom learning, and "researching the impact of computer use on teaching and learning" (p. 1). In 2000, the student-to-computer ratio was 3.6:1 (p. 52); in 2001 when data were gathered for this project, there was a similar ratio, with 12 computers available for 46 children in the two classes. Each computer had a name, signified by a name tag, and children and staff referred to each by name.

Although data were gathered from four classes in the school, data reported here are drawn from two classes (46 children) who were in their second and third years of compulsory schooling. The children worked with two teachers in a double teaching space and most were 7 or 8 years of age. Data gathering occurred for approximately 3 hours per day, 3 days per week, for 9 weeks from July to September 2001 (Term 3). Most data were gathered by a research assistant but the researchers were regular visitors to the classroom. Data included five audiotaped semistructured interviews with the teachers (Cannold, 2001; Glesne, 2006); informal interviews with individual children (Brooker, 2001); observations of children and teachers (Glesne, 2006); detailed field notes (Emerson, Fretz, & Shaw, 1995); audiotapes of incidental conversations with teachers and children; and video records (Silverman, 2000) of children as they used computers to engage with literacy and numeracy. As the research was investigating the intersection of technologies, literacy, and numeracy in everyday classroom activity, short case studies (Yin, 2003) were compiled of five children who demonstrated high and low levels of competency in these areas. One of these children was Nate. However, what are provided here are excerpts from one episode of maze making in the classroom.

During the data-collection period, children used the Microworlds program to complete tangrams and tessellations and to make mazes. They also used Appleworks to undertake a mathematical activity called "Frogs to Ponds." For language and integrated studies, access to the computers was organized on a rotational basis to cover class work. The children also had free time each week during which the computers were able to be used and were popular. The theme for Term 3 was "Past, Present, and Future," and as part of the curriculum the children visited a local historical site. They were required to create a recount of the excursion using Hyperstudio and to make a timeline of their life from birth to the present.

Nate

Soon after we began collecting data in this classroom, Nate was described by his teachers as "struggling with literacy and numeracy." As this was September and the children had been at school since late January, there had been plenty of time for the teachers to form an opinion of Nate's abilities in literacy and numeracy. The following transcript excerpt is drawn from a session where Nate was working on a maze that was to be created using the Microworlds program. Carol is the research assistant for the project who was working in the classroom. She was usually located near the computer and recording equipment used for the study and engaged with the children when they initiated conversation.

1 *Nate:* Do we have to do this?
2 *Nate:* Do we have to use this? (Waved cursor around on screen)
3 *Carol:* Yeah.
4 *Carol:* Unless you can think of another way of doing it … people have been doing all sorts of things.
5 *Nate:* Okay. (Carol begins to move away to assist other students)
6 *Nate:* (To himself) I know what to do. (Chooses the color black and thickness of line draw tool. Draws lines to start constructing a maze) (See Figure 6.1.)
7 *Nate:* Do we have to draw a house?

Figure 6.1 Nate's maze.

8 *Carol:*   You can do whatever you like—whatever your heart desires because it's your maze.

9 *Nate:*   Okay. (Resumes work and changes from black to red. Begins to draw a face with almond-shaped "Spiderman" type eyes)

Nate is reluctant to begin the activity and asked Carol whether "we have to do this" (Line 1) and if we "have to use this [the cursor]?" (Line 2). In this instance, perhaps Nate was wondering about opportunities to create something different than what was required in the task set by the teachers and what other children had already completed. Carol's response (Line 4) indicated that there was scope to experiment and license to invent as "people have been doing all sorts of things." Of significance here is that Nate talked with Carol, probably because she was handy, and not the teachers. When Carol moved away, Nate chose a color (black) and the line thickness he wanted, and began to draw lines for the maze (Line 6). When Carol returned, Nate sought guidance again from her when he asked whether "we have to draw a house" (Line 7). For the second time, Carol provided encouragement to experiment: "whatever your heart desires because it's your maze" (Line 8). Reassured, Nate resumed work and immediately changed the color from black to red and began to draw a face with almond-shaped eyes (Line 9).

11   (Picture now has yellow hair. Nate is very carefully erasing the hair with the erase tool. Changes the face to blue. Changes background to bright yellow. The blue face now resembles what the children have been calling a "stamp." The stamps have been used as symbols in the children's work and many children can identify others' work by their symbols.) (See Figure 6.2.)

12 *Nate:*   (To boy next to him) Did you know what? I can open folders and take them away easy!

13 *Nate:*   Now has a new window open and is drawing a person.

14 *Nate:*   (Muttering in response to the boy B1 at computer next to him) It's not his boobs.

15 *B1:*   What are they? (Laughs in amusement)

16 *Nate:*   Now … I'm … (trails off, concentrating and muttering to himself)

17 *B1:*   Oh … jacket?

18 *Nate:*   (Speaking to himself and concentrating intensely) … and now for the eyes . . . (Begins drawing almond shaped Spiderman-like eyes)

19 *B1:*   (Animatedly) What was *that*? You can't draw (laughing) on it …

20 *Nate:*   Huh?

21 *B1:*   You can't draw on that and neither can I.
(Nate continues to work)

Figure 6.2 Maze with "stamp" in top right corner.

22	*B1:*	What is that? Draw hair! Probably gonna be a … (recording fails)
		(Nate colors the eyes of the person in red)
23	*Nate:*	Hair. That would be easy! … Search … (Concentrating and thinking out loud)
24	*B1:*	Do the line one, do the line!
25	*Nate:*	(Speaks assertively) Just wait. (Nate concentrates while manipulating controls and makes quiet beat-box noises to himself. Returns to fix small detail. Colors the figure's shirt in gray). (See Figure 6.3.) (Note the maze behind the window with the action figure on it.)
26	*B1:*	He looks scary.
27	*B1:*	Cool.
28	*B1:*	That's lookin' wicked!
29		(Recording indecipherable)
30	*B1:*	Who is it?
31	*Nate:*	(To himself) Oh damn … the ears are not supposed to be like that.
32	*B1:*	Who is it?
33	*Nate:*	You wait and see. (Sighs)
34	*B1:*	(unintelligible)
35	*Nate:*	You are pretty slack, hey?
36	*B1:*	Shuddup!
37	*B1:*	(laughs)
38	*B1:*	What the heck is that? A bull ant? (laughs) A d-j?
39	*Nate:*	Nuh.
40	*B1:*	That's lookin' ugly.
		(Nate continues drawing his action hero figure)

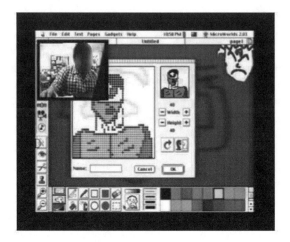

Figure 6.3 Window with scorpion in the foreground; maze is behind.

41 *B1:* How did you do that? (Admiring tone)
      (Nate has drawn a man from chest up. He is wearing a gray shirt with red sleeves. He has black hair and a thick muscular neck and torso. He has red, almond-shaped, slanted eyes) (See Figure 6.3.)

42 *B1:* Oh. A person who robs some … place?

43 *Nate:* No. It's Scorpion … (Recording unclear) Scorpion (Nate keeps working and concentrating) [For a picture of Scorpion, see http://www.yojoe.com/archive/actfig/mk/2scorpion.jpg]

44 *B1:* Who the heck is Scorpion?

45 *Nate:* You don't know him.

46 *B1:* Nuh—don't know anything about him.

47 *Nate:* Do you know why?

48 *B1:* Why?

49 *Nate:* You don't watch MC (?) [Mortal Kombat]…you don't watch it.

50 *B1:* MC? Nuh.

51 *Nate:* You don't watch that, hey?

52 *B1:* Na.

53 *Nate:* You don't like that.
      (A second boy comes up to watch what Nate is doing)

54 *Nate:* Oh crap. I can't get out of here … (Talking to himself).

55 *Nate:* (To the other boys) Do you know how to get out of here?

56 *B2:* Yeah—press the square. (Points to screen)

57 *Carol:* How's it going, Nate?

From Line 14 to Line 53, Nate and the boy (B1) using the computer next to him engaged in a conversation about what Nate was doing, but B1 is not familiar with the character that Nate is creating. For instance, B1 says "He looks scary" (Line 26) and "That's lookin' wicked" (Line 28), and then asked "Who is it?" (Line 30). Nate didn't answer and so B1 asked again (Line 32) but Nate wasn't telling: "You wait and see," after which he sighed (Line 33). Once Nate had established that B1 did not know who he was creating, Nate said: "You're pretty slack, hey?" (Line 35). B1 was not impressed with this comment, telling Nate to "Shuddup!" (Line 36) but remained keen to know what Nate was doing (Line 38). Meanwhile, Nate was creating an action hero figure and B1 was perplexed as to how Nate was able to do it (Line 41). B1 was still not aware of who it was, asking if it was "A person who robs some … place?" (Line 42). Even though Nate named the character (Scorpion) twice, B1 did not know him: "Who the heck is Scorpion?" (Line 44). Nate reinforced his ignorance twice, telling him the reason he didn't know was that he didn't "watch MC [Mortal Kombat]" (Lines 49, 51). When another boy (B2) came to see what Nate was doing, he tried to move to another screen (Line 54) but couldn't, and had to ask the boys how to "get out of here" (Line 55). This could have been because he was unwilling to let B2 see what he had been doing and was in a rush to change the screen. At this point (Line 57), Carol returned and asked how Nate was going. The conversation continued:

58	*B2:*	Press the square. (Points again)
		(Screen reverts to the original maze which has a dark blue background) (Similar to Figure 6.2.)
59	*B2:*	Oh cool—you made one! (A maze)
		(Nate still concentrating and working; responds belatedly)
60	*Nate:*	Yeah … (Chuckles)
61	*B2:*	(Recording unclear)
62	*Nate:*	Well, just wait.
63	*B1:*	Is that … ? (Recording unclear)
64	*Nate:*	Huh?
65	*B2:*	I want *that* picture!
66	*Nate:*	Then watch this—now we'll be able to move it … (Nate clicks on the maze object and drags it through the maze channels)
67	*B1:*	To the side. Side on.
68	*B2:*	You can move that?
69	*Nate:*	Yeah. What you gotta do is draw the line and then start from there. (Nate makes car noises while moving the object through the maze)
70	*B1:*	And can it do pen down? (Refers to instructions for moving the turtle through the maze)
71	*Nate:*	And then you have to go to the [pauses] face.

72 *B1:*   Ohhh.

73 *Nate:*   C'mon man—it's easy! (Nate creates a larger, brighter colored yellow object)

74 *Nate:*   Now—finished! (See Figure 6.4.)

75 *Carol:* Okay, so where do you start, Nate?

76 *Nate:*   Here! (Nate points to the screen)

77 *Carol:* Oh. Okay.

78 *Nate:*   And then you go here …

79 *Carol:* Okay. So, what would you think would be the way to go? (Nate points to the screen, follows maze with finger while making car noises)

80 *Carol:* Ah—that's the shortest way, isn't it?

81 *Nate:*   Well, it's hard.

82 *Carol:* Yes.

83 *Carol:* Do you want to swap with someone else and do their maze?

84 *Nate:*   Yep.

85 *Carol:* Ok—make sure you save yours though!

Nate managed to return to the screen with the original maze and B2 was impressed with it (Line 59). After much concentration with B2 watching closely (Lines 59 to 65), B2 finally exclaimed "I want *that* picture!" (Line 65). Nate responded by dragging the object through the maze (line 66), to the amazement of the boys who were watching (Lines 68, 70, 72). His added admonishment of "C'mon man—it's easy!" came just before his triumph of "Now—finished!" (Line 74) and the return of Carol to discuss the more mundane aspects of where to start, the shortest way through the maze, and a reminder to Nate to save his maze (Lines 75, 80, 85). After making and saving

Figure 6.4 Finished maze.

their mazes, the children were encouraged to try their skills on others' mazes. Figure 6.5 shows two of the other mazes constructed by boys in the class and these examples depict the contrast between Nate's work and the others. The other two examples (Figure 6.5) used icons that were available from the program whereas Nate constructed his own stamp of Scorpion and also used color. Nate also chose to use the line draw tool to make the lines for his maze and the other boys used commands for Terry Turtle. This was evident in parts

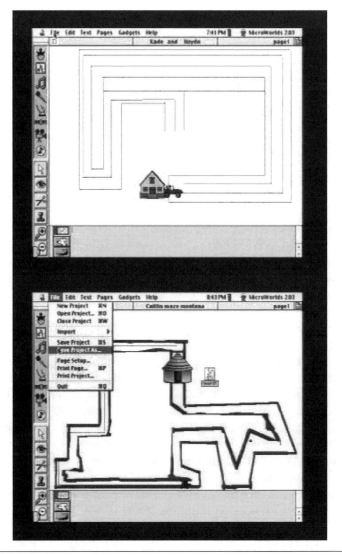

Figure 6.5 Mazes by two other boys.

of the conversation when B1 asked "And can it do pen down?" (Line 70), one of the instructions needed to move Terry Turtle and make the maze.

Although Nate is in his third year of schooling and there is no suggestion that he is displaying latent gangsta tendencies, Moje's (2000) work offers a lens for analyzing Nate's actions and thinking when using the Microworlds program. I discuss two points: Nate's creation of a stamp that resembled Scorpion in the top right-hand corner of his maze as the end point (Figure 6.2); and his use of a window to produce a more detailed picture of Scorpion (Figure 6.3). Both these actions can be seen as a way of claiming a space in the classroom, of constructing an identity, and of taking a social position and writing himself into the life world of the classroom (see also Moje, 2000). Nate's stamp of Scorpion can be likened to the practice of tagging, or the drawing of colorful characters by individuals who are members of tagging crews (Hunt, in Moje, 2000). According to Hunt (as cited in Moje, 2000), tagging is done by individuals to show their ability or "to claim a position as an artist" (p. 686). Tags can adorn "bodies," personal items such as notebooks, and also school and public property such as "desks, walls, [and] lockers" (Moje, 2000, p. 661). Nate's stamp or "tag" of Scorpion was the topic of conversation among several boys a short time after this episode occurred, relayed by B1 and B2. Such activity is an integral part of how Nate was constructing an identity within the class as well as establishing a social position for himself among the boys. As well as the evidence in the transcript, the conversation later indicated Nate was revered by several of the boys for his knowledge of Mortal Kombat, a game that few, if any, of the others knew, and for his ability to create Scorpion using the line draw tool, as well as his design of Scorpion on the additional window that he opened.

Nate complied with the set task of making a maze but took it to another dimension when he opened a window (Line 13) and began to make a representation of Scorpion from the chest up. His terminology was not entirely accurate as he referred to opening a new window as "open[ing] folders and taking them away" and that such action was "easy!" (Line 12). Opening a window to make the representation of Scorpion suggests Nate may have been aware that he was engaging in an unsanctioned practice. He had indicated that it was easy to open folders (windows) and take them away, so may have been prepared to take the risk and be ready to move quickly from the window back to the maze should it be necessary. This occurred when another boy came to watch what Nate was doing (Line 53) and Nate tried to switch back to the maze but realized he couldn't make the move as quickly as he would have liked: "Oh crap. I can't get out of here" (Line 54). He asked the other boys how to "get out of here" and was assisted by the boy who had just come to look at what he was doing (Line 56). It was also at that point that Carol returned and asked Nate how he was going (Line 57). For much of this transcript (Lines 13 to 58), the focus was Nate's unsanctioned but sophisticated construction of Scorpion and the ongoing conversation between Nate and B1 about Scorpion. It is unsanctioned literacy (and numeracy) practices such as these that Moje (2000) contends are the source of potential for transforming "thought and experience" (p. 652) for those who are marginalized. It is also these practices that enable children like Nate to move from passive roles as "watchers or listeners of someone else's story … to be actors in a story" (Moje, 2000, p. 680). What Nate was doing was writing himself into his own story using more complex and sophisticated practices than his teachers had given him credit for previously. However, neither teacher was aware of what he was doing at the time, nor did they mention his maze in later teacher interviews. Nate was not only positioning himself more powerfully with the boys, but he was also writing his own story, as opposed to watching and listening passively to the dominant story as it played out in the classroom. This is what Moje (2000) understands as the transformative potential of unsanctioned literacy practices—the opportunities they provide for children such as Nate to write themselves into the story and become an integral part of it.

As well as being marginalized by the status ascribed by his teachers to his literacy and numeracy learning, Nate's ethnicity and skin color also marked him as different from the dominant group. However, while there was no evidence of this distinction being made by the other children in the transcript excerpt, it is highly likely that there would have been instances where his ethnicity and skin color worked against him in the classroom and the playground, simply because these physical characteristics set him apart from the dominant group. This was the case for Mick (Campbell, 2005), as discussed earlier, although Mick was younger than Nate and was also an English-language learner. What might be done to advance the cause of social justice in instances such as those of Mick and Nate, as well as others, is to capitalize on Nate's interest in literacy and numeracy practices that are not officially sanctioned in the classroom. Nate's motivation is not in question; however, his ability to perform at the required level in tasks that are legitimate in the classroom is, and has been shown wanting.

Possibilities and Certainties

Moje (2000) alerts us to the huge potential that exists to create learning opportunities where children such as Nate can succeed, and Larson and Gatto (2004) tell the story of one teacher who subverted the standardization and accountability that accompanied the No Child Left Behind policies to create a space where third-grade children in an urban school could engage and learn meaningfully. The teacher (Gatto) "does not follow the mandated lesson plan format … does not use the text-books … and the spelling, grammar, phonics, and math workbooks are sent back to the book room" (p. 19). Instead, Gatto and the children constructed a "tactical space within the prescriptive space of school in which traditional power relations are transformed and all languages, literacies, and knowledges count" (p. 37). Gatto's curriculum strategies are based on inquiry as a social practice; multiliteracies are privileged and what transpires is "a fluid, non-linear interaction among the class members, including her [Gatto] ... which in turn transforms the social relations" (p. 21). So in this classroom it was not only the fact that all languages, literacies, and knowledges counted, but it was also that the social relations had been transformed to enable the children to make meaning in ways that were meaningful to them.

But providing opportunities for learning through traditionally illegitimate practices and remaking the power relations in classrooms is by no means the end of the story or all that is needed; nor are these simple options. The link between popular culture and literacy practices can be a persuasive stimulus for children to explore issues of power and identity. Although the superhero story lines and children's use of the identities depicted in Dyson's (1997) research provide powerful ways for children to experience the triumph of good over evil, Dyson noted that these story lines are limiting in their often stereotypical rendering of race, class, gender, culture, and ethnicity; more significantly, unless teachers worked closely with them, the children used these story lines to marginalize or privilege others in relation to race, class, or gender. With the support of their teacher, the children worked through the limitations and challenges of commercial media culture to learn about participating in the classroom as a community of difference, not only in their peer relations but also in their writing. Nate and others like him need to learn to use their unconventional knowledge to "navigate other social spaces and challenge the ways that their social and cultural spaces are positioned in society" (Moje, 2000, p. 683). To learn to do this means that they need to be taught how. One way is to find out what children know (and be sure to use what they know), thus emphasizing the fact that children's knowledge does count in the classroom. But not every teacher is a Gatto (Larson & Gatto, 2004) and can reject the mandated lesson plan format, refuse to use the textbooks, and construct his or her own space of resistance to the demands of standardization and accountability. There are many teachers like Glenys (Comber & Nichols, 2004) who identify successful children in their class as those who understand their instructions and carry "them out with precision" (p. 50).

To complicate matters further, teachers are increasingly positioned by contradictory discourses of literacy: on the one hand, literacy is defined as a "set of specified skills" and on the other as "repertoires of social and cultural practices" (Comber & Nichols, 2004, p. 45). The former definition certainly casts Nate as unsuccessful and may have prompted the description of Nate by his teachers as "struggling"; the latter provides opportunities for making what children know count in the classroom. And what of Nate's out-of-school knowledge? Despite the community being "wired" and the school's overt engagement with technologies, Nate's cultural capital seemed invisible to his teachers. His "unschooled" practices did not count and the teachers may not have even known about them.

We know from this short excerpt that Nate's practices were empowering, productive, and integral to his potential to transform himself to an actor in his own story, as opposed to a passive onlooker of the dominant story. If, as Dyson (1997) and Moje (2000) claim, literacy practices are tools for transforming thought and experience, and, as Gee (1996) has argued, literacy practices are fundamental for identity construction and representation, then what is needed is a makeover or reinvention of what is understood as legitimate literacy practices in early childhood classrooms. In the current climate of No Child Left Behind and moves in Australia to test (or assess) children nationally each year of their elementary schooling except year 1, such a large-scale change seems out of the question. What, then, is the future for Nate and others like him? Given the impending testing regime in Australia and the fact that nobody ever grew taller by being measured, what hope is there that Nate's alternate multiliterate practices will be encouraged, let alone thrive—especially when his teachers do not appear to know about his abilities? The odds are that his story will remain relegated to the classroom underground, that space for illicit activity that occurs on windows that disappear as soon as the literacy and numeracy police materialize.

On a more hopeful note, however, the work of Dyson (1997, 2002) and Larson and Gatto (2004) confirms that there are early childhood teachers who are using nontraditional and unconventional practices to teach literacy and numeracy in the early years of schooling. Pedagogically, there are a number of things that teachers can do in these years. Knowing children holistically, not just academically or cognitively, provides for meaningful engagement with individual children, and meaningful engagement is an integral part of good pedagogy. The importance of knowing, understanding, and respecting children's families should go without saying, but in the daily complexity of classroom life, it can be easily forgotten. Genuinely valuing and respecting children and their families can make a huge difference to what is learned in the classroom. Children's out-of-school knowledge and what is seen as important by schools are often two different things, but the substance of this chapter is that what children bring to school is too valuable to ignore. Thus, making children's knowledge count in the classroom means that it is visible (and therefore valued) and can be used productively for further learning.

Note

This research was made possible by a Queensland University of Technology (Brisbane, Australia) Research Encouragement Award.

References

Alloway, N. (2000). Exploring boys' literacy performance at school: Incorporating and transcending gender. *Contemporary Issues in Early Childhood, 1*(3), 333–337.

Australian Association of Mathematics Teachers (AAMT). (1997). *Numeracy = everyone's business: Report of the Numeracy Education Strategy Development Conference.* Adelaide: Australian Association of Mathematics Teachers.

Brooker, L. (2001). Interviewing children. In G. Mac Naughton, S. A. Rolfe, & I. Siraj-Blatchford (Eds.), *Doing early childhood research: International perspectives on theory and practice* (pp. 162–177). Crow's Nest, Australia: Allen & Unwin.

Campbell, S. (2005). Secret children's business: Resisting and redefining access to learning in the early childhood classroom. In N. Yelland (Ed.), *Critical issues in early childhood education* (pp. 146–162). Berkshire, England: Open University Press.

Cannold, L. (2001). Interviewing adults. In G. Mac Naughton, S. A. Rolfe, & I. Siraj-Blatchford (Eds.), *Doing early childhood research: International perspectives on theory and practice* (pp. 178–192). Crow's Nest, Australia: Allen & Unwin.

Comber, B., & Nichols, S. (2004). Getting the big picture: Regulating knowledge in the early childhood literacy curriculum. *Journal of Early Childhood Literacy, 4*(1), 43–63.

Cooper, T. J., McRobbie, C. J., & Baturo, A. R. (Eds.). (n.d.). *Final ACOT report: Parts A, B, C, D & E* (2nd draft). Brisbane: Queensland University of Technology.

Copley, J. V. (2004). The early childhood collaborative: A professional development model to communicate and implement the standards. In D. H. Clements & J. Sarama (Eds.), *Engaging young children in mathematics: Standards for early childhood mathematics education* (pp. 404–414). Mahwah, NJ: Lawrence Erlbaum.

Cummins, J. (2004). Foreword. In S. Nieto, *Affirming diversity: The sociopolitical context of multicultural education* (4th ed., pp. xv–xvii). Boston, MA: Allyn & Bacon.

Dyson, A. H. (1997). *Writing superheroes: Contemporary childhood, popular culture, and classroom literacy.* New York: Teachers College Press.

Dyson, A. H. (2002). *The brothers and sisters learn to write: Popular literacies in childhood and school cultures.* New York: Teachers College Press.

Emerson, R. M., Fretz, R. I., & Shaw, L. L. (1995). *Writing ethnographic fieldnotes.* Chicago: University of Chicago Press.

Florida, R. (2003). *The rise of the creative class: and how it's transforming work, leisure, community and everyday life.* New South Wales: Pluto Press.

Foucault, M. (1972). *The archaeology of knowledge.* New York: Pantheon.

Gee, J. P. (1996). *Social linguistics and literacies: Ideology in discourses* (2nd ed.). London: Falmer.

Gilbert, R., & Gilbert, P. (1998). *Masculinity goes to school.* New York: Routledge.

Glesne, C. (2006). *Becoming qualitative researchers: An introduction* (3rd ed.). Boston, MA: Pearson Education.

Gorard, S., Rees, S., & Salisbury, J. (1999). Reappraising the apparent underachievement of boys at school. *Gender and Education, 11*(4), 441–454.

Kress, G. (2003). *Literacy in the new media age.* London: Routledge.

Larson, J., & Gatto, L. A. (2004). Tactical underlife: Understanding students' perceptions. *Journal of Early Childhood Literacy, 4*(1), 11–41.

Marsh, J. (2000). Teletubby tales: Popular culture in the early years' language and literacy curriculum. *Contemporary Issues in Early Childhood, 1*(2), 119–133.

Marsh, J. (2005). Ritual, performance and identity construction: Young children's engagement with popular cultural and media texts. In J. Marsh (Ed.), *Popular culture, new media and digital literacy in early childhood* (pp. 28–50). Oxon, U.K.: RoutledgeFalmer.

Moje, E. B. (2000). "To be part of the story": The literacy practices of gangsta adolescents. *Teachers College Record, 102*(3), 651–690.

New London Group. (1996). A pedagogy of multiliteracies: Designing social futures. *Harvard Educational Review, 66*(1), 60–92.

Perry, B., & Dockett, S. (2004). Mathematics in early childhood education. In B. Perry, G. Anthony, & C. M. Diezmann (Eds.), *Research in mathematics education in Australasia: 2000–2003*. Sydney: Mathematics Education Research Group of Australia.

Silverman, D. (2000). *Doing qualitative research: A practical handbook*. London: Sage.

Thorpe, K., Tayler, C., Bridgstock, R., Grieshaber, S., Skoien, P., Danby, S., & Petriwskyl, A. (2004). *Preparing for school: Report of the Queensland preparing for school trials 2003/4*. Brisbane: School of Early Childhood, Queensland University of Technology.

Titus, J. J. (2004). Boy trouble: Rhetorical framing of boys' underachievement. *Discourse: Studies in the Cultural Politics of Education, 25*(2), 145–169.

Weedon, C. (1997). *Feminist practice and poststructuralist theory* (2nd ed.). Oxford: Blackwell.

Yin, R. C. (2003). *Case Study Research* (3rd ed.). Thousand Oaks, CA: Sage.

7

Thought-Provoking Moments in Teaching Young Children
Reflections on Social Class, Sexuality, and Spirituality

LESLIE R. WILLIAMS AND NADJWA E. L. NORTON

Why would you want to spend time thinking about social class, sexuality, or spirituality in designing curricula for young children? Young children don't even notice social class, discussion of sexuality is not appropriate in the early childhood classroom anyway, and spirituality isn't something that young children are capable of talking about. It's far too complicated for them to grasp. There are many more important elements to focus on in multicultural education, like dealing with the diversity that children bring with them into the classroom as a foundation for their learning new things. (Reaction of a teaching colleague to our chapter proposal, August 2005)

The response of our colleague to the proposal for this chapter was not unexpected. Although she had over the past several years become involved in the redesign of teacher preparation programs to incorporate both multicultural and inclusive orientations, she shares with others common misconceptions about young children's sophistication in their observation of the human diversity that surrounds them. Social class is, in her perception, far too abstract to raise questions in the minds of young observers. It is not like obvious characteristics, such as the color of one's skin. As the conversation continued, she reminded us as well of how controversial anything to do with sexual orientation in publicly funded curricula for young children in New York City has been.[1] The notion of introducing thinking about spirituality in activities with young children was even more disturbing to her. She felt that most educators and families alike would equate attention to spirituality to a focus on religion, and that would very much limit the audience for our work. Moreover, she could not recollect ever having heard young children raise "spiritual" concerns aside from elements of their families' specifically religious beliefs or practices, so the possibility that this was of interest to young children appeared moot to her.

Our own experience as teachers, members of families, and teacher educators, however, had given us a different perspective on these arenas of diversity in the lives of young children. In an early childhood center where we frequently observe, the preschool children are annually involved in both food drives and toy collections around the holidays. They not only help in the collection of goods, but they go with their teachers to the venues where the collections are delivered; and we have heard of their comments on the way back to the classroom about "lazy daddies" and "dirty people." Similarly, children do display their sexuality from a young age, some more obviously than others. What meaning they derive from their behaviors remains an important, unexplored question, as it relates to the formation of one aspect of children's identities. And finally, children's spirituality permeates many parts of their lives, as they struggle with the unknowns of their existence just as adults do.

Even though these three dimensions of diversity may be very powerful in children's lives, they may be the three dimensions that are most frequently ignored by teachers, administrators, and families in early education programs because they are difficult to address and are subject to public opprobrium. People in the United States like to maintain the myth that we are a classless society; from Victorian times onward, a common preference has been to see young children as "sexless." Introduction of the topic of spirituality often causes educators and families to shudder, and staff people are reminded (further acting out the common misconception) that in public schools, at least, we must maintain a separation of church and state. In polite conversation, we are told, one should never raise the specters of politics, sex, or religion!

Thus, children's natural introduction of these aspects of their daily lives presents us with difficult moments in teaching. How might we respond to these issues that are salient in children's lives? What tenets do we have to guide our thinking about these moments? What are alternatives to some of our usual silencing and exclusion of children voices in these areas?

Tenets of Multicultural Education in the Context of Schooling

For many, multicultural education has been a reform movement premised upon the ideas of accepting and respecting cultural differences, exploring and welcoming numerous ways of seeing and believing, and including multiple voices and awarenesses (Rogovin, 1998, 2001). We stand among those who construct culture as an intricate dynamic process that shapes and is shaped by how people live and experience their everyday realities. Like Nieto (2004) and Hernandez (2001), we work to illuminate how culture is composed of explicit, visible, and implicit, taken-for-granted elements that signify the artifacts, behaviors, and values of people. In light of these understandings, we define culture "as a total way of life, including the history and traditions of a group, and the experiences and ways of living, perceiving, and thinking" (De Gaetano, Williams, & Volk, 1998, p. 7). Thus, within this chapter, culture and multicultural education are far more inclusive than a focus on race, class, and gender. Rather, they also encompass spirituality, ability, language, nationality, citizenship, sexuality, education, and age.

As multicultural educators, we advocate for teaching strategies that highlight diverse perspectives in order to foster consciousness and acceptance of the vast range of cultures that have been created by human agency. Our multicultural education pedagogies counter prejudice and ignorance by building communities that highlight marginalized voices, make visible ignored images, and reflect a range of lived experiences (Ramsey, 2004). Increasingly, our teaching and learning practices signify the need for people to interact with various cultures by interviewing and conversing with others; engaging with diverse texts, including books, music, food, materials, and social gatherings; and exploring commonalities and differences among and within cultures (Ford & Harris, 1999; Kendall, 1996). We assert that multicultural education does not merely explore the joys and celebrations of culture but investigates the ways cultures and understandings of cultures operate to sustain inequities and discrimination (Banks, 1996).

This idea of inequities and discrimination is particularly important to us because we recognize that despite all the research that has been done about children, many people and educational structures continue to position children, particularly young children, as beings without knowledge and voice (Norton, 2005). This positioning denies the experiences and agencies that young children bring with them into their classrooms. In order to challenge such understandings, we continually search for teaching and learning possibilities that sustain opportunities for children to utilize their voices, make sense of experience, and act upon their worlds. We contend that creating and maintaining educational contexts inclusive of children's voices requires an understanding and valuing of collaborative and reciprocal teaching and learning between teachers and children, teachable moments, and the need to let children's questions and investigations shape and direct curriculum (Rogovin, 2001; Vasquez, 2004).

Pursuing multicultural education from this point of view necessitates understanding that the execution of comprehensive, ongoing, integrated, institutionalized multicultural education is the most possible way to maintain success for all children (De Gaetano et al., 1998; Kendall, 1996). The efficiency and strength of multicultural education lies in its implementation as a pervasive philosophy of teaching and learning that permeates practice and provides a foundation for all decision-making processes within teaching and learning. In light of this knowledge, we see a welcome challenge in discerning how educators enact such practice within and throughout their own personal lives, across all academic content areas, within the social ethos of the classroom, and in relationships with the child's family and community.

This challenge is acknowledged not only by us but also by multicultural educators who understand that the ability to effectively permeate such teaching and learning practices is affected by the structures, organizational policies, and systematic practices of institutions, including schools. Scholars such as Nieto (2004) and Weil (1998) reveal how power intersects with teaching philosophies and practices by hindering or facilitating individual and group positionings and access to resources. Thus, we have joined those who are undertaking the hard work of illuminating how components such as school structures, assumptions, policies, curriculum, assessment, and materials privilege certain cultures over others and disproportionately restrict the assets and means of people who are constructed as nonvaluable (Knight, Norton, Bentley, & Dixon, 2004).

Working within these understandings, we begin in this chapter to explore ways that young children's social class, sexuality, and spirituality may present formidable barriers to their full participation in the educational process, when their identities are constructed negatively by their teachers. By social class we are referring to the social stratification that results from individuals' and groups' (limited) access to material resources and the consequent unequal distribution of power favoring the upper classes (McLaren, 1997). Different cultures may construct social classes differently according to their histories (conflict and conquest), their cosmologies (their understandings of the nature of the universe), and the availability of valuable resources to particular individuals within their group (entrepreneurial activity). Inherent in the construction of social class is the assumption of the superiority of some and the inferiority of others, just as the same is inherent in views of race and ethnicity or other aspects of culture. Thus, social class intersects with these other constructions with ever more powerful negative effects on the lives of the children in the lower echelons (Ramsey & Williams, 2003). What is true of social class also holds for sexual orientation.

Sexual orientation refers to the portion of a person's identity having to do with his or her physical and emotional attraction to others. We assume that all human beings are born with a position on a continuum of sexuality that is determined genetically but that the eventual manifestation of a person's sexuality is influenced by a variety of societal factors and, like social class and other such constructions, intersects with various aspects of culture, race, and class (Ramsey & Williams, 2003). Although the majority of people are attracted to people of the opposite sex, a not inconsequential portion of any population develops differently, with attraction to persons of the same sex. Depending on individuals' abilities and opportunities to be open with others about their orientation, they may or may not have a lifestyle that reflects this aspect of their identity. The possibility of being able to pursue a gay or lesbian lifestyle is very important to many gay and lesbian people. In contrast, lifestyle does not appear particularly salient in consideration of people's spirituality.

Although discussing the term *spirituality* often evokes contentious and amorphous meanings and brings about exclusivity, disagreement, separateness, and elusiveness, our use of this concept seeks to provide an inclusive general definition that incorporates understanding a vast array of world perspectives. We work with a definition of spirituality that denotes two components of connectedness with (un)seen forces that are beyond human power, including but not limited to nature, the universe, constructs of God, spirits, souls, and religious deities. The first component involves the connectedness of an individual's mind-spirit-body in relationship to (un)seen force(s). The second component of spiritualities highlights how spiritualities also connect people's minds-spirits-bodies to the other entities created by or related to those (un)seen forces. For many individuals, spiritualities entail figuring out ways to be in relationship with entities such as humans and other living creatures, as well as geographical features such as mountains and trees. Therefore, children's spiritualities are informed by multiple factors, including family, religion, geography, race, and personal histories (Coles, 1990).

Making Class, Sexuality, and Spirituality Visible in Classroom Practices

We have both incorporated long-standing reflective processes about multicultural education within the various dimensions of our life work that has been integral in assisting us to change and strengthen our teaching practices. What we have come to know is that our reflections upon the communities in which we participate and our educational practices sustain how we advocate for diversity and equity issues. It is in light of past, present, and future reflection that we encourage early childhood educators and scholars to become aware of and make visible to others the silences of class, sexuality, and spirituality. This chapter is intended to support early childhood professionals in reflecting upon and revisioning the assumptions and knowledge that are within our field. In that vein we ask you to read this chapter as a reflective activity that encourages you to critique and question your current practices and to examine how you both facilitate and restrict the experiences of young children. We encourage readers to see through the eyes of the children, as well as through those of the teachers included, and through their own eyes in order to build the necessary bridges that will expand perspectives, teaching practices, and ways of understanding the diversity that is among us.

Making Social Class Visible: Scenario 1

Each year in an independent preschool classroom largely serving middle-class to upper-middle-class children in a large city, the teachers encouraged the children to go out into the community where the center was located to become familiar with all of its resources. In that way, teachers and children would discover interests that could be made into short- or long-term projects for the children's integrated curriculum. Among the resources explored was a large church that sponsored a soup kitchen each day for the many homeless families within the area it serves.

In the autumn of the year, the teachers in the classroom would talk with the children about how many families there were that did not have enough food to eat and help the children to organize and participate in a small food drive. Once a wagonload of food had been collected, a teacher, a director, and several of the children would walk the several blocks to the church with the wagon of food and deliver it to the food kitchen. The church kitchen staff would always receive the little group warmly, and usually the children would see some of the families already standing in line for the lunch that would be ready soon.

On the way back to the center from one such trip, a director overheard two of the children talking about what they had just seen:

Jack: Those kids were dirty.
Robbie: Yeah … dirty.
Jack: I bet they are hungry.
Robbie: That's because their daddies don't work for them to get them food. Their daddies are lazy. My daddy isn't lazy. He works to get us food.
Jack: It's a good thing for them that we got them food.
Robbie: Yeah. … They should get to work … and take a bath!

After the group had returned to the center, the director shared what she had heard with the teachers. Together, the classroom teaching team and the directors began to consider how they might address the misconceptions that the children had shown. The food collection activity had been done routinely for several years, but the teachers realized that there had never been a period of thoughtful preparation for it in which the issues of homelessness had been discussed with the children. Instead, the preparation had focused on the mechanics of food collection and on pronouncements that food was needed. Thus, the children were displaying views untrammeled by any attempts at intervention on the part of the teachers. How and where had the preschool children developed their present attitudes? What was the effect of the media in presenting these issues, and what conversations had the children heard in their own homes?

The teachers have a variety of ways that they could use to begin to develop the children's awareness of the terrible oppressions that can come with being homeless. One alternative would be for the children and teachers to consider how it is that a family might have become homeless in the first place. What can happen to hard-working people's jobs that could cause such a thing? Where do people stay when they no longer have their own home? What sort of access do they have when they are "on the streets" to facilities such as bathrooms and showers? Who is at fault here—the families themselves or something else? Is the issue of "fault" relevant? How are the people in the food line different from or the same as children and families associated with the preschool center? Any of these inquiries could precede or form the foundation for the food collection project.

Once the food had been collected, the teachers wondered, would it be possible for the children to go to the food kitchen to have a meal and time to play with some of the children who ate there? Could this be done more than once, so that the children could begin to get to know each other? Would this help the preschool children to see the children whose families use the food kitchen as people like themselves who had had some difficulties in their lives but who had similar interests to their own? This process surely would not answer all the children's questions, but could it move them beyond the attitude of "noblesse oblige" that seemed presently to be permeating their perceptions?

Just as importantly, how might the preschool children's families become involved in planning activities for the children that would offer a larger view of homelessness and hunger in America? Should this be the subject of one of the ongoing family meetings at the center? How might such a meeting be done so that it does not look as if we are blaming the families? Given the fact that the values displayed in the children's homes may be one of the sources of their misconceptions about homelessness, creating an exploration that involves families, teachers, and children may offer the best chances of growth in the understanding of all involved.

Making Sexuality Visible: Scenario 2

Three-year-old Hugh had been in the 2 to 3's classroom of an early childhood center, and he was due to move to one of the center's preschool rooms. For some time now his teachers had been observing his strong interest in fantasy play and certain scenarios that he liked to reenact. Often when he entered the room in the morning he would head straight for the "dress-up corner," even before greeting the teachers or other children present. There he would select one of the gowns hanging on the wall pegs. His especial favorite was the Cinderella costume, with a long, puffy yellow taffeta skirt and a blue satin bodice. He sometimes would request help with the buttons, while he wiggled his feet into the "glass slippers" and selected a "diamond" tiara to complete the outfit.

Once he was completely outfitted, Hugh would greet the teachers and perhaps sit down for a breakfast snack before joining other children in an activity. In all conversation that followed, he would insist that he be addressed as "she" and would remind both other children and teachers that he was a girl. He especially loved to initiate or join others in role-plays around the storybook character he was representing where he could be the "mother" or the "pretty sister." He would not take off the costume until the end of the day, even taking his nap and going to the outside play area while wearing it. On the occasions when teachers said he must take it off in order to share it with another child,

Hugh would find an alternative costume such as "Sleeping Beauty" or create one from the many dress-up clothes available in the corner.

It was the philosophy of the center, and strongly applied in that particular classroom, to give the children full latitude in their cocreation of the curriculum. Fantasy play was an important part of the children's creation, and the teachers would sometimes participate in an improvisational way, following the children's leads. Most of the children were deeply engaged in these activities and showed as high a degree of enthusiasm and interest as Hugh did.

Recently while sitting a corner of the classroom near two parents, one of the teachers had overheard the parents speaking softly together. They had noticed Hugh's activities and appeared to be uncomfortable with what they had seen. One mother said she was glad that her husband was not observing then, because he would pull his son out of the program if he saw what the center teachers let Hugh do. The other mother said that she found the role-play disturbing too, and that she didn't understand why the teachers didn't just take the costume away from Hugh and give him some "more suitable" toys. She felt Hugh would never have any friends among the boys if he continued "to act that way."

The teacher who had overheard the parents' comments later described her discomfort with Hugh's interests and her feelings of uncertainty about what to do. She felt that Hugh was a happy child now but that he would not soon be, if adults kept pushing their own agendas on him. Yet she was worried about how he would get along in the world if his predilection persisted. She was aware that Hugh's mother was worried about Hugh's behaviors in general, but it was not clear if his mother was aware of the other parents' reaction to their observations or whether she was focusing on these particular behaviors over others.

Another teacher was also struggling with her beliefs that homosexuality was morally wrong. She thought that the teachers should make clear that they did not accept these behaviors, while simultaneously showing Hugh that they cared about him as a person. She was also afraid that the center would "lose its credibility" if Hugh were "allowed to go on as he was."

Hugh appeared to be following deeply felt impulses. On one hand, most of the teachers felt that it was important to support all the children in their continuous development of their identities. On the other hand, the teachers were aware that his possible sexuality would not make life easy for Hugh or his family, and that perhaps they should be trying to interest him in other activities. Perhaps, some thought, Hugh was too young for sexuality even to be relevant in the discussion. Was this perhaps a developmental phase rather than a life condition that Hugh was demonstrating? Hugh's mother was experiencing a number of difficulties in her life. The teachers did not feel comfortable about pointing out their current concern if she, in fact, did not notice it or was not upset about it.

The teachers continued to support Hugh in his choice of fantasy activities while also encouraging him to join the many other activities that were going on in the room as well. No special mention of the matter was made in parent conferences. No deliberate exploration of Hugh's thoughts on his choices was made in conversation with him. Thus, no further insight was added to their consideration.

The directors at the center felt that there might have been other ways to work with Hugh, the teachers, his parents, and the other children in the center. What might they do in the future, should a similar occasion arise? What was the teachers' knowledge base regarding current theory and research around the appearance of homosexuality transgenderness in young children? Without an understanding of the possible biological as well as the possible sociological origins of homosexuality transgenderness, it may be difficult for people to "hear" what a child is telling them. Were there ways for the staff to look at their reluctance to speak with and listen to Hugh's mother about any concerns she might have had about the development of Hugh's sexual identity? What was she thinking, and how might the staff have supported her in her own deliberations? Staff development sessions in these areas might have been useful, as well as some modeling of ways to engage Hugh in conversation about what he was doing.

What was the center staff as a whole doing in terms of presenting alternative images of family compositions, choice of occupations (moving beyond gendered expectations), and varieties of artistic expression? How might the center community be involved in the larger discussion of the "appropriateness" of these curriculum developments? How might family privacy be protected in the midst of public discourse? All of these represented possible directions for future conversations, recognizing that they were not likely to be easily resolvable into a completely clear course of action but also seeing their value in moving the staff and the center as a whole toward support of all the emerging identities of the children in the program.

Some time later, after Hugh had left the center, a teacher saw him and his mother walking home from school one day. Hugh was dressed in a Spiderman costume and was enthusiastically leaping from a small stone parapet and swinging from the uprights on a wrought-iron fence. He was shouting, "I am king of the world!"

Making Spirituality Visible: Scenario 3

Nap time was a daily component of the curriculum within the 5–6's classroom at a New York City school that supported young children's needs to sleep, rest, engage in solitude, and interact quietly with a peer. Students and teachers collaborated in choosing both location and partners. This teaching practice allowed for shared decision making between children and teachers, respected preferred intimate relationships formed between children, and also made space for children to extend their boundaries by occasionally sharing space with a child who was not a preferred social acquaintance. As the school year progressed, children found themselves using their 20–30 minute nap time as a venue for other stimulating activities beyond sleeping, including reading books on rugs, hugging stuffed animals, drawing on paper, writing on a clipboard, or chatting with a friend.

One afternoon, Nyla (the teacher) had paired Lisa, a 6-year-old white middle-class girl, with Matt, a 5-year-old white middle-class boy, who was a self-identified atheist and the son of atheist parents. Lisa and Matt were not friends and did not often choose each other's company, but they were both very verbal children who evidenced strong opinions. As was customary, Nyla walked around the room checking on children and listening to their conversations. She stopped within earshot of Matt and Lisa's conversation.

Lisa:	God is real.
Matt:	There is no God.
Lisa:	Yes there is, I know because I go to church.
Matt:	God is something people just make up.
Lisa:	No, my grandfather is a pastor.
Lisa:	(Crying) Nyla!
Nyla:	Yes.
Lisa:	Is God real?
Nyla:	Well, that's a hard question, because people believe different things. Are you asking me what I think? Stop crying, calm down. Some people like Matt don't believe in God.
Lisa:	But I know God is real. I go to church. My grandfather is a pastor.
Nyla:	Yes, and some people like you who go to church believe in God. I didn't know you went to church. Do you go a lot?
Lisa:	Yes!
Nyla:	There are Christians and Muslims and Jewish people who believe in God. There are people who believe God is real who don't go to the church or the mosque or the temple. And there are people who don't believe in God; they are called atheists.
Matt:	Yes, my family is atheist. We don't believe in God.
Nyla:	One of my best friends is an atheist—she doesn't believe in God either. I know lots of people who don't believe in God. And I know lots of people who do believe in God. I believe in God but I don't go to church anymore.

As a multicultural educator who believed that spirituality was an aspect of culture and that children were spiritual beings, Nyla immediately acknowledged Lisa and Matt's conversations as important and relevant experiences in the classroom. Like many other multicultural educators who work with young children, Nyla demonstrated multicultural teaching practices that first made space for the voices of young children. Rather than censor the spiritual conversation because of its complexity or Lisa's emotional state, Nyla participated in the conversation with the understanding that young children can talk about such abstract issues. Second, Nyla acknowledged and made visible not only the experiences of these two culturally diverse children but also brought in the belief systems of others. Instead of personally distancing herself from the conversation, she also self-identified as a spiritual being and shared part of her seemingly invisible culture with her students. Her behavior affirmed the knowledges and abilities of children to dialogue about their lived realities and to shape their perspectives on the world.

Nyla's teaching practices provided opportunities for Lisa and Matt to develop and sustain knowledges through her interaction with them, yet these opportunities were also limited by the political context of the United States. There exists a popular misconception that religion and spirituality are synonymous and interchangeable concepts, while in actuality, religion is a subset of spirituality. Further, a large majority of the American population believes that religion and spirituality cannot be part of the school's discourse because of the constitutional separation between church and state. In actuality, however, teachers and students alike are able to discuss and observe spiritualities and spiritual practices, as long as they are not proselytizing to others.

How might Nyla's and the 5 to 6's teaching and learning have been strengthened if she had better understood how spiritual and academic content could be blended to meet curriculum standards? How could she have created more spaces for discussion of spirituality to permeate curriculum and provide access to resources for children that would expand their understandings and knowledges? What might have transpired if Nyla's lesson planning had focused more on connecting spirituality to the class inquiry curriculum with the theme of jobs and work?

It is in light of spiritual discrepancies, misconceptions, and diversities that multicultural educators like Nyla must attend to the spiritualities of children in their classrooms. To what degree would she have been able to diversify the social studies and literacy components by exercising more spiritual awareness in her choice of people to interview, exploratory trips, and books to borrow from the library that incorporated diverse notions of spirituality? How might Nyla have also woven spirituality into the math explorations of Venn diagrams and graphs that often stemmed from the children's questions and conversations? How might she have explored patterns in spiritual images, buildings, and artwork? Multicultural educators have to explore how (in)visible spirituality within curriculum invites and alienates children from their classrooms.

Implications for Practice

Readers of this chapter may be feeling some frustration at this point. We have raised far more questions than we have answered. Our doing so has verified what many thoughtful teachers may have suspected, that is, that multicultural theorists and practitioners are in their infancy regarding effective practical work with these issues. The first step surely is to recognize—to name—the issues with as much clarity as possible. We hope that our descriptions have moved this process forward.

The next step is to consider some guidelines for building practice. How might responsible teachers, parents and families, and administrators organize their discussions and decision making as they plan curriculum around these areas? The suggestions that follow arise from our own attempts and continued reflection on these difficult moments in our recent teaching experience:

1. Make time in our daily and weekly schedules to listen to and hear what the children in our classrooms, homes, and centers or schools are telling us about their conceptions and concerns in any or all of these areas.

   - Note instances when the children reveal their conceptions about social class, sexuality, or spirituality in their play, and write them down for consideration by colleagues.
   - Take a walk or arrange a separate lunch so that you may have individual conversations with children about a few of the important matters that you hear them discussing.
   - Build in shared moments where you bring in a special item like a book, photograph, or keepsake that will prompt discussion about the selected issue.
   - Set aside opportunities in classroom team meetings, small-group family meetings, or other professional get-togethers for careful discussion of what the children have actually said or done. Note that confidentiality should be a critical part of these discussions. You may wish to disguise the particulars for protection of children and families, when possible.
   - Reflect on the information collected. Reflection may involve self-reflection (self-confrontation when necessary) and collective reflection. Some strategies may include discussion resulting from audio- or videotaping of your own practice, collegial observations of your teaching, and using such means as metaphors or role-plays to clarify and deepen discussion of the issues.

2. Consider the intended or unintended messages we have been giving the children about social class, sexuality, or spirituality—our own, theirs, or those of other people in general.

   - Lay out evidence of those messages, looking at the ways the children have received them.

- Check and work with the perceptions of other adults about these messages to discover how they have experienced them in their lives.

3. Search out resources intended to guide us as teachers or to use directly in work with children. Include nonprint materials such as posters, songs, and improvisational play techniques that can deepen and focus practice.

   - Work to expand our knowledge to include the most current research on these areas done with children across ethnicities, races, social classes, sexualities, and spiritualities in America and in other parts of the world.
   - Consider what our own values and dispositions are regarding the questions such explorations will raise.
   - Practice the skills involved in handling discussions in these areas, including the skills involved in discussion with families, community members, and colleagues in raising what are considered by many to be "sensitive" or "inappropriate" issues with young children.
   - Think about how we might challenge ourselves and grow as human beings trying to work constructively in enabling children to strengthen their identities and sense of worth as human beings.

4. Talk with children and respond directly to their expressed concerns. Seek proactive ways to engage young children in organized, active discussion of their present knowledge of these aspects of human life. Develop strategies to build curricula that not only explore these areas but also present and encourage visions of social justice and opportunities for action.

   - Plan guided role-plays that help children to explore life alternatives and to understand how different people experience life. For example, present a cot and create different sleeping conditions. Then ask: How did you feel sleeping inside with a roof when it was raining? What was it like sleeping with a roof with a hole in it while it was raining? What was it like sleeping outside with no roof while it was raining?
   - Systematically incorporate images around issues of diversity into classroom activities. Ask children what they think about these images. For instance, how might this child with holes in her shoes feel walking to school in the snow? How does this boy feel when his holiday is not celebrated in school?
   - Include a direct question in the morning meeting that raises children's consciousness and diversity awareness. For example,

how would you feel if your family never had money to go to eat out or order food in?

- Participate in hands-on puppetry, storytelling, and creation of posters depicting issues that children can connect with. Relate these issues to everyday issues that have an impact on children's lives. Suppose that you believed that whenever you passed a garden you had to talk to the vegetables and help them grow. Imagine that you told your teacher and he didn't stop at the garden when you walked past on the science nature walk.

- Stop children and address their conversations with each other in order to highlight typically taboo conversations and to clarify incorrect information.

- Plan lessons that integrate diversity issues throughout all academic content areas and that are tiered through levels of intensity. This might entail having a range of images in the block area, surveys about same-sex families, weekly poems that highlight different class lifestyles, nonfiction reading about different people's experiences in communities, and interviews with diverse people.

- Frequently read books and listen to songs that introduce new cultures, show cultural conflict, and promote problem solving.

- Develop mini-inquiries where children can formulate a question and explore uncertain and unknown topics, such as: What do people do after a pet dies? How do people get better when they aren't well?

These guidelines are intended to help us move beyond occasional forays into unexplored areas of human difference toward institutionalization of their recognition into our ongoing multicultural curriculum. The aim is integration of these concerns in nonspectacular, everyday ways into the range of topics and activities common in early childhood practice. This cannot happen until we ourselves comfortable with working in "difficult" arenas, transforming what we find hard to consider into simply another part of life requiring our attention. Through such action, we hope to continue facing and removing the oppressions that limit opportunities for our children's growth, development, and learning, as well as our own.

To assist us in this endeavor, we have begun the search for resources and listed those we found below. While many of these were originally intended to guide work with children older than those in early childhood programs, they can suggest directions for us that we can adapt for work with young children.

Teacher Resources

Films

Chasnoff, D., & Cohen, H. (1996). *It's elementary: Talking about gay issues in school.* San Francisco: Women's Educational Media. (video)

Web Sites

Electronic Magazine of Multicultural Education, http://www.eastern.edu/ publications/emme.

Multicultural Pavilion, http://www.edchange.org/multicultural/.

Discovery Education, http://education.discovery.com/.

Gay, Lesbian, and Straight Education Network (GLSEN), http://www.glsen.org/ cgi-bin/iowa/home.html.

Oxfam, http://www.oxfam.org.uk/coolplanet/kidsweb.

Live Wire Media, Resources for Character Education, Guidance, Lifeskills, http:// www.goodcharacter.com/SERVICE/webresources.html.

Public Education Regarding Sexual Orientation Nationally (The P.E.R.S.O.N. Project), http://www.personproject.org/.

National Association for Multicultural Education Resource Center, http://www. nameorg.org/resources/plans.html.

Guidelines and Texts

Allen, J. (Ed.) (1999). *Class actions: Teaching for social justice in elementary and middle school.* New York: Teachers College Press.

Casper, V., & Schultz, S. (1999). *Gay parents, straight schools: Building communication and trust.* New York: Teachers College Press.

Cushner, K., McClelland, A., & Safford, P. (2000). *Human diversity in education: An integrative approach* (3rd ed.). New York: McGraw-Hill.

De Gaetano, Y., Williams, L. R., & Volk, D. (1998). *Kaleidoscope: A multicultural, bilingual approach for the primary school classroom.* Columbus, OH: Merrill/Prentice-Hall.

Ramsey, P. (2004). *Teaching and learning in a diverse world: Multicultural education for young children* (3rd ed.). New York: Teachers College Press.

Children's Literature

Bunting, E. (2000). *December.* New York: Harcourt.

de Haan, L., & Nijland, S. *King and king.* Berkeley, CA: Ten Speed Press.

Garden, N. (2004). *Molly's family.* New York: Farrar, Straus and Giroux.

Landowne, Y. (2004). *Selavi, that is life: A Haitian story of hope.* El Paso, TX: Cinco Puntos

Muth, J. J. (2002). *The three questions.* New York: Scholastic.

Newman, L. (1993). *Saturday is Pattyday.* Norwich, VT: New Victoria.

Oppenheim, S. L. (1997). *Hundredth name.* Honesdale, PA: Boyds Mills Press.

Polacco, P. (1999). *I can hear the sun.* New York: Penguin Putnam.

Shaw, M. (2003) *Thich Nhat Hanh: A spiritual biography for young people.* Woodstock, VT: Skylight Paths.

Stuve-Bodeen, S. (2003). *Babu's song.* New York: Lee & Low Press.

Williams, V. B. (2004). *Amber was brave, Essie was smart.* New York: HarperCollins Children's Books.

Wood, D. (1999). *Grandad's prayers of the earth.* Cambridge MA: Candlewick Press.

Wood, D. (2001). *Old turtle.* New York: Scholastic.

Wood, D. (2003). *Old turtle and the broken truth.* New York: Scholastic.

Wood, D. (2005). *A quiet place.* New York: Aladdin Paperbacks.

Note

In the 1980s, a team of early childhood teachers and administrators in New York City designed *The Rainbow Curriculum* for New York's citywide prekindergarten and kindergarten programs. *The Rainbow Curriculum* included brief references to same-gender parents and cited a few children's books about families with two mothers or two fathers. In a series of explosive community meetings, parents and other concerned community members blocked the finalization of the curriculum and eventually brought about the demise of the whole project.

References

Banks, J. (1996). *Multicultural education, transformative knowledge, and action: Historical and contemporary perspectives.* New York: Teachers College Press.

Coles, R. (1990). *The spiritual life of children.* Boston: Houghton Mifflin.

De Gaetano, Y., Williams, L. R., & Volk, D. (1998). *Kaleidoscope: A multicultural approach for the primary classroom.* Upper Saddle River, NJ: Merrill Prentice-Hall.

Ford, D. Y., & Harris, J. J., III. (1999). *Multicultural gifted education.* New York: Teachers College Press.

Hernandez, H. (2001). *Multicultural education: A teacher's guide to linking context, process, and content.* Columbus, OH: Merrill.

Kendall, F. (1996). *Diversity in the classroom: New approaches to the education of young children.* New York: Teachers College Press.

Knight, M., Norton, N., Bentley, C., & Dixon, I. (2004). The power of black and Latina/o counterstories: Urban families and college-going processes. *Anthropology and Education Quarterly, 35*(1), 99–120.

McLaren, P. (1997). *Revolutionary multiculturalism: Pedagogies of dissent for the new millennium.* Boulder, CO: Westview.

Nieto, S. (2004). *Affirming diversity: The sociopolitical context of multicultural education* (4th ed.). New York: Addison Wesley Longman.

Norton, N. (2005). Permitanme hablar: Allow me to speak. *Language Arts, 83*(2), 118–127.

Ramsey, P. (2004). *Teaching and learning in a diverse world: Multicultural education for young children* (3rd ed.). New York: Teachers College Press.

Ramsey, P., & Williams, L. R. (with Vold, E. B.). (2003). *Multicultural education: A source book* (2nd ed.). New York: Routledge.

Rogovin, P. (1998). *Classroom interviews.* Portsmouth, NH: Heinemann.

Rogovin, P. (2001). *The research workshop: Bringing the world into your classroom.* Portsmouth, NH: Heinemann.

Vasquez, V. (2004). *Negotiating critical literacies with young children.* Mahwah, NJ: Lawrence Erlbaum.

Weil, D. (1998). *Towards a critical multicultural literacy: Theory and practice for education and liberation.* New York: Peter Lang.

Part II
Rethinking Policies and Programs

8

Digital Literacies for Young English Learners

Productive Pathways toward Equity and Robust Learning

ALTHEA SCOTT NIXON AND KRIS D. GUTIÉRREZ

Every Monday, Tuesday, and Wednesday, young children, siblings, and friends crowd the hallways outside the library of Morris Elementary School, waiting eagerly for their amigas/os to arrive and to enter the magical world of Las Redes. But the excitement is not one-sided. Undergraduate students trade accounts of their weekend events, their course readings, and share stories about the children at Las Redes Fifth Dimension after-school club as they make their way down the crowded 405 Freeway from a west coast university to Morris Elementary. The traditional barriers of age, educational experience, social class, and language differences are re-mediated as the naturally occurring ensembles of undergraduates and children take shape across the 10 weeks of the quarter, as these new friends collaborate on board and computer games, and on the newest addition to Las Redes, digital storytelling.

In this after-school program in a California elementary school, children in kindergarten to fifth grade work with college undergraduate students on digital storytelling, the creation of short movies about something significant in the children's lives. In this space, children, with the assistance of others, engage in meaningful and complex learning activity that utilizes play, imagination, technology, and rich language tools. For example, on any given day around the digital storytelling tables, one could observe children writing scripts, importing relevant photographs into the computer, and recording their voices while narrating their stories. Background music as the soundtrack for their digital story and digital effects created with computer software programs, such as Adobe Photoshop and Final Cut Pro, add the finishing touches to their proud creations.

Often, these digital stories were created using both Spanish and English, as Spanish is the home language for many of the children in the after-school program. In this biliterate-bicultural space, the home language functions as an unmarked language and is considered legitimate in its own right, as well as a tool to build new literacy practices. During digital storytelling, these hybrid language practices helped children share their stories and lives while learning multimodal storytelling with digital technologies. In this context, we see the kind of literacy learning that is possible when children are allowed access to their full linguistic toolkit to make meaning of the world around them.

We use this example to illustrate the importance of language in accomplishing everyday activities and to contrast literacy learning for English learners in programs that use their home languages as tools for learning with the literacy learning for English learners in today's schools in California. Since the 1998 passage of Proposition 227: English for the Children, a California initiative to end bilingualism in schools, regular classroom teachers in California have no longer been allowed to provide instruction in the students' home language.[1] The consequences of restrictive language policies are further exacerbated by reductive literacy programs that provide children a narrow scope of reading and writing skills and state-mandated assessments offered only in English, even to speakers of other languages. And increased attention has been given to accountability and scripted programs. Such practices are buttressed by the regulatory policies and ideological beliefs of No Child Left Behind as elementary schools are pressured to meet achievement targets measured solely by state-mandated assessments, especially in literacy. In this current sociopolitical climate, nonformal learning environments, especially after-school settings, are considered one of the few spaces where productive, meaningful literacy practices can occur (Hull & Schultz, 2002). This chapter describes one such environment.

We draw from a long-standing after-school program, rich in learning activities and forms of participation and assistance, including what we call hybrid language practices (Gutiérrez, Baquedano-López, & Tejeda, 1999) to illustrate a case of productive and meaningful literacy learning for children from non-dominant communities.[2] We focus on the role digital literacies play when they are a part of an activity setting that is organized around robust notions of literacy and learning that extend the rich biliteracy practices that were once part of everyday life in the school.[3] Specifically, we discuss how the use of cultural tools involved in a digital literacy practice at Las Redes helped create zones of proximal development for children's identity and literacy development. We discuss the importance of these concepts in designing this practice, as well as its implications for classroom learning.

The Context

Morris Elementary School has been the home to Las Redes Fifth Dimension, the context for this chapter, for over a decade. Morris, like so many schools populated by immigrant Latino students, struggles to preserve a social justice agenda in the context of backlash politics with anti-immigrant and English-only sentiments as their centerpiece. And programs such as Las Redes, which are oriented to equity and robust learning, have increased importance. Las Redes is part of a growing network of Fifth Dimension sites in California, across the United States, and internationally. Researchers at the Laboratory for Comparative Human Cognition started the first Fifth Dimension site in San Diego, California (Cole, 1996) as a design experiment (Brown, 1992; Collins, 1992; Design-Based Research Collective, 2003) based on principles of sociocultural theories on learning and development (Vygotsky, 1978) and cultural-historical activity theories (Cole & Engestrom, 1993; Engestrom, 1990). Of relevance to classroom educators, this theoretical perspective privileges the social context of learning and development, including tools involved in goal-oriented activities and interpersonal interactions of the larger community.

Guided by these learning principles, children at Las Redes learn through game play with new technologies as they coparticipate with undergraduate students enrolled in a practicum university course on language, culture, and learning. Digital storytelling is one such practice begun at Las Redes designed with the goal of encouraging meaningful and empowering multimodal literacy learning for the students. Digital storytelling provides children the space to be expressive, using not just written or oral modalities but multiple media as well to express themselves. By blending image, sound, and print in a dynamic, real-time environment (Center for Digital Storytelling, 2005), children use these different media to help them tell a story about an important aspect of their lives and then digitize their stories into a movie format. In this process, digital storytelling "integrates technology with communication, language arts, and literacy skills" (Hathorn, 2005, p. 32).

Because the tools used in digital storytelling (i.e., computers, cameras, digital media, etc.) may be novel for many of the participants, children have the opportunity and motivation to learn new literacy skills. As Gee (2004) points out,

> These new technologies and media may well recruit forms of thinking, interacting, and valuing that are quite different from—and again, more compelling and motivating than—those children find in today's schools. (p. 38)

This is an important point because digital storytelling and the tools it employs help children extend their repertoires of literacy practices (Gutiérrez & Rogoff, 2003). In other words, the children learn not only how to craft personal narratives utilizing their full linguistic toolkit but also how to use technologies such as computer software programs and digital hardware, skills that are becoming more important for success in higher education and the increasingly technological workforce (Warschauer, 2003).

In addition to multimodal literacy learning, digital storytelling allows children, who are at a developmental age when issues of identity are particularly salient, to reflect on questions of who they are and who they might become. Through this reflection, children engage in identity play with events in their lives and their future, possible selves (Markus & Nurius, 1986). In this way, digital storytelling can be a particularly important literacy practice because literacy learning becomes most powerful when children participate in practices that have meaning for them and relate to their identities (McCarthey & Moje, 2002).

Identities as English learners are salient at Las Redes because Morris Elementary School, situated in a port-of-entry immigrant community, has many students who use Spanish as their home language. The students of Las Redes may employ Spanish and English hybrid language practices (Gutiérrez, Baquedano-Lopez, & Tejeda, 1999), as they participate in digital storytelling. The opportunity to employ hybrid language practices is important in the children's identity constructions because creating, speaking, writing, and performing digital stories using multiple language tools empowers the children to think about their linguistic toolkit as meaningful to their identities as learners. Although hybrid language practices mediate students' learning, they also counter the hegemonic, English-only discourse of current educational arrangements in California. Digital storytelling provides a medium for children to construct identities in the practice of telling their personal stories (Davis, 2004). In addition to the relevance of storytelling in conveying one's identities (e.g., Ochs & Capps, 1996; Rymes, 2001; Sfard & Prusak, 2005), digital storytelling has the potential to provide the children with opportunities for new sense-making of who they are and who they might become using digital stories that incorporate images, text, and sound. This sense-making is not additive; instead, it is qualitatively different:

> Multimodal composing ... is not simply an additive art whereby images, words, and music, by virtue of being juxtaposed, increase the meaning-making potential of a text. Rather ... a multimodal text can create a different system of signification, one that transcends the collective contribution of its constituent parts. More simply put, multimodality can afford, not just a new way to make meaning, but a different kind of meaning. (Hull & Nelson, 2005, p. 225)

Holland and colleagues' work is useful in helping us understand that identity construction is a social practice: "Identities are lived in and through activity and so must be conceptualized as they develop in social practice" (Holland, Lachicotte, Skinner, & Cain, 1998). In this way, we can examine multimodal, digital storytelling to learn how to extend children's literacy development as well as show a variety of ways in which cultural tools are used to construct their identities in activity (Penuel & Wertsch, 1995).

Studying identity through the multimodal literacy practices of digital storytelling therefore involves a reconceptualization of what literacy means. From a New Literacy Studies perspective (Gee, 1996, 2003; Kress, 2003; Lankshear & Knobel, 2003; New London Group, 1996), a new theory of literacy moves from linguistics to semiotics—from a theory that accounted for language alone to a theory that can account equally well for gesture, speech, image, writing, 3D objects, colour, music and no doubt others. (Kress, 2003, p. 35)

Given these additional communication features, words are not the only or most important means for expression in digital worlds. Researchers studying literacy practices in the context of new technologies should take into account multimodal ways of communication so as not to miss the richness and depth of expression the many tools afford us.

We study identity through the entire repertoire of literacy practices children take up as they express themselves through the creation of digital stories. This repertoire includes the everyday uses and meanings of literacy in the practices of digital storytelling, such as how children learn to tell stories with different genres, use images and music to depict various messages, understand online media, and use various technological tools to digitize their stories. In the following section, we detail how an expanded set of tools available in the cocreation of digital stories extended the ways children could express themselves and tell their stories, redefined literacy as a meaningful practice both personally and in terms of academic literacy, and encouraged children's authorial stance and new identities as meaning makers. We begin with a discussion of one set of tools, the imaginary world or "tertiary artifact" (Wartofsky, 1979), and explain how it helped create a collective zone of proximal development that helped organize and sustain new forms of literacy activity and new identities for children at Las Redes.

Play, the Imaginary Situation, and Identity Development

Although play and the imagination are often hallmark characteristics of instruction in the early grades, the way learning is organized in many classroom settings does not treat play as a zone of cognitive and social development. We believe this is a significant missed opportunity because children, especially English learners, benefit from the rich learning afforded by play and the imaginary situation. Drawing on the work of Wartofsky, Las Redes is organized as an imagined, "autonomous 'world,'" what Wartofsky (1979) calls a "tertiary artifact." What is key about the role of play and the imaginary situation in development is that it allows for participation in new activities that are often not available to children in learning environments organized around "readiness" or scripted models of learning, or where play is just simply play unincorporated into the classroom learning activity. Participation in such imaginary worlds can support learning and development by changing how individuals see the world, how they act on the world, and how they think about possibilities for the future. Digital storytelling was facilitated by the imaginary world promoted in Las Redes—a world that encouraged play and the reorganization of rules, traditional roles, conventions, and outcomes of learning activity. But the playful imagination was neither limited nor centrally organized by digital storytelling. It is the long-standing practice of writing to and corresponding regularly with a mischievous and playful cyber and hybrid entity known as El Maga that provides participants sustained participation in an imaginary world.

In his (or her) playful and provocative omniscient way, El Maga interacts with the children daily through text, drawing on knowledge of their everyday practices, behaviors, incidents, and predispositions.[4] El Maga also played an important role in mediated learning and identity development in the digital storytelling process by reading about the children's digital stories, asking them questions about their digital stories, and encouraging them to think about their experiences in new ways. For example, 7-year-old Angelica, who has a dog named Rascal whom she loves very much, took a picture of Rascal and brought it to our after-school program to use in a digital story about him, her love of animals, and her dream to one day become a zookeeper. Over several weeks, she found other online pictures of her favorite animals to use in her story, and superimposed a picture of herself feeding one of these animals. She then recorded her voice narrating her story and put text on the screen to emphasize the reasons she loves animals and what she does to take care of them. Throughout this process, she wrote and read a series of letters to and from El Maga about her digital story:

5/2/05

Dear El Maga,

Today I wrote a story and I was talking about what I want to do when I grow up. When I grow up I want to be a zoo keeper because I like animals. All of my family has one pet, but my aunt has two pets. Her hamster only comes out at night. Today I am happy. I haven't written to you in a long, long, long, long, long, long, long time. Do you have a pet? I will tell you a jokes. What do you call a dog that's hot a hot dog?

Sincerely,

[Angelica]

5/3/05

Hello [Angelica],

It's been such a long time. I am happy to hear from you again. I didn't think you would remember me. You only have one pet? That's enough to keep you busy I'm sure. What kind of animal is your pet? Well, imagine when you become a Zoo Keeper. You are going to have hundreds of pets!!! Which animal is your favorite? I have some animals too. I have a pet cockroach and a dog, named Juice. I also like lizards and bunny rabbits. As a matter of fact, I think I like most animals. I have a joke for you too. Where can you catch a man-eating fish?

Sincerely,

EL Maga

P.S. Welcome Back

5/4/05

When i grow up i want to be a zoo keeper. What is the answer to your joke? I have a chiuawa.

goodbye,

[Angelica]

5/4/05

The answer to my riddle is: A seafood restaurant. The best place to catch a man-eating fish is at a seafood restaurant. So you have a Chee Gua Gua? Chee Gua Guas are a handful. If you take care of a Chee Gua Gua, then you are ready to take care of anything, even a lion! What are your chores when it comes to taking care of the dog? What is your dog's name?

El Maga was here

5/9/05

Dear El Maga,

Today I was working on my story, I got all of the animals that I put on my story from the internet. Today I wrote my story with [Sarah]. My favorite animal is a seal.

Sincerely,

[Angelica]

5/10/05

Hello [Angelica],

I can't wait to hear your story, especially because it's going to have lots of animals. Can you tell me some of the plot? Is the seal the main character? I like seals too. They can breathe in water and in air, just like dolphins. Let me know when the story is complete.

Bye for now,

EL Maga

5/16/05

Dear El Maga,

Today I was working on my story. I put more pictures in it. Now, I am making the pictures bigger. Today I was working with [Michelle]. I am only going to do my story on Mondays. The seal is not the main character, I am the main character, ME!!!! Do you know any jokes?

Sincerely,

[Angelica]

5/17/06

Hello [Angelica]!

I still can't wait till your story is complete. I am so excited. I am extra excited now that I know you are the star of [your?] story. Can't wait. Can't wait. Can't wait. Of course I know jokes. I have plenty. What's a wizard without a good joke? Here is one: What kinds of keys taste best? Cookies. HA!

Do you have any jokes?

As illustrated in the exchange above, Angelica wrote to El Maga that her digital story was about wanting to be a zookeeper when she grows up because she likes animals. In a series of letters that followed, El Maga responded to Angelica with questions that encouraged her to imagine herself as a zookeeper, to think about the responsibilities she would have as a zookeeper, and to relate these responsibilities to what Angelica already does to take care of her pet dog. El Maga wrote, "Well, imagine when you become a Zoo Keeper. You are going to have hundreds of pets!!! ... If you take care of a Chee Gua Gua, then you are ready to take care of anything, even a lion! What are your chores when it comes to taking care of the dog?" Angelica took El Maga's questions and incorporated into her digital story how she takes care of her pet dog and what she'll do with animals as a zookeeper.

Digital Story: When I Grow Up

I like animals. I like to cuddle with my puppy Rascal.
I like all types of animals. I like lions, tigers, bears, crocodiles, giraffes, and birds.
My favorite animal is a seal.
When I grow up, I want to be a zookeeper because I like taking care of animals—the ones at my house. I feed them, take them a bath, brush their hair, pet them, and take them for walks with my dad.
When I am a zookeeper, I want to work with the animals, so that I can feed them and have them do tricks.

By suspending her disbelief in the wizard El Maga, Angelica was able to participate in an imaginary world where she communicated almost daily to El Maga in detailed letters about her love of animals and her dreams for the future. Letter writing helped promote zones of proximal development by helping Angelica engage in identity play to imagine what it would be like to be a zookeeper and by modeling for Angelica the relationship between being a zookeeper in the future and taking care of her pets in the present. As described above, El Maga is instrumental in getting children to revise their texts, to elaborate, to add specific detail, and the like. Recall that El Maga encouraged Angelica to describe the plot of her digital story. El Maga asked, "Can you tell me some of the plot? Is the seal the main character"? With this question, Angelica replied vehemently, with capital letters and four exclamation points that she was the main character: "The seal is not the main character, I am the main character, ME!!!!" This response showed the importance for Angelica and for the identity she was constructing where she was the main character. El Maga replied, affirming Angelica's role as the main character: "I am extra excited now that I know you are the star of [your?] story. Can't wait. Can't wait. Can't wait."

El Maga encouraged Angelica to keep working on her story and to write more until it was complete by repeatedly telling her, "Can't wait," and "Let me know when the story is complete. … I still can't wait till your story is complete." In order to have the children's stories finished in time to be shown at the end-of-the-year digital storytelling festival at a west coast university, El Maga used playful dialogue and questions about work, life, and their ideas to encourage all the children, including Angelica, to continue working on their digital stories to meet the festival deadline. However, in contrast to many classroom assignments, creating meaningful digital stories for viewing to the Las Redes community provided an authentic and exciting opportunity for the children and the undergraduates who work with them. These tools and practices have implications for many classrooms where students must also complete assignments within limited time frames and oftentimes under strict deadlines, even when the outcomes are not particularly meaningful or productive for the children.

Joint Activity and Literacy Learning

An important aspect of learning in the Fifth Dimension after-school program is that it not only utilizes play but also organizes learning around activities that promote engagement and motivation. These key activities, known as leading activities, include play, formal learning, peer affiliation, and work (Griffin & Cole, 1984). These leading activities can be understood to be important ontogenetically—that is, across a person's lifespan—based on the primary cultural experiences of the child, adolescent, and adult. For example, the leading activity for young children is play, and the leading activity for older children in school is formal education. For adolescents, the leading activity is peer affiliation, and for adults, the leading activity is work (Griffin & Cole, 1984). However, these leading activities are not attached to particular stages of life; instead, they are simply primary at particular points in the life span and do not disappear as we get older.

As such, Las Redes is designed to have all of the leading activities available to the participants. The two leading activities of play and formal learning were intentionally embedded in the design of Fifth Dimension so that children would want to volunteer to participate and adults would want to support the programs (Cole, 1996). In addition to the leading activities of play and formal learning, the leading activity of work is evident in the different projects children make. For example, the work involved in the digital storytelling activities includes all of the steps needed from playing with one's ideas for the story to writing the script, taking pictures, and importing all of the media into a movie-editing software program for the final digital story creation. In this way, the children play games in the after-school program, but they also have formal learning activities, such as using the required task cards that guide game play. By designing environments with a range of leading activities available, sustained engagement and motivation are increased.

A central characteristic of Las Redes is its participation structure. Of focus is Las Redes's emphasis on joint activity. Children do not work on digital storytelling or any other project by themselves, because it is one of the norms of Las Redes to have children and undergraduate students jointly engage in gaming activity, what we refer to as joint-mediated activity. Joint or coparticipation helps to create the leading activity of peer affiliation. Participants know the participation script that they must play with a buddy, or an amigo/a (Gutiérrez, Baquedano-López, & Álvarez, 2001), whenever they play games or work on projects. The focus on participants as ensembles of children and undergraduates working jointly as copartners to accomplish the task at hand is a hallmark characteristic of Las Redes where strong affiliations develop across any given quarter. The undergraduate students and children at Las Redes worked together across the 10-week quarter, sometimes working with the same child over time or collaborating with different children depending on the needs of the site and children. What is unique about this study's cohort is that a group of especially trained undergraduates worked with the same child or children in the creation of the child's digital story across of number of sessions throughout the academic quarter. This extended collaboration provided an opportunity for the undergraduate students and children to learn more about one another, and in particular for the undergraduate students to learn about the child's interests and skills in relation to the child's digital storytelling goals. The goal of digital storytelling was for children to tell their story—a meaningful story about their lives—and the extended and close collaboration resulted in undergraduates who were better prepared to assist the children in accomplishing their own goals.

Of significance, the emphasis on the children's central role in decision making in the creation of their own stories in the undergraduate students' training helped reorganize the traditional teacher-student relations so that the undergraduates' expertise in digital technology was not instantiated in authoritarian ways or in ways that hypermediated learning activity (Gutiérrez & Stone, 2002). Instead, the back-and-forth sharing of knowledge and ideas allowed the undergraduates to provide meaningful and strategic assistance to the children who always had the final say across the various stages of their stories' development. We argue that such forms of joint activity promoted zones of proximal development and new agentive roles in literacy learning.

There was not only joint activity between undergraduate students and children but also among the children themselves, who at times decided to create shared digital stories. For example, two third-grade students, Laura and María (pseudonyms), who are cousins, created a digital story about being a family with their pet mice and dog. Their story detailed where their pet mice were born, what they eat, and how they play together. Their digital story is in Spanish, entitled "Los Ratones Sesi y Osita." Both girls shared the task of narrating their digital story, beginning with the birth of their pets. They used a digital camera to take pictures of themselves with their pets, and they found online pictures of Petco and a hospital as well as a musical soundtrack of the Mickey Mouse song to play in the background. Their digital story was the following:

Spanish Version of Digital Story

Osita nació en Petco y Sesi nació en una veterinaria y Laura y María nacieron en un hospital. Yo dejo a Sesi caminar en mi casa por la noche. Ella anda abajo de la cama a dormir. Y juegan de pesca, pesca, y ellas le gustan jugar. El otro ratoncito se llama Osita porque es un hamster oso. No tiene una cola, y ella es muy juguetona. Algunas veces ella muerde porque quiere comer la comida que tienes y te alcanza a morder. Ellos se muerden juntos pero a mi perro no le duele porque tiene mucho pelo. Su papá de María se llama Antonio y su mamá se llama Lupe. Sesi está agarrando la comida del perro y se va abajo de la cama y brinca como canguro. Y ella no pelea con mi perro porque ella es muy cariñosa. Sesi y Osita se quieren como amigas. Sesi, Osita, María, Laura y Peluche son una familia feliz.

English Translation of Digital Story

Osita was born in Petco, Sesi was born at the veterinarian's hospital, and Laura and María were born in a hospital. I let Sesi walk at night in my house. She walks under the bed to sleep. The other little mouse is called Osita because she is a hamster bear. She does not have a tail, and she is very playful. Sometimes she bites because she wants to eat the food that you have, so she reaches to bite you. They bite together but she does not hurt my dog because my dog has a lot of hair. María's father is called Antonio, and her mother is called Lupe. Sesi holds the dog's food and she goes under the bed and jumps like a kangaroo. She does not fight with my dog because she is very affectionate. Sesi and Osita love each other like friends. Sesi, Osita, María, Laura, and Peluche are a happy family.

Discussion

At Las Redes, there is no privileging of one language over another; therefore children could participate in digital storytelling using multiple languages. As shown above, although María and Laura created a digital story in Spanish, they used both Spanish and English throughout the digital storytelling process, thus incorporating their full linguistic toolkit to make meaning. It was important to be all-inclusive in language choice to encourage participation so that everyone could learn the multimodal literacy practices of digital storytelling and so nondominant English speakers would not be limited to less rich, less complex, and less rigorous literacy practices simply because of their lack of English proficiency. Although many educators may agree that bilingualism in schools is important, *participation structures* facilitate joint activity and distributed cognition in ways that enrich student learning. The affordances of multimodal, collaborative learning used in digital storytelling highlight how participants can use multiple artifacts particular to a setting—not just one innovation or tool—to mediate learning and development.

We also recognize that the types of literacy practices developed in digital storytelling are not the practices that are favored by traditional notions of academic literacies. Work would therefore need to be done to show how these after-school literacy practices can benefit and inform school-based literacy practices in ways that help children expand their repertoires of practice. Given the importance of identity in literacy learning (McCarthey & Moje, 2002), what has been learned from the work on digital storytelling can shed light on how new technologies of digital storytelling, which growing numbers of students use (Salpeter, 2005), contribute to their identity and literacy development in ways that begin to give nondominant students richer and more equitable opportunities to build strong literacy toolkits that will support both academic achievement and identities as productive learners and meaning makers.

Notes

1. See Gutiérrez, Asato, Santos, & Gotanda (2002) and Gutiérrez, Baquedano-López, & Asato (2001) for an elaborated discussion of the effects of English-only policies in California.
2. Hybrid language practices refer to the use of the student's complete linguistic toolkit used in the service of learning and meaning making. We use the term "nondominant" to describe students who historically have been marginalized linguistically, economically, and culturally.
3. It is important to note that we are not describing traditional bilingual settings as the intervention here; rather, we describe an environment where learning is organized in ways that utilize students' full linguistic toolkits in sense-making activity.
4. El Maga has direct knowledge of what children do and say, their personalities, language practices, preferences both by observing them in everyday activity at Las Redes and through the undergraduates' field notes that document in detail what took place in interaction with the children during every visit. In this way, El Maga's information is current and highly personalized while also remaining anonymous to the children. The intrigue of who is El Maga, where is El Maga, and so forth is a practice that requires collusion from the adults and the children, even though they all know in reality that El Maga is a mythical figure.

References

Brown, A. L. (1992). Design experiments: Theoretical and methodological challenges in creating complex interventions in classroom settings. *Journal of the Learning Sciences, 2,* 141–178.

Center for Digital Storytelling (2005). Retrieved July 14, 2007, from http://www.story center.org

Cole, M. (1996). *Cultural psychology : A once and future discipline.* Cambridge, MA: Belknap Press.

Cole, M., & Engestrom, Y. (1993). A cultural-historical approach to distributed cognition. In G. Salomon (Ed.), *Distributed cognitions: Psychological and educational considerations* (pp. 47–87). New York: Cambridge University Press.

Cole, M., & Griffin, P. (1983, October). A socio-historical approach to re-mediation. *Quarterly Newsletter of the Laboratory of Comparative Human Cognition, 5*(4), 69–74.

Collins, A. (1992). Toward a design science of education. In E. Scanlon & T. O'Shea (Eds.), *New directions in educational technology.* New York: Springer-Verlag.

Davis, A. (2004). Co-authoring identity: Digital storytelling in an urban middle school. *Then, 1*(1). Retrieved July 14, 2007, from http://thenjournal. org/feature/61/

Design-Based Research Collective. (2003). Design-based research: An emerging paradigm for educational inquiry. *Educational Researcher, 32*(1), 5–8.

Engestrom, Y. (1990). *Learning, working and imagining: Twelve studies in activity theory.* Helsinki: Orienta-Konsultit Oy.

Gee, J. P. (1996). *Social linguistics and literacies: Ideology in discourses.* London: Taylor & Francis.

Gee, J. P. (2003). *What video games have to teach us about learning and literacy.* New York: Palgrave MacMillan.

Gee, J. P. (2004). *Situated language and learning: A critique of traditional schooling.* New York: Routledge.

Griffin, P., & Cole, M. (1984). Current activity for the future: The Zo-ped. *New Directions for Child Development, 23,* 45–64.

Gutiérrez, K., Asato, J., Santos, M., & Gotanda, N. (2002). Backlash pedagogy: Language and culture and the politics of reform. *Review of Education, Pedagogy, and Cultural Studies, 24* (4), 335–351.

Gutiérrez, K., Baquedano-López, P., & Álvarez, H. (2001). Literacy as hybridity: Moving beyond bilingualism in urban classrooms. In M. de la Luz Reyes & J. Halcón (Eds.), *The best for our children: Critical perspectives on literacy for Latino students* (pp. 122–141). New York: Teachers College Press.

Gutiérrez, K., Baquedano-López, P., & Asato, J. (2001). English for the children: The new literacy of the old world order. *Bilingual Review Journal, 24* (1&2), 87–112.

Gutiérrez, K. D., Baquedano-López, P., & Tejeda, C. (1999). Rethinking diversity: Hybridity and hybrid language practices in the Third Space. *Mind, Culture, and Activity, 6,* 286–303.

Gutiérrez, K. D., & Rogoff, B. (2003). Cultural ways of learning: Individual traits or repertoires of practice. *Educational Researcher, 32,* 19–25.

Gutiérrez, K. D., & Stone, L. (2002). Hypermediating literacy activity: How learning contexts get reorganized. In O. Saracho & B. Spodek (Eds.), *Contemporary perspectives in early childhood education* (pp. 25–51). Greenwich, CT: Information Age.

Hathorn, P. (2005). Using digital storytelling as a literacy tool for the inner-city school youth. *Charter Schools Resource Journal, 1*(1). Retrieved July 14, 2007, from http://www.ehhs.cmich.edu/%7Ednewby/article.htm.

Holland, D., Lachicotte, W., Skinner, D., & Cain, C. (1998). *Identity and agency in cultural worlds.* Cambridge: Harvard University Press.

Hull, G. A., & Nelson, M. E. (2005). Locating the semiotic power of multimodality. *Written Communication, 22,* 224–261.

Hull, G. A., & Schultz, K. (Eds.). (2002). *School's out! Bridging out-of-school literacies with classroom practice.* New York: Teachers College Press.

Kress, G. (2003). *Literacy in the new media age.* London: Routledge.

Lankshear, C., & Knobel, M. (2003). *New literacies: Changing knowledge and classroom learning.* Buckingham: Open University Press.

Markus, H., & & Nurius, P. (1986). Possible selves. *American Psychologist, 41*(9), 954–969.

McCarthey, S. J., & Moje, E. B. (2002). Identity matters. *Reading Research Quarterly. 37*(2), 228–238.

New London Group. (1996). A pedagogy of multiliteracies: Designing social futures. *Harvard Educational Review, 66,* 60–91.

Ochs, E., & Capps, L. (1996) Narrating the self. *Annual Review of Anthropology, 25,* 9–43.

Penuel, W. R., & Wertsch, J. V. (1995). Vygotsky and identity formation: A sociocultural approach. *Educational Psychologist, 30*(2), 83–92.

Rymes, B. (2001). *Conversational borderlands: Language and identity in an alternative urban high school.* New York: Teachers College Press.

Salpeter, J. (2005, February). Telling tales with technology. *Technology and Learning.* Retrieved July 14, 2007, from http://www.techlearning.com/shared/printableArticle.jhtml?articleID=60300276.

Sfard, A., & Prusak, A. (2005). Telling identities: In search of an analytic tool for investigating learning as a culturally shaped activity. *Educational Researcher, 34,* 14–22.

Vygotsky, L. (1978). *Mind in society: The development of higher psychological processes* (M. Cole, V. John-Steiner, S. Scribner, & E. Souberman, Eds.). Cambridge, MA: Harvard University Press.

Warschauer, M. (2003). *Technology and social inclusion: Rethinking the digital divide.* Cambridge, MA: MIT Press.

Wartofsky, M. (1979). Models: Representations and the scientific understanding. Dordrecht: Reidel.

9

Listening to the Voices of Immigrant Parents

JENNIFER ADAIR AND JOSEPH TOBIN

A significant and growing percentage of the children enrolled in preschool in the United States are children of recent immigrants, but the field of early childhood education has conducted too little research on the experience of immigrant children and their families. Moreover, almost none of this research includes the voices of immigrant parents. (Exceptions include studies by Cornfield and Arzubiaga, 2004; Diaz-Soto, 1997; Goldenberg and Gallimore, 1995; and Uttal, 2002.) In an effort to address this imbalance, 2 years ago we organized a group of researchers in five countries to study approaches to working with children of recent immigrants in early childhood education and care settings. At the heart of this study, which is being conducted in England, France, Germany, Italy, and the United States, is a comparison of ideas about preschool held by practitioners and immigrant parents. A basic assumption of our research project is that preschool programs can better serve immigrants when parents, teachers, and other stakeholders engage in dialogue. Our project aims to serve as a catalyst for dialogue among parents, practitioners, scholars, and policymakers about the problems and possibilities of creating preschool programs that reflect the values and beliefs of both immigrant communities and of the societies to which they have immigrated.

The practice we are advocating is not any particular approach to the early childhood curriculum but instead a process that relies on the willingness of preschool teachers and directors to enter into dialogue with immigrant parents. In this chapter, we explain the method we have developed for facilitating such a dialogue, give examples of the kinds of things immigrant parents bring up about their children's early childhood education when given the opportunity, and discuss implications for practice. Our approach is a combination of ethnography and Bakhtinian discourse theory. Mikhail Bakhtin's (1990) work on dialogism and heteroglossia suggests that we pay attention to the heterogeneous voices and diverse ideological positions that interact in such inherently hybrid sites as preschool classrooms serving children of immigrants. Our work is also informed by the theoretical work of decolonizing critics, including bell hooks (1994a, 1994b), Gloria Anzaldúa (1987), and Linda Tuhiwai

Smith (1999), who call for researchers to include the voices that are too often ignored or silenced, voices such as those of preschool teachers and immigrant parents. This combination of Bakhtinian and decolonizing theories, in positing the vitality of the voices of immigrant parents and preschool teachers, will allow us to challenge the deficit models that have dominated scholarship on immigrant parents and children and to demonstrate the potential for meaningful dialogue between immigrant parents and the teachers who educate and care for their children.

Research Method

The core method of this study is straightforward and follows and extends the approach taken by Tobin, Wu, and Davidson in *Preschool in Three Cultures* (1989). Research teams in each of the five countries make 20-minute videotapes of typical days for 4-year-olds in preschools. We then use these videotapes not as data but as tools to stimulate a multivocal dialogue. The videotapes are used as an interviewing cue to draw out the beliefs and concerns of both immigrant and nonimmigrant parents; of teachers and administrators who work in programs that serve children of newly arriving immigrants; and of community leaders, early childhood education experts, and policymakers concerned with early childhood education and care. By showing the same set of videotapes to these key stakeholders in each of the five nations, we highlight similarities and differences in how each nation approaches the challenge of integrating immigrant children and their families into the larger society and differences and tensions within each nation. In the tradition of ethnography, in this study the parents and teachers are positioned as experts/insiders, providing an emic perspective missing in most studies of preschools.

We are experimenting with different approaches to structuring the focus-group discussions. In our pilot work, we tried mixing parents and teachers but found that parents are more comfortable expressing their feelings about their children's experience in preschool when the teachers are not present. We tried mixing immigrant and nonimmigrant parents in focus groups but found that the simultaneous translation required by this arrangement interrupted the flow of conversation and also that the two groups of parents sometimes hesitate to speak freely in front of each other. We have had our liveliest discussions in homogeneous focus groups. In this chapter, we present examples of statements made by Mexican immigrant parents in focus groups conducted in Spanish, which we later transcribed and translated into English. We use these examples to show the kinds of understandings that can come from engaging with immigrant parents about their children's early education and care needs.

Solano Preschool

In the U.S. portion of the study, we focused on a preschool run by an urban school district. Solano Preschool, in Phoenix, Arizona, is a state-supported program for children of parents at or near the poverty line. About half of the children at Solano are children of recent immigrants from Mexico who speak Spanish at home. There are also children in the school whose families are recent immigrants from Vietnam and Iraq, as well as nonimmigrant white, African American, and American Indian children. The teachers, director, and other staff members all speak Spanish as well as English, and the program is bilingual, with teachers and children speaking both Spanish and English. Lolie, the head teacher, emigrated to the United States from Mexico as a young adult. Having a teacher who is an immigrant and teaching in a bilingual classroom, while not all that unusual, is not typical of U.S. early childhood education. We nevertheless chose Solano preschool for our stimulus tape because we believe that the program's emphasis on bilingual instruction would work to provoke dialogue among parents and staff about issues of language, culture, and curriculum. The bilingual emphasis aside, Solano is a typical American preschool of a certain type (public, half-day, serving low-income children). It is also accredited by the National Association for the Education of Young Children, the primary organization for early childhood education in the United States

The Stimulus Videotape: A Day at Solano Preschool

We edited our Solano videotape so as to both capture the flow of a typical day and to highlight key issues we wanted parents and teachers to talk about in the focus-group discussions. The video opens with children arriving at school. As parents and grandparents sign in their children, the head teacher, Lolie, her assistant, Azalea, and the school's social worker, Roberta (who spends 1 day a week in Lolie's classroom), chat with the parents in both Spanish and English. Michael, who is having a hard time separating from his mother, cries; Lolie takes him in her lap and comforts him. During the free-play period that follows, we see Michelle, a girl from Vietnam who is learning English, engage in an argument in the dramatic play area about a fancy dress with Isabel, and Lolie coming over to mediate the dispute. The teachers move around the classroom during free play, interacting with the children in English and Spanish. During circle time, Lolie reads a book to the class in English, adding brief Spanish translations, and asking follow-up questions in both languages. Circle time is followed by a trip to the playground, an activity in which children draw pictures about the story Lolie read them, more free play, and a second circle time, with dancing and songs. At the end of the day, Lolie hugs each child good-bye.

In the focus-group discussions, the Mexican parents talked about these scenes, about their feelings about the teachers and the preschool, and also about issues not directly present in the videotape but connected with their concerns about their children's early childhood education. We organize our analysis of the parents' comments around key themes: caring, curriculum, bilingualism, and racism.

Caring

Parents responded favorably to the way in which Lolie took care of Michael and held him when he arrived in the classroom crying:

Adair:	What do you think about the way the teacher helped Michael? Do you remember that he was sad when he arrived? What do you think about that?
Mother 1:	That's good, because some teachers, I mean, they don't even talk to the children. I liked it because she even hugged him.
Mother 2:	She made him feel confident.
Adair:	And do you feel comfortable with this?
All:	Yes.
Mother 3:	Yes, and I also agree that the teachers should take care of the child when he's crying when the mom is leaving. So the child feels better for the rest the day because someone comforted him.
Mother 1:	Yes, and we leave the place so worried because the children are crying. Maybe she doesn't like the classroom, or something is happening. Maybe she doesn't like how the teacher treats her. Maybe she doesn't like to be there and every time she's taken there, she cries. This can be a sign that something isn't OK.

In our conversations with Mexican parents at Solano and other preschools in the Phoenix area, Lolie was praised for her treatment of Michael and more generally for her displays of care and affection. Many said that a teacher should be *cariñosa* (a concept discussed by Angela Valenzuela in her 1999 book, *Subtractive Schooling: U.S.-Mexican Youth and the Politics of Caring*). Parents communicated a desire for preschool to be safe, comfortable, and caring for their children. Most of these immigrant parents, who were going through their first extended separation from their children, approved of Lolie's nurturing and parent-like qualities. Lolie's director pointed out that Lolie is the most physically affectionate teacher on staff.

Curriculum

In the focus groups we conducted with Mexican immigrant parents at Solano and other preschool sites, we find a good deal of disagreement about the curriculum. Many parents think the balance of activities at Solano is just right while others want more academics and less play. Only a few want a multicultural curriculum, explaining that teaching about Mexican culture is something that "We can do at home." As one parent commented,

The school should teach children to respect the U.S. If we ask them to do the same for Mexico, that's hard, because there are people here from Guatemala, Salvador, and many other countries. It's better done at home, by each family.

In one focus group we conducted with Mexican parents, all of the parents praised the teachers, with some noting the respect Mexican parents expect children to show towards their *maestras*. There was an interesting debate on the question of whether the preschool should give more emphasis to Mexican culture, with one father saying that it would be nice if his children were taught a bit about Mexican holidays and cultural traditions so his son could talk more easily with relatives back in Mexico. Most parents made the point that, given the shortness of the school day (2.5 hours in either a morning or afternoon session in Arizona's Early Childhood Block Grant preschools), they want the school to emphasize academic and social readiness and the learning of English, saying teaching Spanish and Mexican culture is parents' responsibility.

In discussing how the teachers deal with children's misbehavior in the video, parents made an interesting distinction between *enseñar* and *educar,* both of which are usually translated into English as "to teach," but which in Spanish carry related but distinct meanings of "to point out or show" (*enseñar*) versus "to raise or bring up" (*educar*), some suggesting that the second responsibility is more theirs as parents than it is teachers', and thus if their children misbehave at school this calls for intervention more from them (the parents) than from the teachers (Reese et al., 1995; Valdés, 1996).

Bilingualism

The parents at Solano began discussion on this topic by telling us that they appreciate the program's bilingual approach. But as the discussions continued, parents' positions became more complex and conflicted. Many parents expressed concern about whether their children will be ready for the English-only kindergarten environment they will face next year. One mother, for example, described the bilingualism of the Solano classroom as a kind of paradise from which her child would soon be expelled:

> I think that they are fine in the way they are here. Personally, we would prefer that this would continue in the same way in kindergarten. But, if there's a law [referring to Arizona's "English-only" proposition], we can't do anything about it. We just have to accept it.

Emphasizing the importance of their children becoming fluent in English by the time they entered elementary school, many parents argued that it was the school's job to teach English and theirs to teach and maintain Spanish.

As researchers who are advocates of bilingual education, we were surprised and a bit disappointed to hear Mexican immigrant parents expressing such ambivalent support for bilingual education and so little worry about their children's potential loss of Spanish language fluency. To make sure we were hearing them correctly (and also, perhaps, in an attempt to change their minds), we asked a series of follow-up questions focused on language loss. Looking across transcripts of these discussions, we can see a clear three-step pattern to parents' responses on this topic. The first response was a denial of the possibility that their children would lose their ability to speak Spanish. The second response came in the form of a story about a friend or a relative who has a child who stopped speaking Spanish and could not communicate with his relatives or handle himself when visiting Mexico. The third response came in the form of a statement of the position that it was up to the school to teach English and the parents to teach Spanish.

Adair: Aren't you afraid that they will lose their culture, their language?

Mother 1:   I don't think that they are going to lose it, because that's what I speak. And in the school they learn English.

Mother 2:   I know a family and they brought their children when they were younger. They have been living here for 12 years. They just got back from Mexico and there, they didn't speak Spanish. I mean, they know how to, but they don't know the vocabulary because they know it just in English. And they don't know how to write Spanish.

Mother 3:   So, that depends, on us, not the teachers, I have to pay attention so my son learns Spanish. I'm not leaving the teachers to do it for me. They don't have the responsibility for that. But, if I want my son to learn it, that's my duty, not the teacher's.

Mother 4:   It depends on you. You need to educate them about the culture, to talk about the country, the place we come from.

We find a similar pattern in a second example:

Adair: Are you afraid that they maybe are going to lose their language? That they are going to lose their Spanish?

Mother 1:   Speaking at home?

Adair: Maybe they don't want to speak Spanish in class and their friends don't speak it. Maybe one day they will not want to speak it or maybe they are going to lose it.

Mother 2:   They won't lose it if we speak it at home, and demand them to speak in Spanish.

Mother 3:   I have two nephews who have been living here since they were little and now they don't want to speak in Spanish at their house. When they talk and watch a movie and do homework they are speaking in English, and when they talk to their mother, they do it in English, despite the fact the parents are Latino and speak Spanish.

Adair:	Does this make you a little afraid?
Mother 3:	Yes, because when he grows up he may not want to speak Spanish at home, or he wants to give us back the words in English and Spanish.
Mother 1:	Spanglish?
Mother 2:	Yes, and they will use words in English because it's faster, because they have more time speaking it in English than in Spanish.
Gabriela (another interviewer):	What do you think about jumping from English to Spanish and vice versa?
Mother 1:	I don't like it.

Guadalupe Valdés (1996) discusses the divide between the worlds of home and school and notes that immigrant parents have to make delineations between what is learned at home and what is learned at school that middle-class English-speaking parents do not have to make. The Mexican parents we have interviewed, perceiving great linguistic and cultural discontinuity between their homes and the larger society, look to their children's teachers to help bridge this gap by teaching them English and the skills needed for success in an English-only school system and society, while they assign to themselves responsibility for teaching their children Spanish and Mexican cultural values. Although some worry about their children losing their Spanish fluency when they get older, they are more focused on the more immediate concern that their children learn English quickly enough to be ready for the English-only kindergarten classroom that awaits them.

Although parents expressed ambivalence about bilingual education, they were very clear about their appreciation of the preschool having teachers and other school staff members who speak their language. The Solano parents are particularly appreciative of the ease of their communication with Lolie:

> The teachers treat us well and we feel good here. I feel good here because I can talk and ask freely about what I need to do, about the papers they give us, which are written in both Spanish and English. And when I have a concern, I trust them, I feel good with them. They haven't ever given me a reason to feel bad here.

Parents told us that if schools cannot provide bilingual teachers, they should provide translators.

Adair:	What can teachers who don't speak Spanish do to help your children?
Mother 1:	Provide a translator.

Lirio (another interviewer):	So, for you, it's important that there's somebody there to speak Spanish to your kids?
Father 1:	Or a translator.
Mother 2:	It's about understanding what our children are doing, to help them in any way.

The clarification/correction this mother offers—that a Spanish speaker is needed at school for the parents but not necessarily for the child—reflects the concern of immigrant parents that teachers and other authorities fail to give them the status due them as parents. Immigrant parents in our focus groups told stories of English speakers ignoring or demeaning them in front of their children, of cashiers who make sarcastic comments in English about them to their children, of being confused at school gatherings about light-hearted comments made by other parents they do not fully understand, and of a teacher who asks the young student to act as a translator at a parent-teacher conference. Immigrant parents want the opportunity to exercise their parental role in society and at school. Teachers listening to and taking seriously the words and concerns of immigrant parents is a form of social justice. It is also good practice: A study of Mexican immigrant children by Goldenberg and Gallimore (1995) shows that Mexican immigrant children do better academically when the classroom teacher is Latina. Regression analysis they conducted suggests this effect is mostly due to the ease of communication and trust these teachers have with parents and with parents' confidence that the teachers understand and respect parental beliefs.

This helps us make sense of the apparent inconsistency in the Mexican parents' comments on language policy: The Mexican parents at Solano all told us that they appreciated having bilingual teachers but some did not necessarily want a bilingual program for their child. This apparent contradiction makes sense when we realize that the parents want a teacher who can communicate in Spanish as well as one who understands their child's Spanish, especially at the beginning of the school year, before their child learns English, but not necessarily a teacher who will teach in both languages.

Cultural Identity

At the end of one of our focus groups, after we thanked the group and turned off our recording equipment, the discussion suddenly became heated. One mother, who had argued during the session that Mexico should be given more credit for the strides it was making in education, accused the other mothers of being too critical of Mexico and too enthusiastic about the United States. Several other mothers responded that Mexico could not compare in education or in the opportunities that the United States provides. One mother stated with emotion, "This country has done more for me than Mexico has ever done." In response, the Mexican patriot replied, "Of course we can't compare

Mexico as it is now to where the U.S. is. But Mexico under President Fox is making strides. Don't be such Malinche." (*No sean tan Malinche.*) The other women, insulted, angrily rejected this accusation.

Malinche is still remembered 4 centuries later for her complicity in the Spanish conquest of Mexico. The daughter of a noble Aztec family, Malinche was given to Cortes. She knew the Aztec language (Nahuatl) and Mayan and learned Spanish. She served as an interpreter to Cortes and bore him a son, Don Mahin Cortes, whom Cortes recognized and is the first Mestizo written about in history. Malinche has come to signify traitor, harlot, and the mother of the Mestizo race. As Cherie Moraga writes,

> The sexual legacy passed down the mexicana/Chicana is the legacy of betrayal, pivoting around the historical/mythical female figure of Malintzin Tenepal. As a Native woman and translator, strategic adviser and mistress to the Spanish conqueror of Mexico, Hernán Cortez, Malintzin is considered the mother of the mestizo people. But unlike La Virgen de Guadalupe, she is not revered as La Madre Sagrada, but rather slandered as ... La Vendida, sell-out to the white race. Upon her shoulders rests the blame for the "bastardization" of the indigenous people of Mexico. (1983, p. 35)

The Malinche comment at the end of the focus-group discussion gives us a glimpse into the psychological and sociocultural complexity of the issues facing Mexican immigrant mothers. We can hear in the accusation "*No sean tan Malinche*" not only a call for immigrant mothers from Mexico to be loyal to Mexican culture but also a concern about the cultural identity of their children. Mexican parents who move their families north and urge them to learn English and live among the *Yanquis* are vulnerable to accusations from their compatriots at home, from each other, and from themselves, for having reproduced Malinche's traitorous act, thereby producing an even more degraded, hybridized version of native Mexican-ness. If Malinche is the mother of the Mestizo race, immigrant Mexican mothers in the United States are the mothers of the new Mestizo—the "Mexican American."

This tension goes to the heart of the problem facing immigrant parents everywhere: How can they raise their children to be able to succeed and feel at home in their adopted country while retaining their heritage language and culture? Mexican immigrant parents want their children to be successful in the United States and to become full-fledged, equal members of American society, but at the same time to hold on to their identity and pride as Mexicans. They appreciate the opportunities the United States presents to them and, especially, to their children—opportunities not available to them in Mexico; but they fear that their children will suffer as they (the parents) do from the racism of U.S. society. And they worry that their children may become so engulfed by American culture that they will lose their Mexican cultural values and turn their back on Mexican culture and society.

Racism

We early childhood educators need to learn to think not only about children in the classroom context but also to comprehend their lives outside of school. We are finding Critical Race Theory (CRT) particularly helpful in this regard. Growing out of Critical Legal Theory, CRT focuses on the ways that racism perpetuates white privilege (Delgado, 1995; Ladson-Billings & Tate, 1995; Villenas & Deyhle, 1999). CRT places high value on stories and "witnessing" and argues that accounts of racism are powerful tools to expose and combat social injustice. Our engagement with CRT led us to include in our interviews not just questions about what goes on in the preschool classroom but also questions about the problems immigrant families struggle with outside of school. In the focus-group discussions, after talking about the Solano videotape, we asked parents, "Are there places where you feel uncomfortable speaking Spanish?" and "Have you experienced discrimination since coming to the U.S.?" In response to these questions, immigrant parents told stories that expressed the pain of being treated disrespectfully and especially of having their authority as parents undermined. For example, one mother recounted,

> I was buying groceries and a woman said to me, "What are you doing here? This store is not for you. Do you have one of these?" And she showed me a license. She said, "If you don't have one of these, you don't have any right to buy here. Go away!" I was with my son. He asked me, "What did that woman say, Mom?" I didn't reply to the woman. She said many things to me. In the store, nobody helped me, not even the manager. He could have gone and asked her to calm down, but he didn't say anything.

Another mother answered our questions about discrimination by naming her mistreatment as racism:

> I think there's a lot of racism. It's called racism and I have felt it here. One time, a woman here, the bus driver, I had a problem with her. I didn't say anything to her because I didn't understand her; but a cousin of mine told me what was happening and I think I didn't do anything bad. But I think there's a lot of racism. When one makes a mistake, one says, "Oops, I made a mistake," but when one didn't do anything wrong, you think, "What happened?" One starts feeling the racism.

A father added:

> I work in the construction field, in cement. I'm a finisher. And when I go out from my work, I'm covered with cement dust. I'm dirty and since I'm Latin, I usually go to Food City because is where the Latinos go. One day I decided to go to Fry's, where the American people go, and see the difference. Inside, they looked at me. They were so clean and me so dirty, buying chicken. I felt them staring at me.

Many parents expressed deep concern about the effect racism will have on their children.

> Last year, I had a problem with a teacher in my son's school. The whole year, when he was in preschool, he was OK. But in kindergarten, he didn't want to go. The whole year I was struggling because of that. One time, the teacher didn't allow him to go to the bathroom and he wet himself. I always noticed that she treated the American children better. I mean, when they left, she hugged them and said, "Bye, bye." But, when my son left, she just said "Bye, Federico" and sometimes she didn't say anything. Fortunately, she's not there anymore.

Conclusions

We hesitate to use the term "conclusions," given the fact that we are still early in our research. Nevertheless, here are some necessarily fragmentary, tentative, and intentionally provocative implications of our work to date:

1. Our research is showing that in many (but by no means all) cases, immigrant parents hold ideas about early childhood education that differ from notions of quality and best practice held by early childhood educators and their professional organizations. For example, many of the immigrant parents we have spoken with say they would prefer a curriculum that gives more emphasis to academic instruction, that they want a stronger emphasis on learning the language of their new country, that they don't expect or want the school to teach about their home culture, and that they would like to see teachers be more directive, for example, in dealing with children's disputes. One possibility is to view these positions as being misinformed or ignorant—if these parents understood developmentally appropriate practice, bilingual education, and constructivism, they would support them. But this position implies a hierarchical relationship between progressive early childhood educators and the communities they aim to serve. We suggest that a better approach is to enter into a dialogue about quality standards with parents and teachers in local settings in which the starting assumption is one of respect for all positions held, viewing critiques of progressive positions not as ignorance but as difference, and suggesting strategies for opening up dialogue with parents about these differences.

2. The research method we are using in this study—giving teachers and parents the opportunity to watch and then discuss a video of a day in their preschool (or another preschool)—can be modified as a strategy for promoting dialogue between preschool staff and parents and between immigrant and nonimmigrant parents. The field of early childhood education needs to develop structures to facilitate

ongoing discussion between preschool staff and parents. Training in early childhood education and care gives too little attention to developing skills in communicating with parents. Too often, when practitioners talk to parents, the discussion is hierarchical rather then reciprocal, with the early childhood expert explaining and (sometimes) justifying her curriculum, giving child-rearing tips, and correcting parental misperceptions.

Dialogue among practitioners and immigrant parents need not be adversarial or contentious. When structured well, these discussions can be a chance for both teachers and parents to talk through their uncertainty and ambivalence about what is best for children, rather than to stake out and defend positions. Discussions between teachers and immigrant parents can take several forms: building connections and trust ("getting to know you"), sharing beliefs, and negotiating differences. We must be careful not to assume naively that just because we early childhood educators invite parents into a dialogue that they will feel comfortable sharing all that they believe or want. They may conclude, wisely, to treat these sessions more as negotiation than as soul-baring and to be strategic about what they say. One useful approach might be to first show a video of a typical day in their child's (or another) preschool to a homogeneous group of immigrant parents to give them the chance to make sense of what they are seeing and to decide in a conversation in their own language among people of their culture how they feel about it, and to strategize about which issues to raise with the preschool staff.

3. Support parents' goals for their children. Early childhood education and care programs need to balance sensitivity to the immigrant's culture and language with the need to help the immigrant child learn the host country's language as quickly as possible, the need to create a common culture, and the need to give all of the children a feeling of belonging to and investment in the country and culture in which they live. Part of the problem we face here is discursive. We lack a positive way of referring to "assimilation into the larger society" as a goal for immigrant children, even though immigrant parents in fact often cite this as a primary goal for their children. In the U.S. context, the terms "assimilation," "melting pot," and even "integration" are scorned by progressive educators—but no other terms for facilitating the efforts of immigrants to become members of the larger society have taken their place. It is unfortunate that the discussion of immigration policy and more specifically about how programs should serve children of immigrants tends to become stuck in acrimonious, overly politicized debates in which multiculturalism and bilingualism too often

are assumed to be inherently progressive or leftist positions, while appeals for a common culture and common language are assumed to be inherently reactionary, right-wing, and anti-immigrant. We need to learn to hear immigrant parents' expressions of desire for their children to become Americans as something other than assimilationism or capitulation to the agenda of the right.

4. Immigrant families deal on a daily basis with racism, discrimination, and, often, poverty. Many teachers of immigrant children are insufficiently aware of their students' experience with poverty, of the racism and discrimination they face, and of the feeling of alienation they experience in response to the racism. Even when practitioners become aware of how these larger social problems are having an impact on the families of the children they teach and care for, we are often at a loss for what to do about it. When faced with the enormity of these problems, a natural response is to conclude that we early childhood educators should stick to what we know and to what we can do best—focus on providing high-quality care and education.

A good early childhood education and care (ECEC) program is necessary but not sufficient to protect children of immigrants from the prejudice and unequal treatment that awaits them out in the larger society. It is naive to think that an ECEC program, no matter how well intentioned and well run, can inoculate children from racism or from the vicissitudes of poverty. Providing an oasis from the prejudice of the larger society is appreciated by immigrant families, but it does not go far enough.

But what can we do in the face of such daunting problems? One response is to develop the potential of ECEC programs to serve as a conduit to social services for recent immigrants, acknowledging the fact that for many immigrant parents, preschool is their first and primary contact with their adopted society. Early childhood education works best when it is integrated with other services, including health, housing, parental education, employment, and economic assistance (Barnett, 1995; Karoly et al., 1998).

We should not feel that we must have solutions to immigrant families' problems in order to enter into dialogue. One reason early childhood educators might hesitate to get into discussions with immigrant children and their parents about the social problems the families face is the fear of being unable to offer a solution or adequate response. We need to answer, but this is not the same thing as having the answer. Answerability, in Mikhail Bakhtin's terms (1990), is the ethical obligation we have to enter into dialogue with each other and, after listening, to in some way respond. We do not need to have answers in advance to enter into dialogue with immigrant parents.

References

Anzaldúa, G. (1987). *Borderlands La Frontera: The new mestiza.* San Francisco: Spinsters/Aunt Lute.

Bakhtin, M. (1990). *Art and answerability: Early philosophical essays* (M. Holquist and V. Liapunov, Trans.). Austin: University of Texas Press.

Barnett, W. S. (1995). Long-term early childhood programs on cognitive and school outcomes [Electronic version]. *The Future of Children, 5*(3). Retrieved November 2005 from http://www.futureofchildren.org/usr_doc/v015n03ART2.pdf.

Cornfield, D. B., & Arzubiaga, A. (2004). Immigrants and education in the U.S. interior: Integrating and segmenting tendencies in Nashville, Tennessee. *Peabody Journal of Education, 79,* 157–179.

Delgado, R. (Ed.). (1995). *Critical race theory: The cutting edge.* Philadelphia: Tempe University Press.

Diaz-Soto, L. (1997). *Language, culture, and power. Bilingual families and the struggle for quality education.* Albany: State University of New York Press.

Goldenberg, C., & Gallimore, R. (1995). Immigrant Latino parents' values and beliefs about their children's education: Continuities and discontinuities across cultures and generations. *Advances in Motivation and Achievement, 9,* 183–228.

hooks, b. (1994a). *Teaching to transgress: Education as the practice of freedom.* New York: Routledge.

hooks, b. (1994b). *Outlaw culture: Resisting representations.* New York: Routledge.

Karoly, L. A., Rydell, C. P., Hoube, J., Everingham, S. S., Kilburn, R., & Greenwood, P. W. (1998). *Investing in our children: What we know and don't know about the costs and benefits of early childhood interventions.* Washington, DC: RAND.

Ladson-Billings, G., & Tate, W. F., IV (1995). Toward a critical race theory of education. *Teachers College Record, 97*(1), 47–68.

Moraga, C. (1983). *Loving in the war years.* Cambridge: South End Press.

Reese, L., Balzano, S., Gallimore, R., & Goldenberg, C. (1995). The concept of educación: Latino family values and American schooling. *International Journal of Educational Research, 23*(1), 57–81.

Smith, L. T. (1999). *Decolonizing methodologies: Research and indigenous people.* New York: Zen Books.

Tobin, J., Wu, D., & Davidson, D. (1989). *Preschool in three cultures: Japan, China, and the United States.* New Haven, CT: Yale University Press.

Uttal, L. (2002). *Making care work: Employed mothers in the new childcare market.* New Brunswick, NJ: Rutgers University Press.

Valdés, G. (1996). *Con respeto: Bridging the distances between culturally diverse families and schools: An ethnographic portrait.* New York: Teachers College Press.

Valenzuela, A. (1999). *Subtractive schooling: U.S.-Mexican youth and the politics of caring.* Albany: State University of New York Press.

Villenas, S., & Deyhle, D. (1999). Critical race theory and ethnographies challenging the stereotypes: Latino families, schooling, resilience and resistance. *Curriculum Inquiry, 29*(4), 413–446.

10
Keiki Steps
Equity Issues in a Parent-Participation Preschool Program for Native Hawaiian Children

MARCI WAI'ALE'ALE SARSONA, SHERLYN GOO, ALICE KAWAKAMI, AND KATHRYN AU

Keiki is the common Hawaiian word for child, and Keiki Steps is a parent-participation preschool program for Native Hawaiian children. Unlike most early childhood programs, Keiki Steps was not the brainchild of early childhood professionals. Rather, it grew from the initiative of a mother of two young children. In 1998 Michelle Mahuka, who resides with her family in the Hawaiian homestead community of Nānākuli, saw a television ad about parent-participation preschool programs (also called play morning programs) and thought that she would like to take her children to participate in such a program. When she called the agency that had sponsored the ad, she was informed that there was no parent-participation preschool program to serve her rural community. Such a program had once been available in Nānākuli but had closed three years earlier (Roberts, 1993). Mahuka learned that the nearest available program was in a suburb several miles down the highway, a cultural context and environment quite different from her own rural neighborhood. She decided to see if a parent-participation preschool program could be started in Nānākuli, to serve all the families with young children in the community.

The agency referred Mahuka to Sherlyn Goo, then the executive director of the Institute for Native Pacific Education and Culture (INPEACE), a small, nonprofit, Native Hawaiian educational services organization. Goo sought funding while Mahuka did legwork in the community and garnered donations from area businesses and organizations. In the meantime, residents of another Hawaiian homestead, Waimānalo, had recognized a similar need for a parent-participation preschool program in their community. Goo was able to move this project forward even more quickly, and the first Keiki Steps site began operations in Waimānalo 6 months before the Keiki Steps site in Nānākuli opened.

The rest, as they say, is history. By 2005–2006, Keiki Steps had grown to 14 sites on three of the six main islands in the state of Hawai'i, with parent-participation preschools operating on a 3-day-a-week schedule coinciding with the public school year. Keiki Steps had a written curriculum for children from ages 1 through 4, built in part on the foundation of Hawai'i's state preschool standards. The program had a training module for entry-level teachers and one for teachers with a year or more of experience with the program. A 3-week summer component, Keiki Steps to Kindergarten, had been added to ease the transition of young children into kindergarten at public elementary schools. In the summer of 2006, 23 elementary schools hosted Keiki Steps to Kindergarten classes, an effort enthusiastically endorsed by both parents and educators.

Theoretical Framework

The theoretical framework that underlies Keiki Steps is related to the two major purposes of the program, as conceptualized by the leaders of INPEACE. First, as with other parent-participation preschool programs, Keiki Steps has the purpose of educating young children about school-relevant social skills and academic concepts, as well as educating parents about how they might support their children's social, physical, and academic development and readiness for school. Second, unlike most other early childhood programs, Keiki Steps serves the purpose of community and economic development. Since its inception, INPEACE has had the policy of hiring residents of the Native Hawaiian communities served by its programs as staff members. The theoretical perspective guiding the curriculum and educational aspects of Keiki Steps is culturally responsive instruction, while that guiding the community and economic development aspects of Keiki Steps is the concept of the caring community.

Culturally Responsive Instruction

Culturally responsive instruction has long been proposed as a way of narrowing or closing the gap between the educational achievement of students of diverse cultural and linguistic backgrounds, such as Native Hawaiian students, and their mainstream peers (Au, 2006, 2007). Reviews indicate that much of the research on culturally responsive instruction has centered on elementary and secondary school classrooms (e.g., Au & Kawakami, 1994; Osborne, 1996). However, culturally responsive instruction provides a valuable theoretical framework for early childhood education as well.

Different labels for this same concept have been used, including culturally relevant pedagogy (Ladson-Billings, 1995; Osborne, 1996), culturally responsive teaching (Gay, 2000), and culturally congruent instruction (Au & Kawakami, 1994). More important than the nuances connoted by these different terms, we believe, are the common assumptions of researchers who conduct studies in this area. One shared assumption is that the goal of culturally responsive instruction is to increase the school success of children of diverse cultural and linguistic backgrounds. Another assumption is that school success is to be achieved by building bridges between children's experiences at home and at school. The idea is to foster (or at the very least, to maintain) children's competence in the heritage culture and language. Finally, these researchers share the goal of promoting social justice through a focus on equality of educational outcomes and a celebration of diversity.

Culturally responsive instruction represents one of two theoretical paths for improving the literacy achievement of students of diverse cultural and linguistic backgrounds, as shown in Figure 10.1 (adapted from Au, 2007). Advocates of the first path, which Au terms the direct or assimilationist approach, believe that early childhood and other educational programs should immerse children of diverse backgrounds in mainstream content and interactional processes right from the outset. This is the dominant view of how the schooling of young children of diverse backgrounds should proceed. The second path shown in Figure 10.1 is what Au labels the indirect or pluralist approach, and this is the path recommended by advocates of culturally responsive instruction. In the indirect path, early childhood programs first affirm and reinforce the cultural identity of young children of diverse backgrounds. Working from this basis of cultural identity, educators then give children access to mainstream content and interactional processes. This second, pluralist path is the one we are attempting to follow with the Keiki Steps curriculum.

The Caring Community

McKnight's (1995) ideas about the caring community, or fostering the ability of diverse communities to recover their capacity to care, serves as the basis for the second theoretical perspective informing the development and operations of Keiki Steps. In his book *The Careless Society: Community and Its Counterfeits*, McKnight (1995) defines community as the site for the relationships among citizens. These relationships lead to care, which he defines

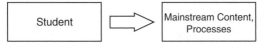

Direct or Assimilationist Approach

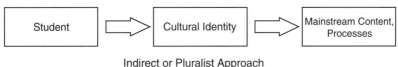

Indirect or Pluralist Approach

Figure 10.1 Two approaches to early childhood education.

as "the consenting commitment of citizens to one another" (p. x). McKnight writes,

> The most significant development transforming America since World War II has been the growth of a powerful service economy and its pervasive serving institutions. Those institutions have commodified the care of community and called the substitution a service. As citizens have seen the professionalized service commodity invade their communities, they have grown doubtful of their common capacity to care, and so it is that we have become a careless society, populated by impotent citizens and ineffectual communities dependent on the counterfeit of care called human services. (pp. ix–x)

McKnight argues that institutions, by their very efforts to provide services, may hamper the community's efforts to supply care. McKnight does not deny that professionalization brings the advantage of greater expertise due to specialized training, but he stresses that it brings the disadvantage of distance, as service providers are seldom dealing with individuals with whom they share the bonds of community.

McKnight's concern for the growing distance between service providers and those served can certainly be seen in the education of Native Hawaiian children today. In precontact times, before 1778, elders in the family—parents, grandparents, and other adults in the extended family—were the teachers of young Native Hawaiian children, along with their older siblings (Kelly, 1982/1991). Children did not attend school but were prepared for full participation in society by observing others, assisting, and attempting to complete the same tasks themselves. These tasks might range from cultivating taro to catching fish to making bark cloth to healing. Adults observed children's progress and made an effort to match specialized training to their talents. For example, a graceful child with a good voice and memory might be apprenticed to a dance expert or *kumu hula*. In contrast, in contemporary times, Native Hawaiian families are often given the impression that the best route is to send their young children to center-based preschools, to be taught by nonfamily members who are usually outsiders to the community and who may have little knowledge of Hawaiian culture.

This theoretical perspective on strengthening the community's capacity to care suggests to us that early childhood programs intended to serve diverse communities need to be developed with an awareness of the extent to which dominant-group perspectives are likely to be privileged over community perspectives, in terms of who can and should be an educator. The privileging of educators from outside the community (even those with outstanding formal training and credentials) over insiders may well contribute to the distancing and commodifying of early childhood education and care. Although statistics are not available for preschool teachers, studies indicate that over three-fourths of the teachers in public elementary and secondary schools in Native Hawaiian communities are neither Native Hawaiians nor residents of the community (Tikunoff, Ward, & Broekhuizen, 1993). Under these circumstances, schooling becomes the process of educating "other people's children," as Delpit (1988) puts it.

These two theoretical perspectives—culturally responsive instruction and the caring community—come together to suggest alternative ways of conceptualizing early childhood efforts in diverse communities. These perspectives give us a framework for countering dominant-group discourse that tends to favor a single solution—center-based preschools—over offering families in diverse communities a variety of options for early childhood education and care (Sarsona, 2004). These perspectives provide grounds for us to challenge the deficit views of young children and their families implicit in the common argument often made for early childhood education as an investment that prevents later social problems (Dahlberg, Pence, & Moss, 1999). Arguments of this nature tend to focus on the role of early childhood programs in socializing young children to dominant-group curriculum content and school routines and away from the family. While we acknowledge the place of such experiences in preparing young children to succeed in school, we believe that assimilationist views need to be balanced by pluralist views based upon assumptions of difference rather than deficit.

In this light, we argue for the potential of early childhood education to strengthen the cultural identity of young children of diverse backgrounds, such as Native Hawaiians, as a means not only to ensure school success but to build vibrant communities and perpetuate the heritage culture and language. Strengthening cultural identity would include encouraging parents and other adult family members to help children learn cultural values and practices, culturally appropriate ways of communicating and relating to others, and the heritage language. A healthy, evolving community can immerse children in the richness of their heritage culture as the basis for preparing them to participate successfully in the educational, social, and economic opportunities offered by a modern, global society.

Keiki Steps Program and Curriculum

As a parent-participation preschool program, Keiki Steps operates three mornings a week, from 8:00 to 11:00 a.m., at locations convenient to caregivers in the community. Although we call Keiki Steps a *parent*-participation program, we should note that young children are just as likely to attend with a grandparent, and to appear with fathers and grandfathers, as well as mothers and grandmothers. Depending on location, each site can accommodate up to 25 children and their caregivers per session. Elementary schools are a good location because parents or other caregivers can see that the older children arrive safely at their classrooms and then bring the younger children to Keiki

Steps. Keiki Steps may be held in a vacant classroom, in the school cafeteria, in a park pavilion, in a community center, or even on the grassy lawn of a school if no sheltered area is available.

The area is set up with a circle-time center, large enough for all the families to gather together, and a variety of smaller centers that let children and their families engage in a variety of learning activities, including reading, writing, art, blocks, thinking games and puzzles, and dramatic play. Outdoor activities are set up as well to allow play with water and sand or balls and hoops, as well as gardening and painting. Keiki Steps is designed to be an economical program, so no expensive furniture or equipment is required. The centers are simply mats, of the kind families in Hawai'i use at the beach, often furnished with a low table and plastic bins containing books, supplies, or toys. Centers change in keeping with monthly themes, which include health and safety, our island, and transportation.

Although Keiki Steps originally targeted young children from ages 3 to 4, families often brought younger children, 1- and 2-year-olds, along as well; they could not leave the youngest children at home while bringing the older ones to Keiki Steps. In response, the curriculum was extended to address the learning needs of very young children, for example, by adding an infant center with toys appropriate for this age group.

The day begins with First Circle, to acquaint families with the program, provide some quick learning activities for caregivers and children (such as a story read aloud or simple song or game), and introduce them to the activities at the play centers. Families are reminded that Keiki Steps is based on Hawaiian values. For example, the value highlighted during the first week of the program is *mālama,* to take care of, while the value for the second week is *kōkua,* to help. Caregivers and children are asked to suggest ways that they can carry out the value during their time at Keiki Steps. For example, with *kōkua,* adults might help set up and clean up the centers, while children might share toys with others. Most of the time is devoted to allowing children and their caregivers to engage in activities at the learning centers.

Some days include a Parent Talk-Story Time. "Talk story" is the term for a Hawaiian community speech event in which individuals share and conarrate personal experiences (Watson, 1974). The site coordinator uses this time to get acquainted with the caregivers' hopes and expectations for the children, as well as to inform caregivers about topics such as different ways of teaching young children (modeling, creating opportunities for exploration), furthering their language development, and determining family needs for which support can be recommended or directly provided, for example, health concerns.

How Keiki Steps Addresses Social Justice

Keiki Steps addresses issues of social justice in ways consistent with the key concepts of its theoretical framework. First, we have tried to make Keiki Steps a culturally responsive early childhood program that will enable young Native Hawaiian children to prosper when they enter kindergarten in public schools. The hallmark of a culturally responsive educational program is that it enables students to experience academic success in school through means consistent with cultural values. A curriculum based on cultural values focuses on learning about cultural identity, proper behavior and cultural protocol, student-created work that exhibits cultural knowledge and values, and an appreciation and fondness for one's homeland (Kawakami & Aton, 1999). These components are evident in Keiki Steps when children learn their names and the names of their family members, are cued and prompted about the proper etiquette for addressing others, engage in traditional crafts such as the making of lei (flower garlands), and explore natural elements—such as stones, shells, or leaves—from the environment in the centers and play areas. These aspects of the curriculum become the content for intergenerational conversations and learning.

Keiki Steps is responsive to young Native Hawaiian children and their families in both content and process. The curriculum is typical of that found in other early childhood settings in providing opportunities for growth in the social, cognitive, and physical domains, along with creative expression. Keiki Steps infuses culturally familiar or culturally relevant activities and objects into parts of the curriculum. For example, children make lei to give as gifts to senior citizens, *ipu* (gourds) are included with rhythm instruments such as tambourines and drums, and *wa'a* (canoes) are created out of cardboard boxes as a model of local transportation or sport. However, for the most part, the curriculum would be familiar to early childhood educators working in other settings throughout the United States. On one hand, we believe that much more can and should be done to bring culturally relevant content and processes into the Keiki Steps curriculum. On the other hand, we know that the curriculum must continue to include content and processes that will prepare the children for the largely Western and mainstream-oriented public school environment.

Second, Keiki Steps addresses social justice by offering families a low-cost, high-quality alternative to traditional center-based preschool programs. Because registration is extremely simple (preregistration and birth/medical documentation are not required) and there is no cost for services other than field trips, Keiki Steps does not pose the institutional and financial barriers to participation that might prove daunting to Hawaiian families and prevent children from entering an early childhood program. The program's location in Hawaiian communities makes it easy for families to participate without having to go far from home.

In Hawai'i in general, and among Native Hawaiians in particular, the 'ohana or extended family may still be intact and strong, as a source of support for relatives. In this situation, grandparents often care for children during the day, even if the family can afford to send the child to a center-based preschool. The belief is that children will benefit from being kept within the family rather than being sent away to be cared for by strangers (Kaomea, in press). Also, grandparents can give children more attention, discipline, and affection than they would receive in a center-based preschool. They can impart cultural knowledge that a preschool teacher might not possess or choose to share as part of an institutional curriculum. For example, grandparents might take children to the beach for a day that includes swimming and gathering *pipipi* (small, edible mollusks) and *limu* (seaweed).

Keiki Steps addresses issues of social justice by offering Hawaiian families enriching educational opportunities without removing the young child from the family. The benefit of intergenerational bonds and the continuity of family stories strengthen cultural identity and bind family members into active engagement with and support for the young child's education. Keiki Steps can provide a wealth of materials—such as books, blocks, and art supplies—that families may not be able to afford, while showing families the way these materials can be used to promote learning.

The program provides an inviting social environment that allows families to interact with other families as well as with the Keiki Steps staff, consistent with the importance of social capital to many Hawaiian adults (Howard, 1974). Typically, Keiki Steps staff members have extensive social networks in the community, and they invite their relatives, friends, neighbors, high school classmates, and other personal acquaintances to bring the young children in their care to the program. Consistency of attendance at Keiki Steps may be enhanced because of staff members' ability to tap into these existing social networks, as well as by the program's evident benefits for young children.

Another way that Keiki Steps seeks to serve the cause of social justice is by giving residents of Native Hawaiian communities jobs in the field of early childhood education, thus contributing to economic and community development. A considerable number of staff members began their association with Keiki Steps as participants who brought their own young children or grandchildren to the program. They were noticed by site coordinators because they consistently arrived early to help set up the learning centers and stayed late to help clean up and put the materials away. Usually these individuals are not seeking employment and express surprise at learning that they might be paid for carrying out such duties. Often, individuals hired as Keiki Steps aides have little or no experience in the workplace. The job is made more practical and attractive because INPEACE has a policy of allowing Keiki Steps employees to bring their own young children with them to the program, and this eliminates the problem of finding child care.

Hiring from the community has definite advantages. Attendance at some sites is high because the site coordinator and aide have recruited relatives, friends, and neighbors to attend. By tapping into existing social networks in the community, Keiki Steps is able to bring new educational opportunities to families and young children. Depending upon their own upbringing, Keiki

Steps staff members may have considerable knowledge of Hawaiian culture to share with program participants. In general, they possess the ability to communicate in a manner that Hawaiian and other local families find inviting and comfortable. This is in contrast to bringing in outside professionals (an element of the commodification of care) who may be unable to gain the confidence of community members. Furthermore, outsiders do not add to the economic well-being of the community, as they live and shop in their own home communities and tend to make contributions there.

The trend toward commodifying care is evident as well in the recent push for center-based preschools as the pillar of early childhood education in Hawai'i. In many Native Hawaiian families, as well as other families in Hawai'i, grandparents often care for young children while parents are at work. This practice runs counter to the mainstream view that children should be sent to center-based preschools where they can learn under the guidance of teachers with credentials in the field of early childhood education. Because the mainstream view is reinforced through the media, the impression may be given that the loving care provided by grandparents is no longer good enough, and that children need to be removed from the family and sent to center-based preschools to lay the foundation for success in kindergarten and higher grades.

We think one way to reverse the trend of commodifying care in early childhood education is by bringing community residents into this field. In common with other INPEACE programs, Keiki Steps has the goal of empowering Native Hawaiians to work in programs serving their own communities and to develop professional skills and networks while on the job. Over time, the residents who work with Keiki Steps should be able to help their communities recover the capacity to care by developing early childhood education solutions tailored to the cultural context. Over the 8 years of the program, several staff members have been nurtured to move into higher paying positions in the early childhood field and higher education. As their children have moved out of the program and into elementary schools, some employees have found the time and mobility to take courses outside of the community.

Due to the hiring policies of INPEACE, almost all of the Keiki Steps site coordinators and aides are Native Hawaiian women from the community. Furthermore, as a condition of employment, INPEACE requires Keiki Steps staff members to complete a series of community college courses in early childhood education (a point discussed in detail below). By furthering their education, the Keiki Steps site coordinators and aides gain transportable job skills while contributing to the support of their families.

Reflections

Our work with Keiki Steps has made us aware of ways in which typical early childhood education policies and practices may run counter to the values and preferences of many families and young children in Native

Hawaiian communities. Three issues of equity strike us as particularly salient. These relate to the questions of (1) what should be taught, (2) what options parents are offered, and (3) who should become early childhood educators.

What Should Be Taught?

We have already alluded to the potential tension between mainstream curriculum content and content meaningful, interesting, or familiar to young Hawaiian children and their families. Obviously, children need access to mainstream content if they are to be prepared for school success. The question is whether children access mainstream content through a direct, assimilationist approach or through a culturally responsive, pluralist approach. We think a good argument can be made for the idea that early childhood programs offer an excellent setting for building children's cultural identity and cultural knowledge. For example, children can be taught to string simple lei and to understand the symbolism of making and presenting lei.

The discourse of public education in Hawai'i, as elsewhere in the United States, has become dominated by concerns about accountability and rigorous academic standards. There is the danger that standards may be written and interpreted so narrowly as to leave little or no space in the curriculum for Hawaiian cultural content likely to be of high interest to Hawaiian children. This danger, plus the poor achievement record of many public schools serving high proportions of Native Hawaiian students, has led Native Hawaiian educators to create a network of charter schools that focus on Hawaiian cultural content, Hawaiian language, and the needs of Hawaiian children. Fourteen of the 27 charter schools in Hawai'i, enrolling 1,700 students, have such a focus (Star-Bulletin Staff, 2005).

Offering Families Alternatives

We believe that all parents, including Native Hawaiian parents, should have a choice of options for providing high-quality early education and care for their children, so that they can make decisions on the basis of their family's values and needs. We know that families are their children's first teachers and that the 'ohana plays the most important role in the education of young children. At the same time, the dominant society, through the media, sends families the message that the best way to ensure that a young child receives quality early learning experiences is by placing that child in the care of others.

Sarsona (2004) reports that, in her own family and among her friends and associates, many young children stay at home with tutu (grandmother) or other family members. As a parent of two young children, Sarsona entrusted her mother with the care of her children. Sarsona writes,

My mother didn't know the meaning of developmentally appropriate practices and she didn't use words like cognitive development, gross motor, fine motor, social-emotional health. But she did know what to do when Wai'ale'ale [Sarsona's daughter] cried, played with her, told her stories, read her books, and let Wai'ale'ale help with preparing lunch and dinner. She even made toys for her, placing beads in a small plastic juice bottle to make a rattle.

Many Native Hawaiians, including Sarsona, believe that high-quality early childhood education and care can be found in many other environments beside the classroom. These environments include parent-participation pre-school programs such as Keiki Steps, family child-care homes, and staying at home with *tutu*. Parents should have the opportunity to understand this range of options, rather than being directed only to enroll their children in center-based preschools.

As Sarsona's experience illustrates, parents may choose different options at different times. Sarsona's family has used the spectrum of options, including parent-participation preschool programs, care by the extended family, care within the immediate family, and a center-based preschool. We argue that what is critical for Native Hawaiian families with young children is the right to choose the option for education and care that they judge to be in the best interest of the child and the family under a given set of circumstances.

In Hawai'i and other states, discussions about early childhood education may become one-sided, in that the issue boils down to whether there can be more money for center-based preschools. As an advocate for the rights of Native Hawaiian children and families, Sarsona (2004) prefers a broader vision.

We need to look beyond the four walls of the classroom to educate and prepare our youngest *keiki* for school. We need to give parents the right to make choices that are best for their children.

Who Is Qualified to Teach?

As noted earlier, INPEACE seeks to hire Keiki Steps staff members from the communities served by the program. Newly hired staff members in Keiki Steps generally have completed little or no college course work. As a condition of continued employment, they are required to complete courses in early childhood education, offered as part of a community college program aimed at preparing individuals to be certified as teachers and aides in preschool classrooms. INPEACE pays all costs related to this certification process and pays staff for time spent taking the courses. Furthermore, INPEACE employs a part-time counselor, an experienced Native Hawaiian early childhood educator, to assist and guide staff members through their course work and make sure that they complete the certification program successfully.

However, while we acknowledge the value of professional development in early childhood education, we do not believe that possessing a college degree is the best or only qualification needed to work effectively with young children and their families in a community-based program such as Keiki Steps. In our experience, the privileging of university credentials tends to create a bias in the early childhood field toward job applicants from dominant-group backgrounds. Yet our Keiki Steps staff members often have other qualifications that may be valuable to a parent-participation preschool program operating in a Hawaiian community. These qualifications include knowledge of the community, its values, and lifestyle; the ability to communicate in a sensitive yet professional manner with Hawaiian families; the ability to serve as a role model to those from similar backgrounds and circumstances; the ability to demonstrate how Hawaiian values can become guiding principles for behavior in an educational setting and workplace; the ability to bring families together as a supportive network to share information and resources; trusting personal relationships built up over the course of many years; and practical knowledge gained through life experience, including that of being a parent or grandparent of young Hawaiian children.

We think the goal should be to support community members in becoming early childhood educators. The transition from a typical Native Hawaiian learning environment to a Western learning environment is a challenge for many youngsters. The Keiki Steps model ensures the transition is a smooth one through a culturally appropriate yet standards-based curriculum, delivered by insiders to the community using culturally responsive approaches.

Conclusion

In concluding, we highlight the benefits of community-based early childhood education efforts such as Keiki Steps. Certainly, there are benefits both in culturally responsive curricula for young children and in opportunities for community and economic development. We are in the beginning stages of exploration to understand how the curriculum of a parent-participation preschool program can build young children's cultural identity as Native Hawaiians, while at the same laying the foundation for success in the mainstream environments of public schools and the larger society. While we realize that our efforts to incorporate Hawaiian values, language, and cultural activities into the curriculum for both parents and young children need rethinking and deepening, we remain convinced of the promise of this approach. We find that Native Hawaiians can and should serve as early childhood educators in their own communities, working in programs that allow children to remain with family members while experiencing the range of educational activities that would otherwise only be available through enrollment at center-based preschools. On one hand, care must be taken to maintain a closeness between early childhood educators and the children and families served, to counter the commodifying of care criticized by McKnight (1995). On the other hand, supports must be in place to promote the professional skills of community members as early childhood educators to ensure that children and parents receive high-quality education and that community members have the opportunity to advance to positions of increasing responsibility and influence.

Because we have emphasized the importance of a Native Hawaiian perspective in Keiki Steps, a question arises about the extent to which Keiki Steps might be an appropriate model for early childhood programs, particularly parent-participation preschools, in other settings. Our opinion is that many of the specific features of Keiki Steps, such as its schedule and location in community settings, would probably work quite well in a wide variety of communities, ranging from urban to suburban to rural. We believe that the benefits of hiring from the community are likely to generalize to other settings, especially when accompanied by the requirement that staff members continue their education in the early childhood field.

Parts of the Keiki Steps curriculum, those not tied to Hawaiian culture and values, could be used with children and families in a variety of settings. For the rest, we would advise curriculum developers to observe the principle of culturally responsive instruction. This means bringing into the curriculum the cultural values and practices of community members, as well as activities and natural materials found in or reflective of the community's environment. We believe that culturally responsive early childhood education may be as welcomed by families in other diverse communities as it has been in the Hawaiian communities served by Keiki Steps.

Native Hawaiians as a group are increasingly determined to stand their ground in the tug-of-war between traditional Hawaiian values rooted in spirituality and the highly competitive and academic nature of schooling promoted by the constant race to get ahead in mainstream, consumerist American society. The ideas we have endorsed—culturally responsive early childhood curricula, community-based parent-participation preschool programs such as Keiki Steps, and offering families a range of options for early childhood education and care beyond center-based preschools—are consistent with this stance.

We see themes of self-determination and the perpetuation of Hawaiian culture echoed in many settings when Native Hawaiians gather to discuss educational issues. For example, while this chapter was being written, the Association of Hawaiian Civic Clubs, the oldest Native Hawaiian grassroots organization in our state, held an education summit. In her opening remarks, Antoinette Lee, the association's president, reminded the audience that she had decided on *kohoia,* to exercise choice, as the cultural value for her term of office (Lee, 2006). Lee declared,

> It is time for Native Hawaiians to determine our destiny. A key component to this self-determination is to build the system we want to educate our children and to carry our values, culture and society forward.

The next day, a *kupuna* (elder) urged members of the audience to bring their young children and grandchildren along when they did volunteer work. Gesturing to her own granddaughter, who had come with her to the summit, she cited the need for youngsters to see adults working together for the good of the community. A grandfather decried the loss of funding for music and art in the public schools, referring to music as "the essence of our being" and arguing that "music should be the *last* thing they cut." Another *kupuna* summed up the sentiments of the group when she declared, "We don't want our children to be materialistic." As these statements suggest, when we speak of diversity in early childhood education, we must remember the importance of allowing families of diverse backgrounds, such as Native Hawaiian families, to exercise their right to choose. These families need and deserve options for early childhood education and care that support their self-determination and beliefs about how deeply held cultural values may be passed on to future generations.

References

Au, K. H. (2006). *Multicultural issues and literacy achievement*. Mahwah, NJ: Erlbaum.

Au, K. H. (2007). Culturally responsive instruction: Application to multiethnic classrooms. *Pedagogies 2*(1), 1–18.

Au, K. H., & Kawakami, A. J. (1994). Cultural congruence in instruction. In E. R. Hollins, J. E. King, & W. Hayman (Eds.), *Teaching diverse populations: Formulating a knowledge base* (pp. 5–23). Albany: State University of New York Press.

Dahlberg, G., Pence, A. R., & Moss, P. (1999). *Beyond quality in early childhood education and care: Postmodern perspectives*. London: RoutledgeFalmer.

Delpit, L. (1988). The silenced dialogue: Power and pedagogy in educating other people's children. *Harvard Educational Review, 58*, 280–298.

Gay, G. (2000). *Culturally responsive teaching: Theory, research, and practice*. New York: Teachers College Press.

Howard, A. (1974). *Ain't no big thing*. Honolulu: University of Hawaii Press.

Kaomea, J. (in press). Failing families? Deconstructing colonial discourses on indigenous child welfare and early childhood education. *Asia Pacific Journal of Education*.

Kawakami, A., & Aton, K. (1999). *Na Pua No'eau curriculum guidelines*. Hilo: Center for Gifted and Talented Native Hawaiian Children, University of Hawai'i at Hilo.

Kelly, M. (1982/1991). *Some thoughts on education in traditional Hawaiian society. To teach the children: Historical aspects of education in Hawaii* (pp. 4–14). Honolulu: College of Education, University of Hawaii.

Ladson-Billings, G. (1995). Toward a theory of culturally relevant pedagogy. *American Educational Research Journal, 32*(3), 465–491.

Lee, A. (2006). *Nana Ma Mua I Loko No'ono'o Kakou welcoming remarks*. Association of Hawaiian Civic Clubs. Retrieved July 9, 2006, from http://www.aohcc.org/docs/ahcc.htm.

McKnight, J. (1995). *The careless society: Community and its counterfeits*. New York: BasicBooks.

Osborne, A. B. (1996). Practice into theory into practice: Culturally relevant pedagogy for students we have marginalized and normalized. *Anthropology and Education Quarterly, 27*(3), 285–314.

Roberts, R. N. (1993). Early education as community intervention: Assisting an ethnic minority to be ready for school. *American Journal of Community Psychology, 21*(4), 521–535.

Sarsona, M. W. (2004, December 2). Early education choices key to family well-being. *Honolulu Star-Bulletin*. Retrieved July 12, 2005, from http://starbulletin.com/2004/12/02/editorial/commentary.html.

Star-Bulletin Staff. (2005, October 11). Hawaiian charter schools get $2.2M. *Honolulu Star-Bulletin*. Retrieved September 17, 2006, from http://starbulletin.com/2005/10/11/news/story07.html.

Tikunoff, W. J., Ward, B. A., & Broekhuizen, L. D. V. (1993). *KEEP evaluation study: Year 3 report*. Los Alamitos, CA: Southwest Regional Educational Laboratory.

Watson, K. A. (1974). Transferable communicative routines: Strategies and group identity in two speech events. *Language in Society, 4*, 53–72.

11

Catching Up with Globalization
One State's Experience of Reforming Teacher Education in the 21st Century

SHARON RYAN AND CARRIE LOBMAN

Globalization has contributed to increased mobility and interaction among cultures. This chapter uses data drawn from a mixed methods study to highlight some of the challenges involved in trying to create a teacher development system that prepares teachers to work with students who differ developmentally, culturally, and linguistically. The findings are used as a springboard to consider some of the reforms required in the field of teacher education if professional development experiences are going to catch up with the effects of globalization.

We are living in a global society in which knowledge, trade, and people move frequently so that there is more contact among cultures than ever before (Barbules & Torres, 2000). As a result, students participating in early childhood programs are increasingly diverse, representing a range of linguistic, racial, ethnic, immigrant, and academic backgrounds. Between 1999 and 2002, there was a 5 percent increase in the number of children with at least one foreign-born parent (Federal Interagency Forum on Child and Family Statistics, 2004). Perhaps not surprisingly, the percentage of children under 18 years of age who are white is decreasing, at the same time as the numbers of children from Asian and Latino backgrounds continues to rise. Thus, educating teachers to be able to individualize instruction and respond to their students in ways that are equitable and culturally relevant is of paramount importance.

Although equity issues and how best to respond to individual and group differences have been a part of the field's thinking and practices for at least 20 years (Bredekamp & Copple, 1997; Derman-Sparks & ABC Task Force, 1989; Ramsey, 1987), what research is available (Graue, 2005; Hyun, 1996; Robinson, 2002) would suggest that early childhood teachers often do not incorporate the kinds of changes to their curriculum and learning environments that are inclusive of students and their families. One reason posited for this lack of responsiveness is that the majority of early childhood teachers are white, female, monolingual, and middle class (Hyun, 1996; Goodwin, 2002). Because of their limited cultural knowledge, many teachers are not able to respond to the multiple cultural, linguistic, and developmental backgrounds of their young students (Hyun, 1996). Another probable reason is that most teachers of young children have had little professional education to perform their work (Bowman, Donovan, & Burns, 2001). Teachers of children under kindergarten age in a large proportion of states have not been required to have anything more than a high school diploma and a few hours of professional development each year (Ackerman, 2004). Consequently, it is quite possible that many teachers may not have received specific training in diversity issues.

The good news is that preschool education across the country is undergoing significant reform, which may lead to a remedy for the limited multicultural expertise of the current workforce. Keen to harness the potential of early education to ameliorate the effects of "disadvantage" and produce social and economic benefits for communities, policymakers are creating coordinated systems of early childhood education (Lobman & Ryan, 2006). These systems bring together various service providers (for example, Head Start, child care, public schools) and employ common standards to ensure quality across setting or auspice. Increasingly, one of these standards is expectations about the professional education of preschool teachers. As the accrued research base demonstrates that those teachers who have attained a bachelor's degree and some additional specialized content in child development or early childhood education are more likely to enact high-quality practices (Barnett, 2003; Whitebook, 2003), policymakers are initiating efforts to help teachers to upgrade their qualifications. Therefore, policymakers are expecting that teachers will now be able to access a responsive system of professional preparation that reflects national standards.

National standards concerning the preparation of early childhood teachers propose that—in addition to education in the foundations of early childhood that includes child development and learning theory, as well as methods courses in both pedagogy and curricular approaches—teacher education programs should prepare teachers to understand how to apply this knowledge in assessing and adapting instruction to meet the needs of individual children, especially those from diverse linguistic and cultural backgrounds. (Bredekamp, 1996, p. 339). As stated in the most recent guidelines for initial licensure, and associate degree programs produced by the National Association for the Education of Young Children (NAEYC), teachers must be able to link children's language and culture to the curriculum and "support and empower diverse families, including those whose children have disabilities or special characteristics or learning needs" (Hyson, 2003, p. 32). Similarly, the Early Childhood/Generalist standards produced by the National Board for Professional Teaching Standards assert that "accomplished early childhood teachers model and teach behaviors appropriate in a diverse society" (Hyson, 2003, p. 156). Given these national expectations governing teacher preparation and the emphasis on improving the qualifications of the workforce, it might be assumed that in the foreseeable future there will be a teaching workforce that knows how to enact pedagogy that addresses the needs of all students participating in early childhood settings. In this chapter, we use the findings of a study of efforts in one state to reinvent its teacher education and professional development system to offer insights into what is happening in practice. We ask whether teacher educators in this state are indeed preparing teachers to work in a global society.

Background to the Study

New Jersey provides a unique context from which to examine the system of professional preparation of preschool teachers because of the *Abbott v. Burke* Supreme Court rulings (1998, 2000).[1] The 31 *Abbott* districts serve the state's most economically disadvantaged students, the majority of whom are from nonwhite backgrounds and whom the Court deemed had not been receiving a thorough and efficient education in comparison to their suburban counterparts. To address this inequity, the New Jersey Supreme Court mandated a set of reforms for these districts that included the implementation of systems of high-quality preschool for all 3- and 4-year-old children beginning in the 1999–2000 school year.

High-quality programs were defined by the Court as those having a class size of no more than 15 students with a certified teacher and teacher assistant per classroom. In addition, each program was required to use a developmentally appropriate curriculum and to provide adequate facilities, special education, bilingual education, transportation, health, and other services as needed. The Court also mandated that all teachers in *Abbott* preschools—unless they already held the Nursery or Kindergarten through Grade 8 Certificate and had 2 years of experience working with preschool-aged children—obtain a minimum of a BA with Preschool–Grade 3 (P–3) Certification by September 2004 (*Abbott v. Burke* VI, 2000).

As there had not been a specialized early childhood teaching certificate in the state, New Jersey's institutions of higher education created specialized P-3 certification programs, utilizing both alternate route and traditional approaches to teacher preparation. Several funding sources (Quality and Capacity Grants, Teacher Effectiveness and Teacher Preparation Grants) were provided by the state government through the Commission for Higher Education to help institutions of higher education expand their early childhood faculties. Further, as school districts were to collaborate with existing Head Start and private child-care programs already offering preschool in their communities, and because many of these teachers had to obtain P-3 certification, a state-funded scholarship program was also initiated to pay for teachers' tuition as they upgraded their qualifications. At the same time as this P-3 preparation system was being created, school districts embarked on a series of initiatives to meet the professional development needs of preschool teachers. These initiatives included the employment of master teachers to provide technical assistance and in-classroom support to preschool teachers with implementing developmentally appropriate curriculum models. Early childhood supervisors were also employed to oversee and implement ongoing professional development experiences for the district's preschool teachers. Thus, within a matter of a few years, a new teacher preparation and professional development system was developed.

Methodology

Between 2002 and 2005, we conducted a series of three interrelated studies that investigated preschool teachers' perceptions of their professional preparation and ongoing training experiences as well as the content and form of the certification and professional development programs being offered to them. In the first study (Ryan & Ackerman, 2005), 457 certified teachers were randomly selected from a list of the total population of 2,823 preschool teachers in the *Abbott* districts. Fifty-one percent of these teachers worked in public schools, 38 percent in child-care settings, and 11 percent in Head Start programs. Most of the teachers who participated in this study are white (59 percent), 21 percent are African American, and 11 percent self-identified as Latina. Teachers had an average of 10 years' experience (with a standard deviation [SD] of 8.04). These teachers were interviewed over the telephone using a protocol that examined four key areas: (a) demographic information, including salaries and retention issues; (b) teachers' efforts to increase their qualifications and the supports and barriers that may be affecting their current educational endeavors; (c) teachers' beliefs and practices; and (d) teachers' experiences with professional development.

The second study (Lobman, Ryan, & McLaughlin, 2005a) was a telephone survey with 135 representatives from the 180 institutions that provide early childhood teacher preparation or professional development. These include the *Abbott* school districts, county resource and referral agencies, 4-year universities, and 2-year community colleges. Utilizing the work of Early and Winton (2001), this survey focused on the kinds of content and experiences being offered to teachers, as well as where and how classes are offered. Another set of questions concentrated on capacity issues, such as numbers of students in various early childhood programs, and numbers and expertise of faculty members.

In the third study (Lobman, Ryan, & McLaughlin, 2005b) qualitative data were collected through a series of eight focus groups with 38 key stakeholders (16 preschool teachers, 6 policymakers, 11 professional development providers/administrators, and 5 teacher preparation personnel). Utilizing a semistructured protocol, these interviews elicited more in-depth information about content of training, capacity of various components of the current system, as well as insights into those aspects of the system that are working well and those that still need to be addressed.

Each of these studies built on the other so that we began with teacher perspectives that could then be cross-referenced with those who were involved in teachers' professional education in some way. The final study provided insights not only from teachers and teacher educators but also from other stakeholders involved in the new P-3 teacher development system. The interrelated nature of these studies allowed us to capture data on the teacher development system from the perspectives of all stakeholders at all levels of the system.

Findings

Each of the data sets was analyzed separately to shed light on particular questions about the content and delivery of professional development programs as well as how the system of P-3 teacher preparation and professional development was working overall. When the findings of the three studies are compared with particular attention to diversity content in teacher education, similar themes become apparent. The first of these is the notable lack of opportunity to access diversity course work, while the second theme is more concerned with the impact of the professional education being offered. Each of these themes is addressed below.

Limited Access to Diversity Training

> I think just in general we need more on diversity. It just needs to be out there more. We probably talk about it in roundabout ways, but never really actually see it.

Participants in both survey studies supported this teacher's perspective that preparation in addressing diversity issues in the classroom was less available than other content. When we asked teachers to indicate whether they participated in course work (a class, part of a class) advocated by the NAEYC standards of professional preparation and endorsed in policy documents concerning preschool education (e.g., *Eager to Learn,* Bowman, Donovan, & Burns, 2001), the highest participation rates for teachers were in classes concerning child development and methods of some kind. For example, 70 percent of teachers reported that they had received classes in child development, 87 percent participated in classes dealing with teaching strategies, and 92 percent in assessment techniques. Content that dealt with teaching special needs children (78.3 percent) and those whose first language is not English (66.1 percent) had the lowest participation rates.

Interviews with representatives from 4-year institutions of higher education corroborated what the teachers said they experienced in their programs of preparation. Across the 19 programs offered at the 12 participating 4-year institutions, teachers were more likely to access course work that is considered foundational to early childhood teaching—child development, early childhood curriculum in general, and play. P-3 students in all but one program receive at least one entire course in child development. Almost 90 percent of programs devote an entire class to curriculum development. Philosophical foundations and developmentally appropriate practice are also well represented, with 100 percent of the programs offering these topics as either part or all of a required class. Course work in addressing the learning and development of children from diverse educational and cultural backgrounds, although available, was less likely to be offered at all institutions. While 38 percent of the programs require their students to take an entire class on working with children with special needs, three programs offer no course work on this topic. Similarly, 70 percent of the programs offer some course work on working with children for whom English is not their first language, but again, several programs do not address this topic at all. However, almost all of the programs (95 percent) provide some preparation on working with families.

These survey responses paint a problematic picture. Apparently, learning about how to work with children who differ academically, developmentally, linguistically, and culturally is, to some extent, dependent on where, when, and how you complete your certification program. Moreover, despite the fact that these P-3 teacher preparation programs were fairly new and presumably teacher educators were aware of the standards, when compared with national data (Early & Winton, 2001), teachers in New Jersey programs at the time of these studies were being provided with less diversity content than their counterparts in other states. Whereas nationwide 60 percent of early childhood teacher preparation programs require students to take a full course in working with children with disabilities, in New Jersey only 30 percent of the schools currently require such a class. Similarly, 43 percent of programs nationwide require a full course on working with children and families from diverse cultural and linguistic backgrounds, while in New Jersey it is only 28 percent.

Perceived Efficacy of Diversity Training

One of the problems with survey data is that it is not always possible to probe deeply into a particular issue. In the focus groups, we asked those invested in preschool teacher education in some way what they thought teachers needed to be able to know and do. Expertise in knowing how to include *all* children was not viewed by many stakeholders as a priority. Teachers and administrators spoke about this issue more frequently than policymakers and teacher educators. However, the responses about diversity often displayed an inadequate understanding of the complex ways culture and context shape children's learning. For example, one child-care director considered diversity as having knowledge of specific cultural groups and what makes them unique. In her words,

I feel that diversity—the teacher must know the culture. Every aspect of that culture, if it's Haiti, Puerto Rico, or anywhere. So they should be able to bring culture into the classroom. It's the only way children connect and bond.

Such a view often leads to what has been termed a "tourist-based" approach to multiculturalism (Derman-Sparks & ABC Task Force, 1989) in which homogeneity within a culture is stressed and is often taught by focusing on customs, food, and dress rather than the values that underpin the ways people interact and how such interactions differ between and within cultural groups.

Some teachers did not even recognize cultural knowledge as necessary for all teachers unless they worked in particular contexts. As one preschool teacher responded, "No, I don't think it should be a part of teacher preparation because maybe you don't have any Spanish-speaking children." Alternatively, one professional development provider implied that teachers did not need a special set of skills on special education, but that they needed support to use the skills they already have.

It takes the same energy to work with a child who has special needs as it does to work with a child who doesn't. And I think the biggest issue for our teachers is they're afraid of it. They're afraid that they don't know what to do. But they really do know what to do and they need to be reinforced and I think this is where the professional development lacks because we're not reinforcing what they already know and how to work with both sets of children.

The *Abbott* districts serve the state's poorest and most diverse student populations, so it is rather disconcerting that some of the educators we interviewed do not seem to see the need for diversity training.

The survey data contradict these responses. When we asked teachers a series of questions about their efficacy to teach particular student populations, a higher proportion reported needing more education; less than 50 percent of teachers felt skilled working with special needs students and English-language learners (ELLs). In contrast, more than 70 percent of teachers perceived themselves to be skilled in child development, developmentally appropriate practices, play, and health and safety issues. Teachers' perceptions of their ability to do a particular task have been found to relate to their effectiveness in the classroom (Darling-Hammond, Chung, & Frelow, 2002). While we did not observe teachers in this study, their responses indicate that they are not as confident in teaching students who differ linguistically, academically, and culturally.

To examine the variables that more accurately explain teachers' self-perceptions of being skilled, we carried out logistic regression with the outcome dichotomously defined as skilled ($Y = 1$) and needing training ($Y = 0$). In this model (see Table 11.1), we examined the variables of route of preparation, auspice, experience, education, age, and ethnicity as well as whether teachers had participated in course work in particular areas. Participation in relevant courses was predictive of teachers' perceived skill level in working with diverse students populations. Of teachers prepared through the same route and having a similar length of time in the classroom, those who had taken courses in teaching special needs children were more likely to feel skilled than those who had not taken courses dealing with this area of practice (odds ratio = 2.70). Similar findings were found for working with ELLs (odds ratio = 2.20) and diverse student populations (odds ratio = 2.2).

Thus, even though some teachers do not perceive that teacher preparation programs should incorporate diversity content unless the context warrants it, many teachers are saying that they need more preparation in these areas. As most of the teachers who reported wanting more education had also received some content in their teacher preparation programs, it might be inferred that the content being offered is not adequate to the complexities they are facing in the classrooms. Although it is impossible to determine the quality of the content of the diversity instruction experienced by teachers in this study, what is evident is that specialized training in addressing differences in the classroom in general, and more specifically with regard to working with students with special needs and ELLs, is not only less available but also not perceived to be as informative as it might need to be.

Discussion

The consistent message of these findings is that even with the opportunity to create teacher preparation programs anew, those who educate teachers are more likely to rely on familiar territory rather than incorporate content to reflect the changing social contexts in which teachers work. Teacher educators in New Jersey appear to be more knowledgeable in the foundational areas of child development, curriculum, and teaching strategies than diversity issues such as special education, bilingualism, and multiculturalism. These results are not isolated to the New Jersey context, however. National studies (Early & Winton, 2001; Ray, Bowman, & Robbins, 2006) have also found that most early childhood teacher preparation programs offer little course work in diversity content of any kind. Thus, despite the fact that we are well into the first decade of the 21st century and residing in a global world, it would seem that early childhood teacher education has made little progress toward providing teachers with the knowledge they need to be able to work adequately with the multiple cultures, languages, and abilities of the children they serve.

One reason for this problem, it might be argued, is a lack of expertise on the part of those who prepare teachers. The demographics of early childhood faculty in higher education mirror those of the teaching population in that the majority of faculty members are white, middle-class females. Although

Table 11.1 Logistic Regression—Variables Predicting Teachers' Self-Perceptions of Being Skilled

Content Area	Overall %	Variable	B	SE B	Odds Ratio
Child Development	81.6	Course work	0.88	0.60	2.40
		Route	−0.27	0.60	0.76
		Auspice	−0.06	0.14	0.94
		Experience	0.21	0.13	1.20
		Highest degree	0.06	0.34	1.10
		Age	−0.14	0.06	0.87
		Ethnicity	−0.09	0.14	0.91
Families	74.0	Course work	0.41	0.31	1.50
		Route	−0.20	0.26	0.81
		Auspice	−0.14	0.12	0.87
		Experience	0.26	0.12	1.30
		Highest degree	0.11	0.32	1.10
		Age	0.05	0.06	1.00
		Ethnicity	0.06	0.13	1.10
Assessment	64.1	Course work	0.42	0.35	1.50
		Route	−0.03	0.24	0.97
		Auspice	0.00	0.11	1.00
		Experience	0.31	0.11	1.40*
		Highest degree	−0.34	0.26	0.71
		Age	−0.09	0.05	0.92
		Ethnicity	0.03	0.12	1.00
Curriculum—Literacy	58.2	Course work	0.14	0.30	1.10
		Route	−0.10	0.24	0.90
		Auspice	0.10	0.11	1.10
		Experience	0.22	0.11	1.20
		Highest degree	−0.50	0.26	0.61
		Age	−0.06	0.05	0.94
		Ethnicity	0.02	0.11	1.00
Curriculum—Science	58.2	Course work	0.68	0.26	2.00*
		Route	−0.03	0.24	0.97
		Auspice	0.12	0.11	1.10
		Experience	0.24	0.11	1.30
		Highest degree	−0.54	0.26	0.58
		Age	−0.07	0.05	0.93
		Ethnicity	0.02	0.11	1.00
Curriculum—Math	58.2	Course work	0.83	0.26	2.30*
		Route	0.02	0.25	1.00
		Auspice	0.12	0.11	1.10
		Experience	0.21	0.11	1.20

(continued)

Table 11.1 (*Continued*)

Content Area	Overall %	Variable	B	SE B	Odds Ratio
		Highest degree	−0.56	0.26	0.57
		Age	−0.07	0.05	0.94
		Ethnicity	0.03	0.11	1.00
Curriculum—Social Studies	58.2	Course work	0.84	0.25	2.30**
		Route	0.03	0.25	1.00
		Auspice	0.12	0.11	1.10
		Experience	0.22	0.11	1.20
		Highest degree	−0.55	0.26	0.58
		Age	−0.07	0.05	0.93
		Ethnicity	0.01	0.11	1.00
Guidance/Discipline	56.2	Course work	0.35	0.30	1.40
		Route	−0.29	0.24	0.75
		Auspice	−0.17	0.11	0.85
		Experience	0.30	0.11	1.30*
		Highest degree	−0.07	0.26	0.93
		Age	−0.04	0.05	0.96
		Ethnicity	0.15	0.12	1.20
Diversity	55.4	Course work	0.79	0.26	2.20*
		Route	0.25	0.24	1.20
		Auspice	0.01	0.11	1.00
		Experience	−0.24	0.11	0.79
		Highest degree	0.28	0.27	1.30
		Age	0.10	0.05	1.10
		Ethnicity	0.19	0.12	1.20
ESL	26.7	Course work	0.77	0.26	2.20*
		Route	−0.31	0.29	0.74
		Auspice	0.18	0.13	1.20
		Experience	0.23	0.12	1.30
		Highest degree	0.41	0.28	1.50
		Age	0.00	0.06	1.00
		Ethnicity	0.47	0.12	1.60**
Special Needs	23.0	Course work	1.00	0.35	2.70*
		Route	−0.40	0.32	0.68
		Auspice	0.03	0.13	1.00
		Experience	0.12	0.13	1.10
		Highest degree	0.48	0.29	1.60
		Age	0.01	0.06	1.00
		Ethnicity	−0.13	0.14	0.88

** Wald statistic shows $p < .01$.

these individuals have attained at the minimum a master's degree, their education is more likely to have focused on developing their skills as producers and readers of research and not necessarily on updating their cultural and pedagogical knowledge. Yet, to reduce the consistent lack of diversity content in teacher preparation programs to a problem of expertise masks what to us is the bigger issue affecting the field. Despite critical research studies that have demonstrated the potential inequities in subscribing to a predominantly developmental view of children (e.g., Blaise, 2005; Mac Naughton, 2001) and the limitations of developmentally appropriate practices (Hatch et al., 2002; Lubeck, 1998), there appears to be little effort in the standards to incorporate knowledge that will help prospective teachers address the multitude of differences that characterize early childhood populations in the United States and elsewhere. To be sure, this statement may seem at odds with the opening paragraphs of this chapter where we assert that national standards for the preparation of early childhood professionals call for teachers to be culturally competent and able to include children with wide-ranging abilities. But upon closer examination of national guidelines and standards, it is evident that while the intent is there, the message about responding effectively to differences in the classroom is vague and fragmented. This fragmentation seems to be the result of the ways various standards are organized as well as the developmental framing of these standards.

All of the national standards concerning the preparation of early childhood teachers at the initial licensure level organize what teachers need to be able to know and do around several key topic statements or standards. However, while the National Board for Professional Teaching Standards has one standard entitled "equity, fairness, and diversity" (Hyson, 2003, p. 156), and those specific to beginning special education teachers of young children have a standard concerned with language differences, there is not a standard produced by NAEYC (the association that encompasses teaching of all children from birth to 8 years) that explicitly states teachers need preparation to work with diverse student populations. Instead, the current NAEYC standards for initial licensure are organized under the topics of: (a) promoting child development and learning; (b) building family and community relationships; (c) observing, documenting, and assessing to support young children and families; (d) teaching and learning; and (e) becoming a professional (Hyson, 2003, p. 51). As can be seen from this example, the wording of current standards at the most basic level does not draw attention to the centrality in enacting an equitable education for young children.

To be fair, much more explicit direction about responding to the wide-ranging abilities, languages, and cultures of children and their families is found within the elaborative statements under each of the key topic areas in the NAEYC standards. Similarly, throughout these explanations, examples drawn from practice and in teachers' words are used to illuminate some of the challenges involved in trying to enact a "developmentally effective education" for all children. Yet, while diversity is acknowledged and integrated throughout most of the standards without it being foregrounded in its own right, it is easy to understand why teacher educators may easily overlook this kind of content when designing their programs. The message being sent is that diversity is not as high a priority for teacher development as these other broader topics.

Not only is diversity less visible, but the developmental and positivist language of the NAEYC standards also masks the complexity of this issue. Much child development theory and research is based on the positivistic view that there are universal laws governing the physical and human world that apply to all populations. As such, children and families have tended to be studied and presented as fairly homogenous groups. Although much of the research base has been conducted predominantly on white, middle-class children and families (Burman, 1994), there is not a lot of recognition within this literature of the variations within this segment of the population, let alone the limitations of using research on one population to generalize to others. There is a danger therefore in using the terms "family" and "children" to encompass the multiplicities of family structures and children's backgrounds present in early childhood classrooms, when most teacher educators have been prepared using a research base that is biased toward one group.

This homogenizing effect can also be seen in the way culture is used as an all-encompassing term throughout national standards to represent what is such a heterogeneous and dynamic set of social characteristics and configurations. Culture is the values, norms, and artifacts that shape and are shaped by a particular group of people. People become connected because of gender, class, race, ethnicity, ability, religion, sexuality, immigrant status, and so forth, and the boundaries that separate such cultures from one another are fluid, resulting in the combination of different aspects. Consider, for example, the diversity of family types in which children are being raised, which can include step, biracial, immigrant, mixed religion, gay, bisexual, and single-parent families, among others. Without spelling out in more depth what we mean by culture, it is very easy for professionals in the field of early education, as the directors and teachers in our focus groups did, to view culture as a clump of characteristics related only to groups of people unlike themselves, usually those who are non-white. Thus, in subsuming so much difference under the general categories of culture, families, and children, the diversity of children's lived experiences are usually relegated to larger, more knowable groupings, and some remain unacknowledged. For example, Goodwin (2002) has argued that very little has been done to address the particular needs of immigrant children, while Robinson (2002) has found that teachers are less likely to consider sexuality issues as diversity concerns of importance.

To be sure, it is important that standards read in a way that our expectations for teachers and those who prepare them are clear. It is also important that teachers believe that they have the knowledge necessary to work with the wide range of students in their care. But as the standards are currently presented, they offer little insight into the kinds of knowledge and understandings that teachers of young children require in order to enact culturally relevant pedagogies. So what might be done to ensure that teacher education catches up with the effects of globalization? How might we ensure that issues of diversity, social justice, and equity are foregrounded in programs of preparation? There are three lessons that we have learned from our experiences studying the New Jersey system that others interested in reforming teacher education might find useful.

First, we would suggest that teacher educators begin by conducting an internal audit. The main purpose of such an audit is to determine what content is being presented to students, how is it being presented, and if there are opportunities for students to observe teachers model culturally responsive instruction with diverse student populations. At the same time, teacher educators need to look inward to evaluate their own expertise and to determine where strengths are within the faculty that might be capitalized on. It might be possible, for example, to coteach classes with faculty with specific qualifications and experiences with ELLs and special education so that faculty with limited backgrounds in these areas might be able to retool. By conducting this kind of evaluation, teacher educators then have a sense of what kinds of messages students are receiving about diversity, where and who they might go to, to build their expertise and improve course content, and how they might begin the task of reinventing their programs.

A second action is to begin to think about what other knowledges might be included within the curriculum to ensure that prospective teachers examine diversity issues in all of their complexity. As we and other researchers (Lubeck, 1998; Mac Naughton, 2001; Ryan & Grieshaber, 2005) have suggested, a developmental lens does not permit teachers to examine learning and teaching as a set of relationships that involve issues of power and concerns about social justice and equity. Without the ability to see politics at work in the classroom, which involves seeing how issues of culture, language, gender, ability, and so forth mediate learning and teaching, educators will continue to respond to children via developmental groupings (e.g., ready or not; smart, socially mature, etc). We would therefore suggest that teacher educators draw on the work of their colleagues (e.g., Genishi, Huang, & Glupczynski, 2005; Lobman, 2005; Ryan & Grieshaber, 2005; Sumsion, 2005; Viruru, 2005) who are incorporating postmodern ideas into their programs of preparation that challenge developmentalist and positivist theories and encourage teachers to critically examine their work from more than one perspective.

The third and final suggestion is the need for more action and communication on the part of early childhood teacher educators. Like many in the profession, we often work in isolation from one another. However, we have found here in New Jersey how fruitful it is to meet together and discuss our work. Much of this work has been done through our local chapter of the Association for Early Childhood Teacher Educators. After presenting the results of our studies to this group for example, members of the association asked a colleague who is an expert in ELLs to share her knowledge. Similarly, we have shared pedagogical ideas we use in our own course work pertaining to particular topics. Although there are potentially many networks teacher educators might utilize, our point is that we need to come together more frequently and talk about how we are trying to address diversity in our programs of preparation.

Just as it is important to share our pedagogical knowledge, it is also crucial that the field begin to generate its own knowledge base. Teacher education is one of most underresearched areas in our field (Horm-Wingerd, Hyson, & Karp, 2000); we need studies that can help inform the field's development in the 21st century and ensure teachers are able to respond effectively to all of the children in their care. This program of research cannot only be about exemplifying what people are trying in practice, although this is important work, but must also target policymakers. Therefore, teacher educators need to consider research that will enable them to show the effects of different approaches to diversity training on both teacher development and child outcomes so that it might be possible to shift the developmental emphasis in current national statements of best practice.

Teacher educators know just how complex an endeavor the teaching of young children is. The current content of our preparation programs, however, is not up to the task of preparing teachers for the effects of globalization. Those of us who prepare teachers need to rethink the content and processes of our programs so that teachers view pedagogy as not only a means of guiding children's development but also as a matter of addressing issues of identity, equity, and power. When diversity as a construct in all its complexity is present front and center in our programs of preparation, then it might just be possible to catch up with globalization.

Note

For information on the *Abbott* decisions, see http://www.state.nj.us/njded/abbotts/dec/.

References

Abbott v. Burke, 153 N.J. 480 (1998).
Abbott v. Burke, 163 N.J. 95 (2000).
Ackerman, D. J. (2004). States' efforts in improving the qualifications of early care and education teachers. *Educational Policy, 18,* 311–337.

Barbules, N. C., & Torres, C. A. (Eds.). (2000). *Globalization and education: Critical perspectives.* New York: Routledge.

Barnett, W. S. (2003). Better teachers, better preschools: Student achievement linked to teacher qualifications. *Preschool Policy Matters, 2.* New Brunswick, NJ: NIEER.

Blaise, M. (2005). *Playing it straight: Uncovering gender discourses in the early childhood classroom.* New York: Routledge/Taylor & Francis.

Bowman, B. T., Donovan, M. S., & Burns, M. S. (Eds.). (2001). *Eager to learn: Educating our preschoolers.* Washington, DC: National Academy Press.

Bredekamp, S. (1996). Early childhood education. In J. P. Sikula, T. J. Buttery, & E. Guyton (Eds.), *Handbook of research on teacher education: A project of the Association of Teacher Educators* (2nd ed., pp. 323–347). New York: Macmillan.

Bredekamp, S., & Copple, C. (1997). *Developmentally appropriate practice in early childhood programs* (Rev. ed.). Washington DC: National Association for the Education of Young Children.

Burman, E. (1994). *Deconstructing developmental psychology.* London: Routledge.

Darling-Hammond, L., Chung, R., & Frelow, F. (2002). Variation in teacher preparation: How well do different pathways prepare teachers to teach? *Journal of Teacher Education, 53,* 286–302.

Derman-Sparks, L., & ABC Task Force (1989). *Anti-bias curriculum: Tools for empowering young children.* Washington DC: National Association for the Education of Young Children.

Early, D. M., & Winton, P. J. (2001). Preparing the workforce: Early childhood teacher preparation at 2- and 4-year institutions of higher education. *Early Childhood Research Quarterly, 16,* 285–306.

Federal Interagency Forum on Child and Family Statistics. (2004). *America's children in brief: Key national indicators of well being, 2004.* Retrieved September 25, 2006, from http://childstats.gov.

Genishi, C., Huang, S., & Glupczynski, T. (2005). Becoming early childhood teachers: Linking action research and postmodern theory in a language and literacy course. In S. Ryan & S. Grieshaber (Eds.), *Practical transformations and transformational practices: Globalization, postmodernism and early childhood education* (pp. 161–192). Stamford, CT: JAI/Elsevier Science.

Goodwin, A. L. (2002). Teacher preparation and the education of immigrant children. *Education and Urban Society, 34,* 156–172.

Graue, M. E. (2005). Who is the child in the child-centered classroom? In S. Ryan & S. Grieshaber (Eds.), *Practical transformations and transformational practices: Globalization, postmodernism and early childhood education* (pp. 39–58). Stamford, CT: JAI/Elsevier Science.

Hatch, A., Bowman, B., Jor'dan, J., Lopez Morgan, C. Hart, C., Diaz Soto, L., Lubeck, S., & Hyson, M. (2002). Developmentally appropriate practice: Continuing the dialogue. *Contemporary Issues in Early Childhood, 3,* 439–457.

Horm-Wingerd, D., Hyson, M., & Karp, N. (2000). *New teachers for a new century: The future of early childhood professional preparation.* Washington, DC: U.S. Department of Education, Office of Educational Research and Improvement, National Institute on Early Childhood Development and Education, Media and Information Services.

Hyson, M. (Ed.). (2003). *Preparing early childhood professionals: NAEYC's standards for programs.* Washington, DC: National Association for the Education of Young Children.

Hyun, E. (1996). New directions in early childhood teacher preparation: Developmentally and culturally appropriate practice. *Journal of Early Childhood Teacher Education, 17,* 7–19.

Lobman, C. (2005). Improvisation: Postmodern play for early childhood teachers. In S. Ryan & S. Grieshaber (Eds.), *Practical transformations and transformational practices: Globalization, postmodernism and early childhood education* (pp. 243–272). Stamford, CT: JAI/Elsevier Science.

Lobman, C., & Ryan, S. (in press). Differing discourses on preschool teacher development. *Journal of Teacher Education.*

Lobman, C., Ryan, S., & McLaughlin. (2005a). Reconstructing teacher education to prepare qualified preschool teachers: Lessons from New Jersey. *Early Childhood Research and Practice 7*(2). Retrieved May 22, 2006, from http://ecrp.uiuc.edu/v7n2/lobman.html.

Lobman, C., Ryan, S., & McLaughlin, J. (2005b). *Toward a unified system of early childhood teacher education and professional development: Conversations with stakeholders.* New York: Foundation for Child Development.

Lubeck, S. (1998). Is developmentally appropriate practice for everyone? *Childhood Education, 74,* 283–292.

Mac Naughton, G. (2001). Silences and subtexts of immigrant and nonimmigrant children. *Childhood Education, 78,* 30–36.

Ramsey, P. (1987). *Teaching and learning in a diverse world: Multicultural education for young children.* New York: Teachers College Press.

Ray, A., Bowman, B., & Robbins, J. (2006). *Preparing early childhood teachers to successfully educate all children: The contribution of four-year undergraduate teacher preparation programs.* Chicago: Erikson Institute.

Robinson, K. H. (2002). Making the invisible visible: Gay and lesbian issues in early childhood education. *Contemporary Issues in Early Childhood, 3*(3), 415–434.

Ryan, S., & Ackerman, D. J. (2005, March 30). Using pressure and support to create a qualified workforce. *Education Policy Analysis Archives, 13*(23). Retrieved August 8, 2005, from http://epaa.asu.edu/epaa/v13n23/Ryan, S., & Grieshaber, S. (2005). Shifting from developmental to postmodern practices in early childhood teacher education. *Journal of Teacher Education, 56,* 34–45.

Ryan, S., & Grieshaber, S. (2005). Shifting from developmental to postmodern practices in early childhood teacher education. *Journal of Teacher Education, 56,* 34–45.

Sumsion, J. (2005). Putting postmodern theories into practice in early childhood teacher education. In S. Ryan & S. Grieshaber (Eds.), *Practical transformations and transformational practices: Globalization, postmodernism and early childhood education* (pp. 193–216). Stamford, CT: JAI/Elsevier Science.

Viruru, R. (2005). Postcolonial theory and the practice of teacher education. In S. Ryan & S. Grieshaber (Eds.), *Practical transformations and transformational practices: Globalization, postmodernism and early childhood education* (pp. 139–160). Stamford, CT: JAI/Elsevier Science.

Whitebook, M. (2003). *Bachelor's degrees are best: Higher qualifications for pre-kindergarten teachers lead to better learning environments for children.* Washington, DC: The Trust for Early Education.

Part III
Rethinking Teacher Education and Professional Development

12

Talk about Children

Developing a Living Curriculum of
Advocacy and Social Justice

BEATRICE S. FENNIMORE

Language is arguably the most powerful tool for social justice available to every early childhood educator. When a language of respect for the hope and resiliency of children is supported by an abiding personal and professional commitment to fairness and equal opportunities, every early childhood educator can enact a living curriculum of advocacy for children. Unfortunately, the opposite is also true. Early childhood educators who are comfortable with the use of deficit terminology that denigrates the abilities and experiences of children who are different from themselves in their economic and cultural lives, even when they express their professional commitment to children, can enable deeply entrenched forms of discrimination that work directly against fair treatment of children. Even the most talented and well-prepared educators can build a wall between themselves and their students with language that reinforces historic and damaging beliefs about children most at risk for institutional harm fueled by discrimination. Such walls can serve to justify teacher decisions and actions that withhold or alter opportunities and expectations for children deemed inferior or deficient.

As a teacher educator, I have maintained a journal for almost 20 years with anecdotal notes on the language about children that I hear in schools. Well-regarded tenured teachers have told me, "If three kids in this class make it in life it will be a miracle" or "This is a really slow group with two disabled kids" or "The population we get in this school can't even think, much less do critical thinking." I was once talking with an elementary school principal on the street when he casually referred to children in another district school as "thugs." Both of my own children had attended and graduated from this school, which had a majority African American population. At a nice luncheon for district administrators, a high-ranking administrator at my table called children from a district elementary school "the dregs of the earth." Another principal informed me during an introductory phone call that I was well advised not to think of the children in her school as "civilized human beings."

In every case above, the educators were referring to children whose schools were in economically poor communities that were either resegregated or had never been desegregated in the first place. My purpose is not to denigrate these professionals but rather to emphasize the fact that educators who are considered to be successful and accomplished and who think of themselves as committed to children can be comfortable using insulting, discriminatory, and damaging language about children. I believe this is a major ethical and professional problem that must be persistently addressed until it is eradicated. However, as an early childhood educator who has dedicated a great deal of time and work to this problem, I am well aware of how elusive the solution may actually be.

The more I have studied and written about language, the more I have realized that the process of understanding how to construct an ethical professional language about children that honors their human dignity and protects them from unjust discrimination is enormously complex. To illustrate this, I will share a recent story about a graduate class I taught at my university. My students, almost all practicing teachers, were assigned an action research project. I made two expectations very clear in the assignment. The first was that the research should focus on *self-improvement* on the part of the *teacher* rather than improvement on the part of the children (although data on such improvement due to teacher improvement would hopefully be gathered). The second was that any descriptions of the children should be based in *documented fact and shared only to the degree that they supported my understanding of the rationale and nature of the teacher action research.*

I emphasized these two expectations because I knew it was all too easy for my graduate students to describe their teaching problems as located in the shortcomings and deficiencies they perceived in their students. I wanted to urge them to find words that reflected interest in and commitment to the potential of their students as well as words that moved them toward greater reflectivity on their own practice. I told them that, when I read their first drafts, I wanted to read a strong sense of respect for children combined with honest appraisal of their documented strengths and needs and a plan of teacher self-improvement to meet needs while recognizing strengths. Here is an example of a description I received in a first draft from one of my students, a kindergarten teacher:

> The students in [school district] are mostly from low-income families. Over 90% of the students receive free and reduced meals. Many of the parents are uneducated and many of the children don't have any skills or have very few skills before they enter kindergarten. The district does not have a pretest for kindergarten. … Over 90% of my kindergarten students do not know all of the letters. Most of them only know a few letters.

This draft contained no evidence of action research focused on self-improvement. The problem throughout was located only in the children and families.

I invited the student to my office before class one day and discussed this description with him. He seemed surprised that I was concerned about his statements and assumptions. When I asked him if he had seen any specific data about the level of education of the parents of children in his class, he indicated that he had not. Further questioning him about his meaning of "uneducated," I wondered if he meant that the parents had graduated from high school or trade school rather from college. Were high school graduates uneducated? Or, although they had not attended college, did they actually have strengths, skills, and accomplishments? It was clear from our discussion that he really had never thought through what uneducated meant or what the level of education of the parents actually was. And, even if he had, the information was not relevant to the intent and purpose of the assigned action research project.

Our conversation continued. Could it be possible, really, that children entered school with no skills? Had he ever attempted to document and recognize the many life skills, apart from alphabet recognition, they undoubtedly did have? My student was not able to articulate specific skills he realized that his kindergarten students did bring to the classroom. Turning to the purpose of kindergarten, I posed the possibility that kindergarten could actually *be* the appropriate environment for all children to successfully learn the letters of the alphabet. Instead of denigrating such young children at the point of school entry, couldn't he possibly generate excitement over the opportunity to teach them the alphabet? Couldn't he better meet the purpose of the assignment by focusing on ways in which he would seek to improve alphabet instruction by tailoring it to the specific needs and interests of the children in his classroom? Although the student continued to respond with some negativity, I hoped that he would successfully reorient his next draft paper to meet the expectations I described above—to focus on self-improvement as a teacher, and to share only information about the children that was relevant to his final project. This is the description that I received in the second draft:

> All the children in my school district are happy and well prepared for school. Also, all the parents are caring and have a high level of education. We teachers are satisfied with the entry level skills of our students, and our kindergarten year is always smooth and successful.

Sadly, when I asked, the student confessed to sarcasm. He further admitted to resenting my challenges to assumptions about his students and parents with which he and many colleagues had grown quite comfortable over the years. However, further discussion also revealed that he really did not understand the difference between fact-based honest descriptions that were important to his study and unfounded peripheral and denigrating generalizations.

I again explained how it would have been fine to describe important and documented information ("My initial assessment indicated that over 90% of my students could identify between 5–15 letters of the alphabet") in the context of his own professional indication of accountability and efficacy in seeking more success in his alphabet instruction. ("My action research will focus on gathering data during my increased use of visuals and letter forms that can be manipulated by the children during language arts.") The student seemed more open to thinking about how stereotypical beliefs about some children can have a negative impact on the way we perceive them and describe them. I also had a sense that he was truly interested in the idea of descriptive language as a form of activism on behalf of his students in their school and community, as well as an avenue to developing more positive responses to their entry level skills. Although I had previously written a book about educational language (Fennimore, 2000), my conversations with this student reminded me once again of the importance of continuing to develop a better understanding of all the dimensions of educational language that could ultimately become a curriculum for social justice in classrooms across our nation.

The problem with educational language is clearly much more complicated than "talk." As the above anecdote demonstrates, there is little to be gained from simply suggesting that teachers "speak in a positive way about children." This suggestion can generate an artificial response that does not indicate attitudinal or behavioral change. Also, again reflected in the above anecdote, it is important to recognize that there are reasons why some educators *want* to retain deficit images of their students and *want* to communicate them to others. These reasons might include force of habit; influence of a home or working environment in which such deficit images had always been the accepted norm; rationalization of failure to improve student outcomes; resentment of difficulties encountered with children and families; frustration with the serious problems of poverty, addiction, or violence in the communities in which they worked; or the desire to retain the social privilege that they and their own families had benefited from over time and that depended on continued stereotypical beliefs about others. Deficit language can serve to preserve a social and cultural status quo in which some people, including some educators and their own children, are very well served.

What does this mean for early childhood educators who seek to embrace social change through their own language about children? If deficit language about children can serve to preserve the social status quo, then use of language to challenge that status quo will inevitably become a form of resistance, creating the tensions necessary for reflection and change. A powerful language about children, one that becomes a curriculum for social justice, thus needs to be strongly fueled by a commitment to child advocacy, a deep *desire* for equal treatment of children, and a sense of moral imperative to stand by the needs of *all* children. It is important to remember that children can encounter problems and sufferings across socioeconomic, racial, and cultural lines. Rather than single out "diversities" that require a social justice focus, I believe that we should see all children as deserving and needing our language of social justice. This helps us to honor each individual child in our presence with respect for her or his unique characteristics. When children suffer greatly, as many do, our habitual use of language to develop social conscience and action can take on even greater power and importance.

How can we early childhood educators work together to restructure the cultural power of language to build a daily practice of social justice in our classrooms? The remainder of this chapter explores that question in terms of theory, critical assumptions, and desired practice.

Theory of Language as Behavior

Quite frequently, educators tell me, "I may speak negatively about my students to other teachers, but when I enter my classroom I treat every one of them equally." These educators seem to think of their language as a benign form of communication that does not actually affect real-life events. In contrast, linguistic theory supports the conceptualization of language as a powerful and event-changing *behavior* in and of itself. Austin (1962), in a remarkable series of lectures at Harvard University in the 1950s entitled *How to Do Things with Words,* elaborated on the *performative* function of language. In answer to the question "Can saying it make it so?" he pointed out that in many cases words were not descriptive as much as they were "actually doing it." As he put it, "the uttering of the words is indeed, usually a, or even *the* leading incident in the performance of an act" (p. 8). Searle, in *Speech Acts: An Essay on the Philosophy of Language* (1969), also wrote extensively on the conceptualization of language as action, and thus described the use of language as a *speech act* that not only made things happen but made it very likely that they would continue to happen in exactly the same way.

If early educators would accept this view of language as a behavior that makes things happen and continue to happen, they would realize that acts such as describing children with the words "talented" or "slow" take on much more importance than many would assume. Such statements would be viewed as actions that make it almost inevitable that the student seen as talented will continue to be treated as talented and thus become more and more talented, while the student described as slow will continue to be treated as slow with a resultant progression of limitations built into the very process of education. These labels and many others are inappropriately rigid and thus fail to allow for the normal balance and variation in human ability. Just as the term "talented" leaves out the ways in which the child might also need to continue to expand in some developmental characteristics and skills, the term "slow" leaves out the many ways in which the child is actually strong and well functioning. Such descriptive labels, when applied to certain children, should never be viewed (as they often are) as *inevitable*. Educators have the power to *choose* the terms they use, based on the abilities they choose to see, and to decide what to include and what to leave out of their descriptions. These decisions have a lifelong impact on the children in their care.

Cultural Power and the Semantic Environment

Every educator works in a *semantic environment,* which is defined as any human setting in which language plays a critical role (Postman & Weingartner, 1969). Within a semantic environment, people continually define their purposes and then *choose language that allows them to achieve those purposes.* If the purpose of educators is the enactment of desire that every child experience optimal growth and development, we would expect to see a language of hope, encouragement, and recognition of potential in all educational settings.

Why, instead, are we so often aware of the use of dismissive, denigrating, discriminatory language about children? Why is this language almost unfailingly present to some degree in schools serving children who are the most economically poor or who represent significant forms of cultural, racial, or language diversity? At first sight, the answer might be that well-meaning teachers and administrators are by habit simply reflecting the deficit-based language that has long been unfortunately present in the field of early childhood education. Another answer might be that teachers who are struggling with their work in teaching a more challenging child population are making a possibly wrong but understandable attempt to analyze their problems through the lens of the problems of the children they teach. A less comfortable answer is that institutions in which teachers and administrators routinely denigrate children with deficit-based talk are fulfilling the actual purpose of maintaining a discriminatory status quo in school and society.

In some cases, this is not the conscious purpose of the educators themselves. Rather, without adequate reflection and determination to become change agents, they are passively leaving unchallenged the ways in which negative linguistic assumptions routinely lead to negative educational outcomes for children. In other cases, hopefully few, it might actually be the conscious if unarticulated purpose of educators to support a status quo that ensures privilege and more access to resources for themselves and their own families. Often, such educators express resentment of the characteristics of poor families, such as a need for public assistance or services such as free meals in school.

Pierre Bourdieu, in his book *Language and Symbolic Power* (1991), describes his theory that language is a form of cultural power that serves to retain and reinforce structures of stratification and privilege. Focusing specifically on descriptive language about children, he explains that it is possible to use language in a way that that might "tell a child what he is" (p. 52) instead of telling him what he might do and how he might do it. Clearly, educational language that labels a child as deficient is never telling that child about his or her talents, abilities, and potential for resiliency.

Within the theoretical context of language as cultural power, early childhood educators must be vigilantly aware of the ways in which they are affected in their thinking about children by past and current theory and research. First, it is important to consider the cultural deficit theories that emerged during research on early childhood programs after the Civil Rights Movement are still in evidence in language used by many teachers (Fennimore, 2000). These theories, deeply affected by the bias of the times in which they were created, located the learning difficulties of children in deficient families and communities rather than in the institutional structures of racism and discrimination.

Likewise, early childhood educators need to be cautious about the ways in which continuing research into the connection between poverty, brain development, and potential for learning is utilized in educational, political, and social arenas (Wolfe, 2003). While such research can help us understand many important aspects of development and learning, it could also in some cases strengthen the argument that poor children who lack early optimal developmental experiences will *never* overcome the resultant cognitive deficits. This unexamined argument might be considered to be socially and politically dangerous if one examines historical roots of many forms of discrimination, exclusion, and even genocide on a global level.

Early childhood educators also need to think carefully about the idea that those who work in large bureaucracies such as urban public school systems may be unable to make personal differences in real school reform (Weiner, 2006).While it is important to be realistic about what individuals can and cannot do in terms of larger school reform, I argue that in even the most challenging bureaucratic situation, the individual teacher can still construct a strong social justice curriculum through language. This may not be viewed as a major movement toward institutional change, but it certainly should be viewed as a realistic commitment to seek social justice for children, as it is possible to do so on a daily basis. Early childhood educators should also carefully evaluate the current discourse about the effects of "social class" on school outcomes, particularly discourse that automatically assigns negative characteristics to people who live in poverty (Rothstein, 2004). Although research can demonstrate significant differences in children, it should neither create overly generalized (and thus discriminatory) views of socioeconomic groups nor be used to validate the routine use of deficit terminology when discussing children who are poor.

In summary, while certain social, cognitive, physical, or emotional deficits in children are real and can be verified, they must never become the *total* definition of who they are and what they might become. To this end, early childhood educators should remember that all research and theory, however competent, is capable of providing language favoring some desired aspects of reality while ignoring others (Bourdieu, 1991). This bias can serve in some cases to place a stamp of objective validity on discriminatory assumptions about children.

> *Saying* someone is inferior is largely how structures of status and differential treatment are demarcated and actualized. Words and images are how people are placed in hierarchies, how social stratification is made

to seem inevitable and right, how feelings of inferiority and superiority are engendered. (MacKinnon, 1992, p. 31)

Clearly, early childhood educators need to understand the choices that they constantly make in using their experiences and their knowledge of theory and research to design their descriptive language about children. Inappropriate or discriminatory application of research or theory to practice can increase stereotyping and undermine the resilient powers of so many children who experience adversity as well as the resiliency and hopefulness of their teachers. All early childhood educators need to acknowledge the power of the descriptive words they use and to be accountable for the ways in which a commitment to social justice should guide their own use of language in their institutions.

Theory of Social Justice

If early childhood educators accept the linguistic theory indicating that their words are not only performative actions but an expression of cultural power, it is then ethically incumbent upon them to consider whether their actions (in the form of descriptive language about children) bring harm to their students (Strike & Soltis, 1998). The work of John Rawls (1971, 2001) serves for the purpose of this chapter as a link between critical conceptualizations of language as a powerful behavior, language as cultural power that reinforces social stratifications, and a sense of basic justice and fairness in the use of language about children in educational institutions. Rawls (1971) initially identifies justice as fairness and "the first virtue of social institutions" (p. 3). In later reflections, Rawls (2001) argued that each person in a just and fair society has the same claim to a fully adequate scheme of equal basic liberties. While his theory of justice is often framed as philosophical in nature, Rawls later emphasized that his work was actually political:

> One thing I failed to say in *A Theory of Justice,* or failed to stress sufficiently, is that justice as fairness is intended as a political conception of justice. While a political conception of justice is, of course, a moral conception … it is a conception worked out for (democratic) political, social, and economic institutions. (2001, p. 38)

What does this theory say to early childhood educators constructing language about children as a social justice curriculum? First, this theory of justice leads early childhood educators to examine their use of language, and that of others, for a sense of basic fairness. The institutions in which they work can and should reflect democratic commitments to equal treatment of children. In this regard, it is useful for early educators to ask themselves how they would feel if their own children were discussed or described with negative labels or derogatory descriptions in their schools. Would they object to such linguistic treatment of their own children, knowing it would almost surely lead to lowered expectations with resultant limitation of equal access to educational opportunities? If so, they are ethically obligated to recognize and rectify harm through language done to the other people's children. Clearly in that case, a greater commitment to fairness in the use of language describing all children must be constructed.

Second, this theory of justice helps early educators who develop a desire to utilize language as a daily curriculum of social justice to understand the *political* nature of their decisions. The open refusal on the part of early childhood educators to denigrate children or to validate stereotypes based on their life experiences is a political act that may very well create discomfort and opposition in others. Educators, administrators, or board members may not be welcoming to language (and thus action) that challenges the discriminatory status quo. It is in the ensuing creative political tension that the persistent early childhood educator can indeed foster social change over time through her or his commitment to a language of fairness, respect, and hope for children. His or her purposeful intent to design a language of hope and curriculum for children ultimately becomes a personal curriculum of social justice in the early childhood classroom.

What Does Language for Social Justice Look Like?

As I have continued to try to develop an applicable blueprint for language that serves as a curriculum for social justice, I have realized that such a language curriculum needs both a structure of *basic assumptions* and a structure of *basic practice*. The assumptions are important to counteract the problem with which this chapter began. As noted in the second response of my graduate student to my suggestions regarding language, it is entirely possible for artificial or "politically correct" changes to be made to deficit language only in certain circumstances. Certainly this is not a desirable goal. Rather, there has to be a significant philosophical motivation fueled by an informed *desire* to change one's own language and counter that of others when necessary. What can create and support such motivation and desire? I believe that once central assumptions are in place, the practice of a language of social justice can be designed and implemented.

Assumptions Supporting a Language of Social Justice

I argue that there are four important assumptions that can serve as a foundation for language as a curriculum of social justice. First, I believe that early childhood educators should recognize that historical attempts to achieve cultural domination over diverse groups in America have been documented up to the present time. This includes the history of education, which has also reflected a persistent theme of dominance and deculturalization of persons of oppressed groups (Spring, 1994). This recognition should lead to the first necessary assumption, which is that *negative talk about diverse children is often an unjust reflection of cultural domination and a refusal to accept and value diversity.*

Second, I believe that early childhood educators should recognize that the labels and terminology of deficiency routinely applied to children who were diverse and poor during the War on Poverty in the early 1960s, many of which have carried over to our present day, were not only inaccurate in many cases but based in large part on a form of political resistance to the revolutionary nature of the American Civil Rights Movement (Fennimore, 2000, 2005). This should lead to the second necessary assumption, which is that *negative talk about diverse children is often a form of resistance to movements that seek to equalize power and opportunity among diverse American groups.*

Third, I believe that all early childhood educators should recognize the fact that their own family, community, and cultural background has almost inevitably reflected, to a greater or lesser degree, the racism and discrimination against groups that is deeply embedded in our American culture. This should lead to the third necessary assumption, which is that *every educator of children must continually reflect upon, honestly recognize, and seek to change bias that may have been assimilated into personal belief systems during childhood and adolescence.* Deeply embedded personal bias is enduring and dynamic, and continually finds ways to emerge and reemerge throughout one's career. Thus, recognition of personal bias is a lifelong job for educators committed to social justice (Irvine, 2003).

The fourth and final assumption relies on teacher belief in the power of a personal sense of efficacy combined with constant willingness to advocate for children through words that are carefully crafted into ethical and professional statements. This leads to the assumption that *the thoughtful, assertive, and persistent desire of teachers to promote social justice for children can become part of daily practice when language about children has intentionality and reflects respect, high expectation, and a basic sense of fairness.*

In summary, I argue that the above four assumptions must be in place to support a fully committed desire on the part of early childhood educators to use their daily professional language as an instrument of social justice. Such use of language is potentially transformational, as it provides a relevant and practical opportunity for vigilant resistance to the forms of educational injustice that can harm the development, hopes, and ultimate outcomes for all too many American children. Early childhood educators whose language is an active curriculum for social justice are in all likelihood better teachers as well as stronger social models because of their positive intentions toward and determined efforts on behalf of all children. These positive intentions are likely to translate into the high teacher expectations that are central to effective schools and effective school research (Irvine, 1990, 2003).

Practice Supporting Language as a Social Justice Curriculum

The strongest focus of this section of the chapter is on the individual early childhood educator who makes a personal decision to use her or his descriptive language about children as a progressive social force. Certainly, groups or even an entire faculty within an early childhood program could make a commitment to ethical changes in the ways in which children are discussed within programs. Ultimately, this could involve the development of an ethical code concerning language within a school or program serving young children, and such a collaborative code is the ideal outcome of a commitment to language as a social justice curriculum (Fennimore, 2000).

However, many committed early childhood educators are working in professional environments that may not be ideal and may involve working with colleagues who do not share similar commitments to equity and social justice for children. Every great social idea, including the conceptualization of early childhood education as a vehicle to counteract a history of unequal opportunities for children, must ultimately be implemented in many cases by individuals who take the risks and opportunities inherent in ascending to a social ideal in an imperfect setting. These settings can involve the potential discouragement of the ramifications of poverty in families that include addiction, imprisonment, and inability to provide adequate nutrition and medical or dental care for children. Further, they can involve inadequate salaries and benefits for the very early childhood educators who are often encouraged in professional literature to be advocates for adequate income and benefits for children and families. Dedicated early childhood educators in these settings may have colleagues or administrators who routinely express disparagement of the child and family populations served by the program. While it is important to stress that there are indeed many outstanding programs and many excellent early childhood educators, true reform for social justice requires recognition of the realistic struggles many early educators will have as they seek to become moral and ethical examples within their programs (Sockett, 1993).

What will we see from dedicated early childhood educators in their positive linguistic practice? First, we will see the discipline of talk that comes from the recognition that professional language about the children we serve in our employment is very different from the casual language we use in family and social settings. Professional language should embody the ethical ideal that no child be harmed in the process of education (Strike & Soltis, 1998). Thus, as children are discussed, a *desire to help them and promote their welfare* is clearly expressed in the words that are carefully chosen.

Second, during each conversation or observation of these dedicated early childhood educators, we become aware of the fact that their own *professional accountability* is central to the ways in which they describe problems or challenges with children. Along with the clear expression of accountability are a sense of *open inquiry* into problematic situations and a *valuing of multiple perspectives on causes* of the problem (Fennimore, 2000). For example, imagine that we are visiting a kindergarten classroom in a community experiencing severe economic and social dilemmas. Many children have incarcerated parents, single parents, or parents on public assistance. Entering the classroom during free play, we notice that some of the children are crying or arguing as the teacher patiently encourages them to peacefully solve dilemmas and to renew their interest in learning activities. As the teacher approaches us, one of the visitors might say, "You certainly have your hands full with these children." This is an example of a somewhat negative comment that might easily elicit a negative answer. Some early childhood teachers, stressed with challenges, might tell the visitor at this point that most of the children are not really ready for school because their home lives are too difficult and their parents do not support the development of skills necessary for success in school. Imagine these words instead:

> I am dedicated to these children, and see them growing in important ways every day. I do need to continually evaluate my own practice to be sure that I do my best to counteract some of the challenges the children face because they are poor or because their parents are addicted or imprisoned. Really, we need the help of everyone in our society to solve a lot of their problems. But, for me, the goal every day is to work hard to understand the lives and concerns of the children and their families and to find the best ways to help the children be resilient as they find their best strengths and abilities. My work is sometimes difficult but I am dedicated to it and enjoy it.

Clearly, in the natural flow of a conversation, the teacher would probably not say all of this at once, but the example as a whole or in parts of conversation embodies the essentials of the use of language as a social justice curriculum. The end result of the statement is that there is no doubt in the mind of the listener that the teacher is dedicated to the children, accountable for their positive learning outcomes, and concerned about the larger social challenges they face. The desire to respect and help the children is clearly expressed, as is a sense of the larger need for social reform. The intention of valuing the different perspectives of children and parents is made clear, as is the sense of inquiry in addressing and solving difficult problems. While this teacher might later appropriately *vent* in private with a trusted friend or colleague ("I had an unbelievable day! Visitors came in and the children were fighting and crying again during free play!"), she understood and demonstrated the importance of using a public and professional language with the visitors that embodied her own commitments to children as well as her responsibility to portray the children in a respectful and positive light. Through the words she used, the teacher thus created a pathway to greater social justice for her students.

Moving more deeply into this example, the early childhood educator who makes a commitment to language as a vehicle for social justice must reflect on three areas that are generally problematic. The first area is that of routinely used *deficit terminology* ("at risk," "parents who don't care," "kids who never saw books at home and come to school delayed") that have worked their way into the everyday habitual language of teachers in the school or program. The second is the way in which a great deal of *confidential information* about children and families (income level, past child abuse reports, family problems, diagnoses of medical or emotional problems) is utilized and communicated within the program and in wider social settings. The third area is that of *classification* of children based on IQ scores, standardized test scores, Individual Education Plans, or other evaluative labels (Fennimore, 2000).

In most cases, routine and unnecessary use of deficit terminology should be scrupulously avoided. Specific discussion of problems of some children ("A few of our children in this program were born to mothers who used crack cocaine during pregnancy") may be necessary during professional discussions that are hopefully taking place to create avenues of help for the children. Casual public use of deficit terminology in discussing these same children ("We have crack babies in our program") would not be appropriate. Likewise, confidential information about children is appropriately shared only in the context of assistance to children. ("It is going to be important to help Charisse deal with the upset caused by her mother's recent arrest.") Unnecessary communication of confidential information in school or community ("A child in our program had a mother arrested for passing bad checks this week") can serve to harm public perception of and respect for children without providing any demonstrable assistance. Finally, talk about classification of children should take place in the context of suspended judgment. It could be necessary to discuss a recent test score with the intention of helping the child ("Paulo surprised us with a score of 90 on his IQ test because he has so many skills. Let's be sure his IEP does reflect his abilities."). Talk about classification without purpose ("Some of these kids have really low IQs") can be very harmful to perceptions of and future expectations for children, and need to be avoided at all times (Feeney & Freeman, 1999).

A final area of language as a curriculum for social justice is that of counteracting prejudiced or discriminatory statements made by colleagues, parents, administrators, or others. Early childhood educators cannot allow silence in such situations to be interpreted as agreement. However, as nurturing individuals, they are often reluctant to be confrontational. A technique that can be helpful in countering prejudiced comments involves four possible steps (Fennimore, 1994): objectively restating the prejudice, asserting personal belief and commitment, saying something positive about the group or person victimized by prejudice, and gently reshaping the conversation in a new direction. For example, a colleague might say, "I've been teaching in this program for 10 years, and this is the worst group of children we've ever had." A response might be:

> It is true that we seem to be experiencing more of the ramifications of economic distress and serious social problems in this school (restate the

prejudice.) However, I am so aware of the needs of these children and determined to do my best for them (asserting personal belief and commitment.) You know, when I really try to observe the children, I see many skills and strengths in them (say something positive.) Maybe it helped me to watch that great show about child resiliency—did you get a chance to see it? (gently reshape the conversation).

The practice of language as a social justice curriculum grows stronger through practice combined with a deep determination to develop a professional presence that enhances the perceptions and experiences of children through the powerful use of words.

Moving Forward

When I speak about language as a path to social justice, I frequently encounter the response that we need to change attitudes before we can change language. To the degree that I believe this is true, I have attempted to identify the beliefs and assumptions that are needed to structure a vision of language as a form of social action. However, I also believe that changes in *behavior* can lead to changes in *attitudes*. As indicated in the beginning of this chapter, a fundamental problem is the fact that many educators who are viewed as competent and successful and who view themselves as committed to children feel comfortable using disparaging, denigrating, or discriminatory language about children. Again, while this language may seem more disturbing when it targets children from groups that have experienced historical oppression, its habitual presence makes it likely that it is also used to describe some children from all economic, racial, or ethnic backgrounds. If early childhood educators could move forward with a larger professional ethic of responsible language about children as fundamental to the expectations of our field, a greater awareness of language could be present in many settings. The more we can establish the idea that it is *wrong* for early childhood professionals to speak negatively and carelessly about children, the more the culture of our programs could change with the result that more educators might reflect on not only their words but also the underlying attitudes that bring their words to the surface.

Early childhood educators must be encouraged to realize that the ways they speak of and describe children go well beyond the walls of their schools and programs. Visitors, parents, student teachers, future teachers, family members, and many others hear and are affected by their descriptions of children. We are responsible for creating enduring representations of children in school and society. In growing more deeply conscious of our linguistic responsibilities as committed educators, we need to continually distinguish "political correctness" from language as a social justice curriculum. To be politically correct, as I think of it, is to be careful about words spoken of certain people in certain settings in which sensitivities might exist. This concept implies an artificial situational caution rather than a genuine commitment to fairness and social justice. As we early childhood educators continue to design and implement a professional and ethical use of language that serves as a powerful force for children, our words must embody an honest recognition of injustices in society, a determined advocacy for children, a deep commitment to working for social change, and a responsible awareness of the impact our words have on the present and future well-being of all our children.

References

Austin, J. L. (1962). *How to do things with words.* Oxford: University of Oxford Press.

Bourdieu, P. (1991). *Language and symbolic power* (J. B. Thompson, Ed., G. Raymond & M. Adamson, Trans.). Cambridge, MA: Harvard University Press.

Feeney, S., & Freeman, N. K. (1999). *Ethics and the early childhood educator: Using the NAEYC code.* Washington, DC: National Association for the Education of Young Children.

Fennimore, B. S. (1994). Addressing prejudiced statements: A four-step method that helps. *Childhood Education, 70*(3), 202–203.

Fennimore, B. S. (2000). *Talk matters: Refocusing the language of public* schooling. New York: Teachers College Press.

Fennimore, B. S. (2005). Brown and the failure of civic responsibility. *Teachers College Record, 107*(9), 1905–1932.

Irvine, J. J. (1990). *Black students and school failure: Policies, practices, and prescriptions.* Westport, CT: Greenwoood.

Irvine, J. J. (2003). *Educating teachers for diversity: Seeing with a cultural eye.* New York: Teachers College Press.

MacKinnon, C. A. (1992). *Only words.* Cambridge, MA: Harvard University Press.

Postman, N., & Weingartner, C. (1969). *Teaching as a subversive activity.* New York: Delacorte Press.

Rawls, J. (1971). *A theory of justice.* Cambridge, MA: Harvard University Press.

Rawls, J. (2001). *Justice as fairness: A restatement.* Cambridge, MA: Belknap Press of Harvard University Press.

Rothstein, R. (2004). *Class and schools: Using social, economic, and educational reform to close the black-white achievement gap.* New York: Teachers College Press/Economic Policy Institute.

Searle, J. R. (1969). *Speech acts: An essay in the philosophy of language.* Cambridge: Cambridge University Press.

Sockett, H. (1993). *The moral base for teacher professionalism.* New York: Teachers College Press.

Spring, J. (1994). *Deculturalization and the struggle for equality: A brief history of the education of dominated cultures.* New York: McGraw-Hill.

Strike, K. A., & Soltis, J. F. (1998). *The ethics of teaching.* New York: Teachers College Press.

Weiner, L. (2006). *Urban teaching: The essentials.* New York: Teachers College Press.

Wolfe, P. (2003). Brain research and Education: Fad or foundation? *mcli Forum, 6,* 4–7.

13

Disrupting the Taken-for-Granted
Autobiographical Analysis in Preservice Teacher Education

A. LIN GOODWIN AND MICHÈLE GENOR

Framing the Study

We believe that the first step in fulfilling the promise of democracy, equity, and social justice is in preparing new teachers to define themselves as advocates for all children. This preparation involves developing a critical perspective in which teachers gain reflective habits that lead them to actively question and work towards changing the inequities that exist in our schools (Britzman, 1986; Cochran-Smith, 2004; Lucas & Villegas, 2002). Yet, having been reared in a country that traces its roots to the subjugation and annihilation of the Taino, the enslavement of people of African descent, the colonization of Mexicans and Puerto Ricans, the exclusion and internment of Chinese and Japanese Americans, and the marginalization and alienation of people of color and women, many teachers-in-preparation cannot help but have been influenced by "the ideological mechanisms that shape and maintain our racist order" (Bartolome & Macedo, 1997, p. 223). They may enter classrooms carrying unconscious yet deeply rooted assumptions that schools are inherently fair, that children's capacities to learn are predetermined and unalterable, and that meritocratic competition is the route to equal educational opportunity. As teacher educators, our primary goal should be to actively and deliberately interrupt this racist ideology and to engage novice teachers in their own processes of self-analysis so they learn to see through new eyes that can recognize injustice and oppression.

As we engage in the preparation of elementary teachers for urban classrooms, our experiences repeatedly show us that that students will enter our program filled with all manner of expectation, preconceived notion, implicit theory, assumptions, and beliefs about education and schools, the children they will teach, and the practices they believe are appropriate (Goodwin, 2002a, 2002b; Maher & Tetreault, 1994; Martin & Van Gunten, 2002). We acknowledge that these tacit beliefs have their roots in students' lives, school experiences, and cultural locations (Brookhart & Freeman, 1992; Calderhead & Robson, 1991; Goodwin, 2002a; Knowles, Cole, & Presswood, 1994; Lortie, 1975; Richardson,

1996; Su, 1992), and hold the power to shape their pedagogical decisions and ongoing practice as teachers (Goodwin, 2002a; Richardson, 1996).

Given the reality that two-thirds of students in our program are white, female, monolingual, middle class, and able-bodied, a reality reflected in most teacher preparation programs across the United States (Cochran-Smith, 2004; Dilworth & Brown, 2001; Gordon, 2000), we cannot assume our students have had extensive or intimate experiences with students "different" from them. Thus, we believe that it is essential to help our students explore their own positions and histories by making explicit their unspoken values and cultural knowledge. Cochran-Smith (2000) points out that it is necessary but not sufficient to immerse students in educational literature that examines race, class, culture, gender, and disability. We agree. Consequently, we intentionally engage our students in a number of reflective, autobiographical assignments throughout their student teaching year; students are asked to continually consider their backgrounds and experiences in relation to issues raised by course readings and discussions. Additionally, we ask our students to think about the possible impact these life experiences may have on their actions, priorities, and choices as teachers. In this way, we seek to disrupt their ideologies and comfort zones by helping them recognize that the ways teachers view students are informed first and foremost by the beliefs teachers bring with them into their classrooms. Therefore, our work with new teachers is undergirded by two central assumptions: (1) that all aspects of one's autobiography have rich potential for analysis; and (2) that regardless of individual background and identities, each person comes to teaching with preconceptions that need to be consciously examined and deliberately disturbed.

In this chapter,[1] we describe our use of autobiographical analysis as a "disruptive strategy" that is deliberately structured to enable preservice teachers to expand their ways of thinking about teaching. Specifically, we (1) describe the ways in which we incorporate autobiographical analysis throughout the program as a tool for initiating preservice teachers' critical examination of biases and assumptions, and (2) present data that document transformations we have seen in preservice teachers' thinking as they engage in these opportunities for critical examination. Using students' assignments, or "texts," as data grounds our discussion and makes this an authentic conversation relevant to all those involved in teacher preparation. This work is especially germane to teacher educators because it seeks to build a more cohesive bridge between educational theory, classroom practice, and the implicit knowledge that preservice teachers bring to their teaching. Our study illustrates how the very process of "positioning" prompts an important analytic examination on the part of preservice teachers, and we argue that teacher educators can use their students' articulation of "position" to more responsively plan curriculum and effectively support and sustain student teachers' work in the field.

Before we go any further, it is important to acknowledge that many teacher educators have been using autobiographical reflections for years (Connelly & Clandinin, 1990; Gomez & Tabachnik, 1992; Goodwin, 1997; McIntyre, 1997). However, the research analyzing these preservice pedagogical practices has primarily concentrated on identifying the themes of teachers' autobiographical experiences (Johnson, 2002); illuminating the essential and complicated questions about diversity that must be taken up by teacher educators (Cochran-Smith, 2000); or helping students locate themselves as cultured, classed, raced, and gendered (Banks, 1991; King & Ladson-Billings, 1990).

Although this paper builds strongly upon this prior work, it hones its focus on the ways that preservice teachers can develop over time in relation specifically to the assumptions they have about children, schooling, culture, difference, power, teachers, schools, and communities. In our study, we see students' stories as content for self-analysis, as lenses for them to look more keenly at themselves and gain awareness of and insight into what one's cultural locations might mean in terms of what one does, how one thinks or perceives, and the actions one chooses as a teacher. In this piece, we demonstrate the ways in which autobiography provides a means to articulate and interrogate these implicit beliefs (Florio-Ruane, 2001; Knowles, 1993).

The Program Context

The Preservice Program in Childhood Education[2] is a graduate-level teacher preparation program for those seeking a master's degree and New York State elementary certification, grades 1 through 6.[3] The curriculum of the program mirrors that of most teacher preparation programs across the country, that is, educational foundations, pedagogical content methods, and student teaching. However, the program is more than a sequence of courses taught by different and individual faculty. Instead, half of the program, and therefore the very heart of the experience, occurs in what we call "Core." Core is a yearlong course that integrates elementary methods, multicultural education, and curriculum development, and explicitly emphasizes inquiry, urban and inclusive education, and teaching for social justice. Beginning in the fall, students enroll in the Preservice Program Core alongside student teaching and reading methods; all three experiences continue side-by-side for the academic year. Students cannot enroll in Core if they are not student teaching, or vice versa, because the experiences, assignments, and activities in Core are deliberately linked to the field and to students' experiences, and are therefore intended to help students blend personal, school, and university-based knowledge. Each year, 75 to 80 students go through Core in cohorts of about 25 students. Each cohort is led by a professor who remains with her cohort for both semesters. The cohort structure supports conceptual continuity—work in the fall simply flows into the spring without interruption. The cohort structure also affords faculty and students the time and space necessary to develop strong working (and interpersonal) relationships. These relationships, in turn, foster trust among community members, so they can freely wrestle with thorny issues in safety.

The Study

Data for this study came from two assignments that engaged students in autobiographical analysis: an autobiographical analysis paper and a social studies critical analysis paper (Table 13.1).

We identified a sample of 10 students for the study, taking care to select a group of students who reflected the 2002–2003 cohort of student teachers registered for Core in terms of race/ethnicity, gender, and nationality.

Table 13.1 Descriptions of Both Autobiographical Analysis Assignments

---

Autobiographical Analysis (Program Syllabus, Fall 2002)

It is often said that we teach who we are. Who are you? What are your biases? Reflect on your autobiography in relation to critical issues raised by (Beatrice) Fennimore and (Patricia) Ramsey. Although you may choose to incorporate pieces of the autobiography that you wrote prior to student teaching, the emphasis for this assignment is on analysis, not storytelling. The purpose of this paper is for you to critically look at the ways in which your life experiences will have an impact on the kind of teacher you will be.

In 10 to 15 pages you should:
(1) provide a careful, detailed, but brief synthesis of critical issues raised by these scholars;
(2) pinpoint a specific issue discussed by each author and use these two issues as a lens to deeply analyze your assumptions, values, perspectives, positions, cultural locations, biases, and limitations;
(3) outline specific and immediate goals for your learning and development in light of your analysis. Describe in detail what you feel you can now do to further your understanding by clearly articulating possible actions you could take to continue this process of analysis and professional development.

Critical Analysis of Social Studies (Program Syllabus, Spring, 2003)

It is often said that we teach as we were taught. How were you taught social studies in elementary school? Reflect on your own experiences in social studies classrooms in relation to dynamic social studies learning and multicultural historical knowledge. Use A Different Mirror: A History of Multicultural America and the National Council for the Social Studies' Vision of Powerful Teaching and Learning in the Social Studies to:
(a) Deeply analyze the assumptions, values, perspectives, positions, cultural locations, biases, strengths, and limitations of your own social studies education. Please note the emphasis on analysis for the purpose of understanding, and not on highlighting and criticizing all the shortcomings of your own social studies education.
(b) Describe, given your analysis, issues that you may face as a social studies teacher.
(c) Outline specific—and immediate—goals, and possible actions for your learning and professional/personal development in light of your discussion. [Page limit: 15]

Thus, our purposive sample consisted of one male and nine females: two African Americans (one of whom was the sole male in the sample), three Asian Americans, one South Asian immigrant, one Latina, and three European Americans. We then collected both assignments from each student and content-analyzed them for the purpose of addressing the following questions:

> How do preservice students locate themselves culturally when they engage in autobiographical analysis?
>
> How do their cultural locations frame their thinking about teaching and learning?
>
> How do preservice students' thinking about teaching and learning change as they engage in critical autobiographical analysis?

Our analysis procedures began with each researcher independently sifting through the critical analyses papers to sort student teacher talk, using the three sections of the assignment as categories that we labeled (a) locations, experiences (or, where am I located?); (b) realizations, dilemmas, assumptions (or, what does this mean?); and (c) goals, actions, resolutions (or, what will I do about it?). Both researchers then came together to discuss and compare categorizing or coding decisions in order to resolve any coding discrepancies—of which there were very few given the fairly unambiguous nature of the initial categories.

In the next phase of our analysis, we focused on the first category, *locations, experiences,* in order to determine what we termed students' primary locations (identifying one or two). We defined location as how students position themselves culturally; primary was defined as the location to which they each devoted the most text in their papers. We then used students' primary location(s) as analytic lenses to look across all the categorized data to identify possible connections between how students located themselves and the understandings and actions they articulated throughout both papers. We charted connections that emerged for each student, using representative quotes as signifiers for locations that ran as themes within each paper and across both papers. Table 13.2 presents an example of one student's matrix (Susie).[4]

Findings and Discussion

This discussion of our findings takes an overall look at the total sample in order to take a "broad strokes" view at the ways in which our data cumulatively responded to our research questions. Throughout, our discussion is anchored by examples from our practice—some of the activities and strategies we use to support students toward ever deeper analysis as they are challenged to confront themselves—as well as by the words students used to tell us what they were thinking.

Table 13.2 Sample Student Data Matrix

Susie	Autobiographical Analysis (Fall)	Social Studies Analysis (Spring)
Where am I located?	Race: "Race is one of the most prominent issues in my mind." Marginalization: "I am still working on overcoming these 'false assumptions' of inferiority. I am happy with myself now but I had a difficult time overcoming my self-hate." "My initial assumption when I come across another Chinese person is that they probably do not speak English."	Race: "Social studies was just viewed through and presented to me through the dominant white male perspective." Marginalization: "My own identity and culture having been left out of the curriculum in elementary school … I was unable to find my place as an American until very recently."
What does this mean?	Race: "I could be more sensitive to these students. I might give them more attention." "Because I understand and identify with what it feels like, I would work even harder to support these students." Marginalization: "Will it [my false assumptions of inferiority] affect how I approach students who are minority?	Race: "Having been raised on the history of white Americans, I feel like I am more prone to think from the perspective of and learn from that view of history." Marginalization: "When a group of people are not able to see themselves as a part of the history, and to not be included in the classroom curriculum, it makes for an unsafe learning environment."
What will I do about it?	Race: "That image [that all black people are criminals] is something I have to check myself of sometimes whenever I am in a neighborhood like mine [i.e., dangerous, inner city] Marginalization: "To instill in all students confidence in themselves and what they are capable of. I want them to be proud of who they are and where they come from."	Race: "Become more familiar with history from all perspectives by reading a lot more history because there is just so much that I do not know." Marginalization: "I will work to include all students from all different backgrounds and those that are not in the classroom as well."

Students' Cultural Locations

As one might expect, the students in our study located themselves in diverse and multiple ways, specifically in terms of race/ethnicity, class, religion, language, immigrant status, able-ness, and nationality. Given our small sample, we sought to discern interesting trends as opposed to generalizations. First, race or immigrant status emerged as most salient for students of color. Four of the seven students of color located themselves primarily as immigrants or within an immigrant culture: "I was from a voluntary immigrant group coming to America for a better life" (Kiran, South Asian American); five of the seven defined themselves as raced or located themselves within their ethnicity/ethnic culture: "My views are from the vantage point of being a Black American" (Carol, Jamaican/Black American). A subtext running through students' discussions of being "raced" was the notion of "otherness" or marginalization framed by their cultural or racial difference. Thus, the narratives of five of the seven students of color included statements such as "I feel I was wrongly labeled as a disadvantaged youth because I grew up in the inner city and because I was black" (Jack, African/Native American); "I was unable to find my place as an American until very recently" (Susie, Chinese American); and "School life was an American thing that all other Americans did. ... The different aspects of my life were so distinct and extreme, it often felt like none of my sides ever met or understood one another" (Sonya, Korean American).

Of the three white students, one located herself within her whiteness: "I am white ... my values and biases are ingrained in this issue" (Brittany, Italian/Irish American); the remaining two described themselves as individuals in the process of becoming conscious of their blind spots or prejudices and therefore beginning to explore their own assumptions and biases: "I have always considered myself an open-minded individual, free from stereotypes. More recently, however, I realized that I did and still do have ideas about certain populations of people" (Amy, European American). Interestingly, by engaging in this somewhat "benign" discussion about the importance of being aware of one's own limited perspectives, they were able to avoid specifying a cultural location altogether. Finally, though there were other students in the sample who spoke home languages other than English, Mary was the only student who "focus[ed] on language in the context of my Puerto Rican and Ecuadorian roots" as well as "on religion."

We would not presume to come to any conclusions about why students located themselves as they did even while available literature offers insight into, for example, the salience of race in the lives people of color (Carter & Goodwin, 1994; Tatum, 1997), the "raceless" identity and color-blindness assumed by whites (Fine, Weis, Pruitt & Burns, 2004; Pollock, 2004; Tatum, 1997), or the fluidity and hybridity of culture (Dardar 1995; Goodwin, 2003). However, such questions were not our focus. Rather, the purpose of the autobiographical analysis is for students to become conscious of the notion that all of us *are* culturally located and that these locations are facets of our identity, including our teaching identity. Students' responses also give us, as their teachers, clues about how to reach them through what appears to be important to them and about what we may need to introduce or investigate in class given the silences that may become apparent in students' writings.

Cultural Locations and Thinking about Teaching and Learning

Preservice students' locations were visible in the educational issues and priorities they articulated and the teaching actions they indicated. Of course, this observation is partly a function of the structure of the assignment, the way it directed students to analyze their own autobiographies. Nevertheless, this finding allowed us to see that the assignment was successful in enabling students to use their cultural locations as analytic lenses. In the context of this discussion, however, our emphasis is not on *whether* students used these locations but *in what ways* these locations seemed to inform the issues and actions they highlighted. What became evident as we sorted through the data is that students' locations stood out as themes that characterized the ways they wrote about their teaching and learning. Students used their locations to (1) name realizations, assumptions, and dilemmas that had emerged through the analytic process; (2) articulate their intentions to resist or counter their own experiences, assumptions, and perspectives; and (3) consider what they might do to ensure that the children they teach experience an education different from theirs.

Realizations, Assumptions, and Dilemmas   In Core, students are introduced to a number of texts that scaffold the process of autobiographical examination and support them in critically considering how these realizations will affect their teaching lives. One particular text, *Teaching to Change the World* by Jeannie Oakes and Martin Lipton (2002), illuminates the pervasive inequalities that historically—and still—exist for children, especially in urban school settings. Aided by the perspectives suggested by this foundational reading, preservice teachers examine their own schooling experiences through the lens of their cultural location from a more critical, and sometimes politically conscious, vantage point and express realizations of which they might not have been previously aware. In this study, for example, Jack (African/Native American), looking through the lens of his primary location as black and Native American, realized that he "may be the only black teacher [my students] encounter," and assumed that he "will have a relationship with kids, simply based on race [because] many of the black students will have a dialogue and rapport that I only understand." Yet, despite this assumption, he worries "that many students may have difficulty in accepting their heritage; I fear that I may someday scare a student with unveiling a piece of history that is too difficult to accept," and that "on a professional level, I may be observed and challenged slightly harder than a white teacher because this is the way society operates." His analysis revealed the challenges he speculates he might face as a black teacher from both whites and blacks, challenges that he inserted into the many discussions about race and racial identity that were initiated in Core.

We have found that it is often in the first autobiographical paper that students express some initial awareness of the complexity, contradictions, and paradoxes that naturally characterize their assumptions and positioning. One strategy we have used to render visible complexities such as the one articulated by Jack and create a space where different voices and disparate perspectives can emerge is to create a "Readers' Theatre," where we pull specific quotes from our students' papers into a collective autobiography of sorts. Reading this script aloud as a community allows a variety of authentic talking points to pointedly yet safely enter the classroom environment, which in turn encourages us all to engage in more candid discussions around issues that are often difficult but clearly relevant to our students and indeed come directly from them.

Students in our study also articulated a growing consciousness of all that was missing in terms of content in their education and expressed anxiety and anger over the limited account of history to which they have been exposed. Amy (European American) wrote, "I was exposed to one dominant perspective, the white male of European descent. ... 'He' left out many things I consider meaningful," which led her to realize that "it is almost overwhelming to think about the gap between my social studies learning and the social studies teaching I hope to adopt." Implicit in her statement is a dilemma echoed by many of her peers: "How do I teach what I do not know?" One text we use that particularly illuminates "all that we do not know" (and probably never learned) is *A Different Mirror* by Ronald Takaki (1993). After reading this and other more inclusive accounts of history, students are able to assess their own knowledge base against different benchmarks and quickly verbalize a mission to become more knowledgeable and to seek out the content they "missed."

Clearly, this can be seen as a favorable outcome and one our program supports. Still, it is insufficient, since our intent is not to bring our students to the point where they subscribe to certain goals or repeat what we would like to hear. Instead, our aim is always to spur our students to think, question, and reflect, which is why our response to their newly found fervor is to persistently push them to rethink yet again the images they may in fact have of teaching. In one activity we have used to engender such reflection, we pose two images—that of *teaching as having answers* and *teaching as asking questions*. While we recognize that dichotomizing teaching in this way is problematic to some extent, we find that this activity guides preservice teachers to envision teaching in ways not informed primarily by either their personal experiences or memories. As they begin to revise their image of the teacher as the one "who knows" (indeed, *must* know) to one that defines the teacher as centered on inquiry and on the learner, our preservice students are able to use autobiographical analysis as an important tool in moving beyond the limitations of binaries such as "knowing" versus "not knowing." They are encouraged to adopt a more critical stance and ask different questions such as, "How do I ensure that all my students feel included and safe in the learning that takes place in my classroom?" or "How do we come to know together as a community?" Questions such as these shift the focus from the teacher to learners and raise issues around inclusion and the experiences of "other," those who have been marginalized by normative schooling practices. Kiran (South Asian American) articulates this marginalization all too well when she states, "My school life and my Indian life were separate."

Finally, Jessie (European American), who talked quite generally about how personal assumptions and biases can influence what a teacher does, comes to realize that she has engaged in labeling, "categorizing a child as 'a good reader,' a 'bad math student,' or as having a 'behavior problem.'" She feels she has "slowly become aware of how so many issues are extremely complex" and that she "must constantly remember that my students will come from diverse backgrounds from me and from each other." Even while she raised no particular dilemmas in her analysis, her ability to recognize her own unconscious labeling is perhaps honed by the child inquiry assignment. This assignment requires each student to closely observe and document one child for the duration of his or her student teaching placement. The primary purpose of the assignment is to help our students mistrust their initial assessments of learners—which often represent hasty and uninformed judgments—but instead to rely on different kinds of data collected from multiple sources in order to come to know children intimately. The assignment consists of several components that are completed over the course of the term. This means that the child inquiry becomes a dialogic process whereby student teachers and faculty talk back and forth in a recursive feedback loop. The child inquiry also allows faculty to introduce explicit in-class opportunities to air students' assumptions. For example, one activity uses raw data drawn from child inquiries to help students differentiate description from judgment, and to engage them in generating as many possible explanations for the documented behaviors. This activity is always very enlightening to students as they recognize how quickly they were ready to generalize and categorize children without really having much information.

Another strategy we have used integrates autobiographical analysis into the inquiry project and asks students to compose a reflective paper where they compare themselves to the child they are following. By using their data and stories to construct Core discussions, we find students are easily and authentically engaged in examining the possible implications of their assumptions in their current student teaching placements, and are then guided to consider more specifically how to confront these inclinations in their practice.

Stepping outside Oneself: Intentions to Counter One's Own Assumptions and Experiences Students in our study sample talked at length about not allowing their own assumptions and experiences to limit their vision and actions as teachers. Jessie (European American) described her intention to make

> a great effort to recognize when this [labeling others/making assumptions] happens and ultimately prevent myself from separating and focusing on only one aspect of a person's personality whether it is a disability

or some other characteristic … by being extremely cautious and critical of my impressions of a person and the reasons for these impressions.

Mary (Puerto Rican/Ecuadorian American) stated she will "have to work on really listening to what others say and sometimes even to the things they don't say" because she has begun to "gain an understanding of the power of our words and the indelible mark they leave on the children that we teach." Carol (Jamaican/Black American) located herself very deliberately within her racial/ethnic culture and talked extensively about how her "heritage [gave her] a unique perspective into the notions and stereotypes of others." She also defined herself as someone who was marginalized in school by "having to deal with the ramifications of speaking differently and of being Jamaican" but who resisted and defied stereotypes of her because "school seemed to come easily." Her own experiences led her to

worry that my successful school experiences may cloud my judgment in that I believe you can do anything if you put your mind to it, almost to the exclusion of appropriately considering the burden (i.e., racism, low expectations) you may be required to carry to get there … [she hopes] to become more sensitive in terms of recognizing and respecting cultural differences.

Again, it is important to reiterate that the two autobiographical assignments that we use as data for our study represent, in some ways, the culmination of numerous discussions, readings, and activities that faculty integrate into Core for the express purpose of engaging students in a continuous autobiographical analytic process. As indicated earlier, we use situations presented by our student teachers' personal experiences to connect them more directly to the possible impact of their beliefs and personal histories on classroom practice. For example, we have asked students to create brief vignettes that document cultural dilemmas or conflicts that they have witnessed in their classrooms. These vignettes then become fodder for serious discussions about stereotypes, misconceptions, racism, and culturally responsive pedagogy. Strategies generated from these discussions are then collated, typed up, and distributed to all the students across the three cohorts. Cultural vignettes have also been used to structure professional development opportunities for supervisors. In bimonthly group meetings typically used to share students' progress in the field, we have introduced these vignettes to our supervising staff, involving them in the critical analysis process as well. This helps us ensure that supervisors will actively seek analytical thinking in student teaching journals and will continually challenge our students to pose alternative interpretations and a variety of instructional responses in their classroom practice.

Teaching in Ways Different from Their Own Experiences   When students outline the actions they will take as a consequence of their autobiographical analysis, they typically speak in terms of filling the gaps that they now see in their own educations, doing what was not done for them (or not doing what was done to them). Susie's (Chinese American) "identity & culture having been left out of the curriculum in elementary school as well as in later school experiences," coupled with her "immersion in Chinatown for most of my life" led to her feelings of isolation. She "always remember[s] thinking what all this stuff has to do with me," and now intends to

> work to include all students from all different backgrounds, and those that are not in the classroom as well, to promote social understanding in the world outside of their own as well as their own.

She stated passionately, "because I feel cheated, I will work really hard to give my students the experience that I never had access to." Carol (Jamaican/Black American) wrote about "all of the stories that I wasn't told" and described how she "extended my learning with my own choices" by pursuing her interests "outside of school." As a consequence, she hopes to offer her "students opportunities to build on their own interests" and "ensure that a much broader range of people and perspectives are covered." Jack (African/Native American) recalled that "the only time that we studied people of color was during Black History Month" and that the textbooks he read "were not providing us with a truthful depiction of our country's history." He saw that African Americans were "represented negatively" and "that again my people made no contribution to society other than cotton and tobacco." In his analysis he stated poignantly, "If black was tainted and white was pure, what was I?" To ensure a different experience for his students, he aims "to show students that they have a special identity within this world" by providing them with a curriculum "with multiple voices recognized," full of "a richness of materials that pull them closer to knowing their own culture." Jessie's (European American) story offers a final example. She was taught "mainly from our own perspective, namely that of a white American with strong, mostly Eastern European Jewish heritages" and now vows to not "impose my beliefs or any one belief on my students; instead I must present as many perspectives on a topic as I possibly can."

Changes in Thinking

In both assignments, students were asked to "Outline specific and immediate goals for your learning and development in light of your analysis/discussion." Our third research question directed us to compare their responses in each paper to this requirement and identify the possible ways in which our students' thinking about teaching and learning appeared to have changed. Change is, of course, inevitable and is often a function of time passing and the accumulation of additional experiences. Students conduct the first analysis as they are beginning their first student teaching placement, which, in many instances, is also their start in the program; the second analysis occurs after they have acquired a full term of experience in the field, and have completed half of Core and all that it entails in terms of knowledge, skills, and pedagogical content designed to stretch students' thinking and expose them to alterative perspectives. Therefore, it only makes sense that they come to the second analysis with much more insight into teaching, classrooms and themselves as teachers. Still, we were interested in the kinds of changes in thinking that became evident in students' writings, how students' analyses might be characterized when we compared assignment 1 against assignment 2.

In the first paper, we found that students were very vague and framed the actions they would take in terms of their *intention* to "do better." Phrases such as "I will make an effort to …," "I will work hard to …," "I will try to …," "I hope to …," "I have to work on …," and "My goal is to …" peppered their discussions. Overwhelmingly, the majority of the students were not able to specify particular actions they would take in their efforts to fill in any gaps identified during the analysis process or actualize their vision of good teaching. Typical examples of what they said included: "I must view my students as the whole and complete people who they truly are" (Jessie, European American); "I think my main goal … is to create a supportive environment for all students" (Susie, Chinese American); "One of my main goals is to create a classroom community that is inclusive of all my students' needs" (Sonya, Korean American); "I will have to make every student value the cultures and traditions of others" (Shoba, South Asian/International). Our analysis also revealed that students' initial attempts to define ways they would support their own learning and that of their students were marked by rhetorical generalities such as "community," "inclusiveness," and "multiple perspectives." Clearly, students had adopted the "right" language but seemed unable to bolster their rhetoric with substance.

In the second paper, students seemed better able to articulate concrete actions they would take or strategies they would use to enact their aspirations or realize their goals. Carol (Jamaican/Black American), who stated in the first paper her intention to "expose my students to the perspectives of many different cultures, primarily through literature and social studies," was able to specify in the second paper that she would "need to preview the books in my library for cultural sensitivity … to ensure that a much broader range of people and perspectives are covered." Sonya (Korean American) wrote of her intention to "create a classroom community that is inclusive of all my students' needs and one that celebrates our differences." By the second paper, she seemed to understand that one route to meeting this goal might be to "really look at the community in which I teach" and "build a social studies curriculum that speaks to what my kids want to know [which will] eventually lead them to the study of things they didn't realize even connected to their realities." Finally, in her first paper, Brittany wrote that her most important goal "is to relax and be myself in the classroom, allow the students to be themselves (race, gender, class, culture, etc.)." Despite acknowledging her students' differences, Brittany adopted an "I'm ok, you're ok" attitude that she seemed to assume would support harmony and mutual understanding in her classroom. By the second analysis paper, however, she had moved to a more action-oriented and deliberate stance: "to find ways in my classroom to learn about cultures other than the white European" so as to meet her goal "to respect my students ... to make students aware of history through a multicultural lens that incorporates everyone."

A second difference we observed between papers 1 and 2 was in the quality of students' talk. A handful of students began to adopt a more critical tone that emphasized the political nature of knowledge and an awareness of a larger teaching context beyond their own practice or classrooms. Carol (Jamaican/Black American) hopes that "my students come to realize that they can make a difference, individually and collectively." One strategy she plans to employ to empower and ignite them is "discussing how people have historically organized, fought and lobbied to bring about change." Jack (African/Native American) becomes aware that he will be "educating my students about the controversies of American history" and that his "job as a teacher is to unveil and lead my students to their own discoveries, not teach them to work the system and follow standard practices like I did in the past." Shoba (South Asian/International) expressed the need to "visit more classrooms to see demonstrations of powerful teaching and learning" and voiced her desire to "get involved in decision making concerning adoption of curriculum materials."

So What? Implications for "Doing"

In 1970, Ray Rist's groundbreaking study of kindergarten children showed teachers categorizing children in "ability" groups based on appearance and behavior. Attractive, clean, well-dressed children who conformed to middle-class behavioral norms were assigned to the highest group; children who found themselves in the low-ability group were those who did not match the teacher's mental images of "smartness." Rist followed these kindergartners into the third grade and found that the initial "ability" decisions their first teacher had made "stuck"—children's positions in ability groups remained constant, demonstrating the devastating (and long-term) impact of teachers' perceptions and assumptions not only on children's immediate educational experiences and opportunities but on future possibilities.

Volumes have been written about teacher perceptions and expectations and how they can hinder (or support) the achievement of students (e.g., see Brophy & Good, 1986; Dusek & Gail, 1983; Good & Brophy, 1984; Garibaldi, 1988; Goodwin, 2002b; Irvine, 1991). Yet these data have not enabled us to recognize, and interrupt, our own harmful and hurtful practices; too many children who are culturally and linguistically diverse, children of color, poor children, or children who are new immigrants continue to experience troubled and limiting school lives. As a society, we have come to accept too easily as "business as usual" what should stand out as stark aberrations and deep contradictions: race and low socioeconomic status as "predictors" of poor school performance; gifted classrooms that exclude most children of color; "minorities" and the poor always doing less well on standardized tests than those in the white middle class; children of color disproportionately labeled as behavior problems and assigned to special education; and schools serving culturally and linguistically diverse children invariably being resource poor. The current (and historical) sociopolitical-economic climate fosters a "willful ignorance about the impact of race and racism" (hooks, 1995, p. 16), and forwards an "egalitarian discourse [that] is reconciled with the massive inequities of our social, economic, and political lives" (Shapiro & Purpel, 1993, p. 62), a discourse that requires active disruption.

This chapter offers some of the strategies we use to actively disrupt taken-for-granted habits and inclinations, while the research we describe provides an illustration of some of the understandings we have gained about student teacher learning through the course of our work. However, we have also gained insight into ways to support and structure autobiographical analysis that constitute, for us, some basic principles that should underlie this process. First, we delineate clearly for ourselves and our students the separation between analysis and mere storytelling. While the sharing of stories is fundamental to autobiographical analysis, the purpose of the assignments and activities is not to provide students with a cathartic or therapeutic outlet but to push them to thoughtfully and analytically wrestle with and explore possible *relationships* between and *influences* of their prior experiences, beliefs, and assumptions about teaching and learning, on their current and future instructional decisions and interactions with children. Students come to understand that successful papers are based on depth of analysis and application to teaching rather than colorfulness of stories. Second, we make clear to students that we are not looking for particular stories, only the ones they are willing to share and feel will provide the most appropriate context for their analysis. Third, we aim to honor everyone's voices, not just privilege or rely upon those that are spoken aloud—thus our constant search for creative strategies designed to render visible multiple perspectives so that they can be integrated into our larger conversations, without exposing students who may be reticent to speak but still have much to say. Strategies such as the Readers' Theatre, which we described earlier, enable not only diverse opinions to enter classroom discourse safely but contrary ones as well. This allows us to concretely forward the message that all voices count, that there is no universal or "politically correct" position. Fourth, we integrate opportunities for students to engage in autobiographical analysis throughout our assignments and classes—activities, discussions, lectures, and so forth. Autobiographical analysis becomes an expected—and regular—aspect of our curriculum. Finally, we try to be conscious of our own assumptions, beliefs, and expectations. In weekly collaborative planning meetings, faculty weigh ideas, interrogate one another, debate ideas and outcomes, and assess each previous class in terms of student response and impact.

Interruption is no easy task. Even preservice teachers who initially express a willingness to engage in these conversations "are often resistant to rethink their contemporary beliefs about people different from themselves and how one might teach them in ways that are equitable and just" (Gomez, 1994, p. 328). Rarely have our preservice teachers been asked to confront their unquestioned assumptions. As a consequence, "the beginning teacher is an outsider looking through the lens in order to identify with the experiences of students from different cultural, ethnic, and economic backgrounds" (Frykholm, 1997, p. 51). Therefore, teacher education—and specifically, autobiographical analysis—can support this interruption, not only as a sign of growth, but as "foundational to the growth" (Meyer et al., 1998, p. 24). Indeed, preservice students' cultural locations can become sites of "interruption," lenses they can utilize to critically examine how their lived cultural experiences mediate their way of knowing the world, the ways that schools structure inequality, and the ways in which they as prospective teachers could make a commitment to social justice and social change (Ladson-Billings, 1999).

Notes

1. This chapter draws upon some of our earlier work. See M. Genor and A. L. Goodwin (2005), "Confronting ourselves: Using autobiographical analysis in teacher education," *The New Educator, 1*(4), 311–331.
2. As of fall 2006, the program is known as the Preservice Inclusive Elementary Program.
3. Please note that this description of program context reflects the program structure in 2004–2005. The program is one that is constantly evolving and so continually undergoes structural and philosophical changes.
4. All names used are pseudonyms. Pseudonyms selected are culturally representative of respondents' real names.

References

Banks, J. (1991). Teaching multicultural literacy to teachers. *Teaching Education, 4*(1), 135–144.

Bartolome, L. I., & Macedo, D. P. (1997). Dancing with bigotry: The poisoning of racial and ethnic identities. *Harvard Educational Review, 67*(2), 222–246.

Britzman, D. P. (1986). Cultural myths in the making of a teacher: biography and social structure in teacher education. *Harvard Educational Review, 56,* 442–456.

Brookhart, S., & Freeman, D. (1992). Characteristics of entering teacher candidates. *Review of Educational Research, 62*(1), 37–60.

Brophy, J., & Good, T. (1986). Teacher behavior and student achievement. In M. C. Wittrock (Ed.), *Handbook of research on teaching* (3rd ed., pp. 328-376). New York: Macmillan.

Calderhead, J., & Robson, M. (1991). Images of teaching: Student teachers' early conceptions of classroom practice. *Teaching and Teacher Education, 6,* 1–8.

Carter, R., & Goodwin, A. L. (1994). Racial identity and education. In L. Darling-Hammond (Ed.), *Review of research in education* (Vol. 20, pp. 291–336). Washington, DC: American Educational Research Association.

Cochran-Smith, M. (2000). Blind vision: Unlearning racism in teacher education. *Harvard Educational Review, 70*(2), 157–190.

Cochran-Smith, M. (2004). *Walking the road: Race, diversity and social justice in teacher education.* New York: Teachers College Press.

Connelly, F. M., & Clandinin, J. (1990). Stories of experience and narrative inquiry. *Educational Researcher, 19,* 2–14.

Darder, A. (1995). The politics of biculturalism: Culture and difference in the formation of *Warriors for Gringostroika and the New Mestizas.* In A. Darder (Ed.), *Culture and difference* (pp. 1–20). Westport, CT: Bergin & Garvey.

Dilworth, M. E., & Brown, C. E. (2001). Consider the difference: Teaching and learning in culturally rich schools. In V. Richardson (Ed.), *Handbook of Research on Teaching* (4th ed., pp. 643–667). Washington, DC: American Educational Research Association.

Dusek, J. B., & Gail, J. (1983). The bases of teacher expectancies: A meta analysis. *Journal of Educational Psychology, 75,* 327-346.

Fine, M., Weis, L., Pruitt, L. P., & Burns, A. (Eds.). (2004). *Off white: Readings in power, privilege, and resistance* (2nd ed.). New York: Routledge.

Florio-Ruane, S. (2001). *Teacher education and the cultural imagination: Autobiography, conversation, and narrative.* Mahwah, NJ: Lawrence Erlbaum.

Frykholm, J. (1997). A stacked deck: Addressing issues of equity with preservice teachers, *Equity and Excellence in Education, 30*(2), 50–58.

Garibaldi, A. M. (1988). *Educating Black male youth: A moral and civic imperative.* New Orleans: New Orleans Public Schools.

Gomez, M. L. (1994). Teacher education reform and prospective teachers' perspectives on teaching "other people's" children. *Teaching and Teacher Education, 10*(3), 319–334.

Gomez, M. L., & Tabachnick, B. (1992). Telling teaching stories. *Teaching Education, 4,* 129–138.

Good, T. L., & Brophy, J. E. (1984). *Looking in classrooms* (3rd ed.). New York: Harper and Row.

Goodwin, A. L. (1997). Historical and contemporary perspectives on multicultural teacher education: Past lessons, new directions. In J. King, E. Hollins, & W. Hayman (Eds.), *Preparing teachers for cultural diversity* (pp. 5–22). New York: Teachers College Press.

Goodwin, A. L. (2002a). The case of one child: Making the shift from personal knowledge to professionally informed practice. *Teaching Education, 13*(2), 137–154.

Goodwin, A. L. (2002b). The social/political construction of low teacher expectations for children of color: Re-examining the achievement gap. *Journal of Thought, 37*(4), 83–103.

Goodwin, A. L. (2003). Growing up Asian in America: A search for self. In C. C. Park, A. L. Goodwin, & S. J. Lee (Eds.), *Asian American identities, families and schooling* (pp. 3–26). Greenwich, CT: Information Age.

Gordon, J. A. (2000). *The color of teaching.* New York: Routledge/Falmer.

hooks, b. (1995). *Killing rage: Ending racism.* New York: Henry Holt.

Irvine, J. J. (1991). *Black students and school failure.* New York: Praeger.

Johnson, L. (2002). My eyes have been opened: White teachers and racial awareness. *Journal of Teacher Education, 53*(2), 153–167.

King, J., & Ladson-Billings, G. (1990). The teacher education challenge in elite university settings: Developing critical perspectives for teaching in a democratic and multicultural society. *European Journal of Intercultural Studies, 1*(2), 15–30.

Knowles, G. (1993). Life-history accounts as mirrors: A practical avenue for the conceptualization of reflection in teacher education. In J. Calderhead & P. Gates (Eds.), *Conceptualizing reflection in teacher development* (pp. 70–98). London: Falmer Press.

Knowles, J., Cole, A., & Presswood, C. S. (1994). *Through preservice teachers' eyes: Exploring field experiences through narrative and inquiry.* New York: Merrill.

Ladson-Billings, G. (1999). Preparing teachers for diversity: Historical perspectives, current trends, and future directions. In L. Darling-Hammond & G. Sykes (Eds.), *Teaching as the learning profession: Handbook of policy and practice* (pp. 86–124). San Francisco, CA: Jossey-Bass.

Lortie, D. C. (1975). *Schoolteacher: A sociological study.* Chicago: University of Chicago Press.

Lucas, T., & Villegas, A. (2002). Preparing culturally responsive teachers: Rethinking the curriculum. *Journal of Teacher Education, 53*(1), 20–32.

Maher, F. A., & Tetreault, M. K. (1994). *The feminist classroom: An inside look at how professors and students are transforming higher education for a diverse society.* New York: Basic Books.

Martin, R. J., & Van Gunten, D. M. (2002). Reflected identities: Applying positionality and multicultural social reconstructionism in teacher education. *Journal of Teacher Education, 53*(1), 44–54.

McIntyre, A. (1997). *Making meaning of whiteness: Exploring racial identity with white teachers.* Albany: State University of New York Press.

Meyer, R., Brown, L., DeNino, E., Larson, K., McKenzie, M., Ridder, K., & Zetterman, K. (1998). *Composing a teacher study group: Learning about inquiry in primary classrooms.* Mahwah, NJ: Laurence Erlbaum.

Oakes, J., & Lipton, M. (2002). *Teaching to change the world* (2nd ed.). Boston: McGraw-Hill.

Pollack, M. (2004). *Colormute: Race talk dilemmas in an American school.* Princeton, NJ: Princeton University Press.

Richardson, V. (1996). The role of attitudes and beliefs in learning to teach. In J. Sikula (Ed.), *Handbook of research on teacher education* (2nd ed., pp. 102–119). New York: Macmillan.

Rist, R. (1970). Student social class and teacher expectations: The self-fulfilling prophecy in ghetto education. *Harvard Educational Review, 40*, 411–451.

Shapiro, H. S., & Purpel, D. E. (1993). *Critical school issues in American education.* New York: Longman.

Su, Z. X. J. (1992). Sources of influence in preservice teacher socialization. *Journal of Education for Teaching, 18*(3), 239–258.

Takaki, R. (1993). *A different mirror: A history of multicultural America.* Boston: Little, Brown.

Tatum, B. D. (1997). *Why are all the blacks kids sitting together in the cafeteria?* New York: Basic Books.

14

Community College Students Talk about Play and Early Childhood Teacher Education for Social Justice

RACHEL THEILHEIMER

In this chapter, research on the practice of early childhood teacher educators is "the doing"—a way to advance causes of social justice. According to Marilyn Cochran-Smith (2004), teacher educators who work for social justice, first of all, teach about teaching for social justice. Secondly, teacher educators who are concerned about social justice act as politically aware advocates for social justice. Cochran-Smith (2004) says that teacher education for social justice includes a third component, too, one that involves

> taking our own professional work as educators as a research site and learning by systematically investigating our own practice and interpretive frameworks in ways that are critical, rigorous, and intended to generate both local knowledge and knowledge that is useful in more public spheres. (p. xxi)

This third aspect of teacher education for social justice is the focus of this chapter. Isolating one dimension of our work as early childhood teacher educators—how and what we teach about play—I compare theories of cross-cultural play researchers with what one can learn from listening to community college students talk about play. I query the implications of that comparison for early childhood teacher education for social justice.

Practice Enacted: Teacher Education and Listening (or Not) to Students' Stories

Our research project was to understand 10 community college students' perspectives on play.[1] We hoped what we would learn would help us to become better teachers for them. We were also aware that although nationwide the difference between the backgrounds of teachers and children creates a gap that seems to be increasing (Cochran-Smith, 2004), at Borough of Manhattan Community College we teach a pool of prospective early childhood educators whose backgrounds are congruent with those of the growing numbers of children of color in schools. We have the opportunity to learn from our students and to share what we learn towards the goal of early childhood education that is fairer and more responsive to more children.

Many students in our community college early childhood classes write enthusiastically about children's play but indicate during class discussions that they do not believe children really learn through play. When this happens, professors—myself included—react in a range of ways. We may respond to what students say, perhaps arguing with reference to the extensive literature that supports the value of play for young children. We may open up the point for class discussion, perhaps hoping that other students will argue on behalf of the ideas about play that they have heard from us and read in their texts and that may resonate with their experience. Alternatively, we may ignore opposing views about play, as if the student who wrote cogently about the value of play in a paper but spoke disparagingly of it in reference to her job or field experience did not really mean the latter. In all three of these putative instances, the early childhood teacher is not listening to the student to understand more about the gap between a view of play as a vehicle for learning and the way we find that many community college students regard play.

What if, instead, teacher educators were able to see the world from these early childhood students' perspectives? Their college teaching might become more accessible to the students. Teaching and learning might become a more collaborative endeavor between instructors and students. Students could contribute to their own educations, introducing missing perspectives into critical conversations (Cook-Sather, 2002). This is not to overlook the power imbalance in classrooms (Manke, 1997), as instructors make assignments, give grades, and write letters of reference for prospective teachers, nor is it to romanticize students' perspectives. Rather, it is that community college students often have stories that describe marginalization and oppression and that warrant their instructors' attention, particularly for teacher educators in pursuit of teacher education for social justice (Schultz, 2003).

The site of our investigation into future early childhood educators' perspectives on play is a community college that serves upwards of 18,000 students in New York City. Approximately 1,000 students were enrolled in the early childhood education program at the time of our research. Most were women who probably fit the overall self-reported college demographics of 35 percent black, 27 percent Hispanic, 11 percent white, 11 percent Asian or Pacific Islander, and 16 percent other. In 2003, 78.4 percent of the incoming students who responded to a survey reported living in families whose total annual income was under $25,000 (BMCC Factbook, 2003–2004).

Laden (1999) maintains that besides transitioning into academe while retaining their identities, community college students contribute "border knowledge" (p. 174) that can transform an institution. Community college students who study early childhood education have knowledge along the border between at least two ways of thinking. On one side of the border is thinking that originates in the ways they have processed experiences within their families and communities; on the other side is the thinking to which they are exposed in their early childhood classes. Sometimes that border is blurry; sometimes it is more distinct. By learning more about what lies along that border, early childhood teacher educators can go beyond preaching social justice to practicing it informed by students' border knowledge, with its foundation in the families, communities, and broader cultures in which the students have been raised.

Thus, we sought a way neither to buck nor to ignore the apparent contradiction between what students wrote and what they said but rather to understand what lies along the border of the two that is not necessarily visible to their instructors. To listen closely to at least a small group of students, we interviewed 10 about-to-graduate community college students from Latin America, Asia, the Spanish- and English-speaking Caribbean, and the United States to learn what they thought about their early play experiences and about the role of play for the children they teach.

Using Seidman's (1998) in-depth interview approach, one of us met with each student three times. In the first interview, the participant recalled her childhood play and learning, and we became acquainted with each other. In the second interview she spoke about herself in the present, her college experiences in and out of classes, her work with children, and her leisure activities. In the third interview, each student theorized about play and learning based on the experiences she had discussed in the first two interviews.

Although the women we interviewed share some similarities with one another—all of them are women of color or recent immigrants who have chosen a community college education—they differ in many ways; each respondent's background and current situation is unique and interesting. Using the methods we did, we could not generate broad statements about early childhood teacher education (Dyson & Genishi, 2005). Rather, in our repeated rereading of the students' stories, we looked at each narrative for what we could learn from it about listening to students' perspectives on play. In that way, each case informs us about early childhood teacher education. For this chapter, I chose two of them to examine within a framework that to some degree grounds teacher education about play: cross-cultural play research.

The Theory: Cross-Cultural Perspectives on Play

According to Lancy (2002), children of all cultures play, but the amount of time spent on play varies, depending on adults' other expectations of children, including the degree to which children contribute to the household's survival activities. Other factors that constrain children's play are adults' concerns about their safety, gender roles, the play scripts that adult activities provide for children to follow, an ethos of cooperation or competition, the size of the community and consequent range of playmates especially of the same age, and enough time to play. Klein and Chen (2001) discuss the different ways in which families believe children learn, contrasting an interactive approach that calls for play and adult involvement with a belief in direct instruction or observation.

Some cross-cultural research on play constructs a continuum of modern and traditional cultures. In the terms of this continuum, cultures closer to the traditional pole are rural, not literate in the conventional sense, not exposed to technology, and follow traditional and communal beliefs and religious practices. They tend to be collectivistic. The most modern cultures on this continuum are urban, highly literate, technologically advanced, secular, and individualistic (Ariel, 2002). Child development research, then, cannot be the sole source of understanding children's play or adults' views about it, because its explanatory power differs at every point along the continuum (Kieff & Caspergue, 2000).

Roopnarine and Johnson (2001) note that play may not be an indicator of educational or developmental competence for all cultural groups. They speak of differences between parents' and teachers' beliefs and ideas about play and the way in which play does or does not meet children's developmental and educational needs. They also caution that comparisons between groups

> are quick to interpret group differences as being synonymous with cultural differences without delving into culturally contextualized constructions of the meaning of play for the acquisition of skills relative to the social and cognitive demands of individual cultures (e.g. technological vs. social intelligence). (p. 302)

They warn that such decontextualization can lead to stereotyping, particularly of children who are not white, who are members of nondominant groups, and who live in diverse societies.

Listening to community college early childhood students who are different from us and from one another and not representative of any larger group, we wanted to avoid decontextualization, categorization, and polarization. What we heard from the students and the degree to which they believed play indicated educational and developmental competence piqued my interest in how the cross-cultural play continuum applied to them. Two factors isolated by play researchers, the role of adults in children's play and the degree to which adults regard play as a vehicle for learning, serve as starting points as I relistened to what these community college students said about play.

The Doing: Listening to Two Students Talk about Play

The intricacies of Justine's and Fiona's views about play are striking. Justine provides an example of a nuanced, perhaps in flux, but certainly complex attitude toward the teacher's role in children's play. Fiona demonstrates how she assimilates conflicting messages from her upbringing in New York City and from childhood summers in Florida, from early unsuccessful school experiences, from continued struggles with academic subjects in college, from what she learns in her early childhood classes, from what she knows from caring for family members' children, and from input from Jumpstart. Instead of falling neatly on a play continuum, Justine and Fiona seem to hold many views simultaneously, defying such categorizations as traditional, modern, or any specific points in between. Although each of their sets of views may appear contradictory or internally inconsistent to someone else, they are part of an integrated or integrating way of thinking for each of them.

The Adult Role in Play

Lubeck's (1985) landmark study of two early childhood programs—one a private preschool in which the children and teachers are middle class and white, and the other a Head Start center in which the children and teachers are working class and African American—illustrates how people from different backgrounds may regard the adult role in children's play differently. At the Head Start center where Lubeck observed, play occupied children while teachers took care of other business in a different part of the room. The teachers assigned children to play areas that remained nearly the same throughout the year. At the preschool where Lubeck also observed, children moved freely and chose from a wide variety of activities that changed over the course of the year and in which teachers participated along with the children.

Interpreting what she saw, Lubeck shows how historical, social, and environmental issues influence the way teachers provide care and education to young children. She looks at the African American teachers' practices as adaptive behaviors or strategies, not as right or wrong, and regards these women as "active agents in the structuring of a life that is meaningful and shared" (p. 6). She concludes that

> it must be realized that differences among peoples within American society are deeply grounded in a social system that is premised on an unequal distribution of resources, a society that is product, more than people, oriented, one in which verbal facility, abstraction and self-achievement are prized to the exclusion of other values. (p. 146)

Several of the community college students to whom we listened recounted stories of their childhoods in which adults were detached from their play. Some of them seemed to agree with the Head Start teachers in Lubeck's study that play was children's business and did not involve adults. Justine is one such student, at least some of the time, and knowing her personal story and its social and historical context can help her teacher educators learn from it and teach and learn with her within its frame.

Justine was adopted as a baby in Jamaica. When she was 5 and her recently adopted younger brother was 2, her parents moved to the United States. Justine and her brother remained in Jamaica with their grandparents for the next 4 years. While living with her grandparents, Justine took responsibility for her younger brother, who has a disability. When she spoke about early play experiences in her interviews, they seemed intertwined with looking after him. In fact, she had difficulty recalling playtimes in her childhood. As an adult attending community college, Justine worked for an arts service organization and taught Sunday school and dance to 3- to 11-year-olds at her church. She was also a mentor and a music leader for young people, counseling them on Fridays. She referred to all of these experiences, as well as to her fieldwork for the community college teacher education program, when she spoke to us about play.

Justine described a school that she liked whose director is also from Jamaica. The school implements what Justine often referred to as the "British academic curriculum" that she knew from Jamaica and regarded highly. The teacher's role at the school that Justine liked was

> more the instructor, and give some form of guidance. But when they do … free play or they're in the imaginative area … the teacher doesn't facilitate, they don't encourage conversation or things like that. They just kind of let it go.

This was in contrast to Justine's field placement at a progressive nursery school where, in her words,

> no matter what area, there is someone there that is encouraging conversations from children, and you know, really helping them to think, and also the teacher there is a moderator … to kind of intervene when something happens. At the other school, the teachers were mediators when something happens, if they could get over there to them. … [T]he teacher as a mediator in the [progressive nursery school] kind of catches students … before it escalates.

When Justine insightfully contrasted the school she liked and its practices with her observations of another school's practices, she seemed simultaneously to value a teacher's involvement in children's play and to prefer the teaching style of a school where teachers were not involved in children's play. At the school that was similar to what she knew from Jamaica, she could see the teaching at work. Yet from the close observations she described to us of children building with blocks and playing with sand at the progressive nursery school, we could see that she believed children's thinking skills were developing there.

Justine also told us what she did when she was the teacher at her church. Her description of her own practice shed more light on her approach to the teacher's role in children's play:

> For instance, last week, we talked about the two men that built their house, one on the rock and one on the sand and one fell and so forth,

and so it's talking about a strong foundation. And so I got dominos and kind of gave them all seven dominos each. ... First I had them do one simple [activity], where everybody put them right in front of each other, next to each other, and then after I told them, "You build it however you want to, build a structure." And, I'll have them blow it at a certain spot and see which ones will stand, which ones are stronger, and kind of let them predict: Do you think that his is going to stay up if he blows it and depends on where he blew it? Do you think just the top will fall off? And they would kind of guess and so forth, and then they will see theirs fall down and someone did theirs differently, and they would try to build theirs like that one 'cause it stayed. And so that's how I kind of introduced the lesson by doing things like that.

Her role as a teacher, when given the freedom to construct it for herself, seems to blend the two approaches. She did not relinquish her adult authority and simultaneously orchestrated and was involved in children's play activities. While she was teaching a lesson, she set up her teaching so that children played, making their own choices, to learn the lesson. She facilitated their thinking with questions and suggestions to blow on different parts of the building.

What Justine told us about adult roles in children's play did not fall on one end or another of a play continuum. Her responses to our questions seemed full of multiple meanings and are, thus, difficult to place linearly. Justine illustrates a blend of approaches that a professional early childhood educator of color might use (Delpit, 1995; Kieff & Caspergue, 2000) and that we also saw in other participants' responses.

This blend takes into account the social, political, and historical contexts that Lubeck (1985) suggests can lead teachers to direct children's learning so that children will have the knowledge they need. Adults who value interaction with people over objects are also more likely to rely on giving children information versus setting up investigations as children's means of learning.

At the same time, Justine is learning about play and playful learning in her classwork and her work with the arts council. She seems to be in constant negotiation between these ways of regarding play and the British curriculum of her childhood. In this way, Justine and other teachers develop their own ideas about play that honor what they know about survival as a member of a historically oppressed group and that also value children's agency.

Play, Work, and Learning

Lubeck (1985) calls attention to differing images of the child as developing or as learning. In her study of a Head Start center in which children and teachers were African American and a middle-class preschool, she found the use of free play based on these images perhaps "the most striking difference between the two programs" (p. 73) that she studied. The teachers at the preschool thought the children would learn through play and were thrilled that three children were reading by the end of the year. In contrast, the teachers at the center set aside learning time, during which children sat as a group with the teachers who taught specific information (address, phone number, days of the week) repeatedly throughout the year, reinforcing a group ethic and attention to authority, recreating and extending "the same authority structure of which they are a part, socializing children into the reality that they themselves experience" (p. 125). Lubeck points out that the preschool's emphasis on divergence led to individualism, a valued quality for the teachers and the children's parents, while the center's emphasis on convergence led to community, a value for the teachers and families there.

We asked the participants in our study about play and learning and the relationship between the two; once again, some students' responses fell at either end of the spectrum. However, most of the participants' responses did not fall neatly at one end or another or even somewhere in the middle. For example, Fiona by and large saw learning as work and not play—but with certain caveats.

At the time of the interview, Fiona was 23 years old. An African American, she was born in the South Bronx. Fiona and her older brother had lived with their mother when Fiona was young but often stayed with her grandparents and teenage aunts and uncle. When Fiona was about 5 or 6, she and her brother moved in permanently with her grandparents. Fiona described their neighborhood as unsafe. When she started junior high school, she moved to her aunt's house in a safer Bronx neighborhood.

Fiona comes from a family of 13 brothers and sisters, including her father's and her mother's children. She also has a large extended family and spent summers in Florida with her mother's mother and the family there. While attending the community college, Fiona was a Jumpstart corps member for 2 years and was hired by the Head Start program at which she did her Jumpstart service. Fiona became interested in studying early childhood education when she babysat for her younger siblings and cousins but was also interested in pursuing a career as a police officer.

Fiona always struggled in school and had difficulty learning to read. She differentiated clearly between work and play, as when she told us that she wished she had done "more learning than playing" when she was a child. According to Fiona, play is what children do naturally, and the work of learning is an onerous obligation. She said of play:

> It's something that they want to do. And I think from early on, when they start to really use their senses ... from when they're babies, you know. ... And as they get older they just play even more and they just continue most of the time really just playing all the time, until they get

into … day care and Head Starts and go to kindergarten, because that's when the work starts.

Fiona recalled how her family in Florida made her read or complete puzzles before going out to play in the summer. She remembered how she chafed at the work, anxious for the play. She saw children in her Head Start classroom who reminded her of herself:

> We have some children who, if we're sitting down and we're writing with them, you know, they'll write a letter and then say, "Can I go play now?" and then if you say, "No, do more," then they'll do one or two more and then like, "Well, can I go now?" So it's kind of like they're doing it just so that they can go.

Bridging the gap between learning and play, Fiona remembered herself as a child, empathized with the children who did not want to sit still to learn, and tried to think of ways to make such learning more palatable for them. She contrasted her dislike of biology and math classes with her ability to focus in her early childhood classes and said that she can learn what interests her and that the same is true for children.

Fiona also talked about what she called "constructive play" and gave the examples of children's using shaving cream and writing letters in it or making fruit salad and tasting and learning the names of new foods. She saw a relationship between constructive play and learning as she had learned about it through Jumpstart experiences.

She also believed that some children liked work while others did not and that for those children who liked work

> it's something fun for them or interesting that interests them. Or if they're … a child who questions things and wants to know why. If it's something that will give them the answer to something.

She seemed to base that response on what she observed along with what she experienced as an adult. She said that when she eked out a few pages for an English assignment she was "just writing … to write it and be done with it" but could "just keep going and elaborating on whatever the issue is" for an assignment in an early childhood education class.

Fiona reflected thoughtfully on her past and present experiences with play and clearly articulated the Jumpstart and early childhood college classroom approaches to play. At the same time, based on her early and current school experiences, she believed that learning by sitting, listening, practicing, and producing—not play—is what children will need to succeed. While Jumpstart and other early childhood approaches that she learned about in college made sense to her as she considered her love of play as a child and her experiences as an early childhood student in college, they coexisted with the reality of her early and present educational experiences. She was the child in the lowest reading group and remains an adult who memorizes for a biology test with no hope of understanding what the terms mean.

Fiona held what appeared to be contradictory notions about play and learning, but they seemed to reside together in her theory and practice of early childhood education. Rhedding-Jones (2003) calls for a retheorizing of play to reflect diverse cultures, a retheorizing that blurs the dichotomy between work and play for a more complex reading of attitudes toward play that acknowledges the cultural locations of children and teachers. Such a rereading makes a place for Fiona's and other students' experiences, ideas, and practices.

Reflections: Listening to Talk about Play as Teacher Educators for Social Justice

Justine, Fiona, and the other students with whom we spoke raise the possibility of a three-dimensional grid for representing ideas about play instead of the two-dimensional continuum described in the cross-cultural play literature. Their ideas fall simultaneously at different ends of the play spectrum and at points in between. Their talk shows how apparently opposing variables are not mutually exclusive or stable over time (Cooper, 1999). Listening to them helps us to see beyond a binary set or even a continuum of ideas about play and its place in the early childhood classroom. While cross-cultural play research that polarized attitudes toward play gave us a framework with which to compare what we heard in the interviews, we did not find it helpful to limit our analysis of the students' talk to the points on the cross-cultural play continuum (Ariel, 2002).

Justine and Fiona have play histories, school histories, and personal histories that shape the way they learn about play in teacher education classrooms and the way they will use play in the classrooms where they will teach. They are also members of larger cultures with histories and subsequent values that help to shape the way they think about play. Our actions in listening to them expand our vision to include more views that belong to other children, families, and students.

Listening to Justine and Fiona underlines how little a teacher educator might know about the specifics of the contexts students bring to their statements about play in journals and papers, in-class discussions and activities, and multimedia and traditional presentations. While we create reading and written assignments, activities, and, one hopes, supportive classroom atmospheres to elicit students' experiences and opinions and even to share classroom power by enabling students to define and construct knowledge (Manke, 1997), teacher educators might not learn as much about students as one can through in-depth conversations that involve listening closely to students. Students may need to write and rewrite extensively about play in response to probes from their teacher educators and other students to look deeply at and reveal to others their views and the sources of their views. In addition to learning about prevalent theories about play, students can become theory-makers themselves. They can debate theories with reference to existing theories and to their own lives.

Listening for social justice in teacher education includes learning and unlearning, just as it does for students who are learning to teach children in socially just ways (Cochran-Smith, 2004). The students' talk about play challenged not only the cross-cultural play continuum and the distinctions made between traditional and modern views of play (Ariel, 2002) but also the ostensibly open and student-constructed ways in which many early childhood teacher educators usually teach about play. Bringing in play materials, discussing play theory, and even asking students to recall early experiences without delving deeply into them may not get to the heart of students' thinking about play. Considering the ways in which the British academic system served Justine well and the ways in which a more play-based system allowed Fiona to fall through cracks leads to thinking in a more complex manner about play, how we teach about it, and what it might mean for different students in our classes.

To make a more inclusive teacher education classroom for Justine, teacher educators have to recognize the way in which she lives in more than one world. The British academic system of her childhood is an undeniable part of her identity. Although in conversation about play she recalled making balls of mud and articulated in retrospect that she must have learned about scientific principles such as evaporation from that activity, her early memories of school success in an organized and established environment seem to be the most satisfying ones to her.

Justine's early childhood teacher educators can learn about the roles that play and schooling took in her early years from her and from other students with similar experiences. Teacher educators who look from Justine's perspective can credit its validity instead of dismissing it as very different from what they are teaching. If they get to know her well enough, they will find that she is also a dancer who brings a creative sensibility both to her teaching and to the way she thinks about her teaching. She is an active church member who demonstrates her competence weekly in Sunday school. Recognizing the multifaceted nature of what she brings to her teaching, her teachers can join her as she makes sense of it together with whatever she is reading and discussing in the course of becoming a teacher on her own terms.

Socially just teacher education does not deny the experience of children who are in danger or who live in poverty, nor should it deny those experiences when they belong to the future teachers in the classroom. Acknowledging Fiona's history as a player and as a learner, her teachers can join her in demystifying both learning and playing. They can admit to the play/learning dichotomy in her lived experience and, in so doing, add dimensions to their own understanding of play for children who struggle to learn. Teacher preparation can provide her with an opportunity to articulate and sort her beliefs as she did in the interviews.

Like the teachers in Lubeck's study, the students with whom we spoke in depth "have clear ideas about how children learn and about how they should behave" (1985, p. 133). Although Lubeck's teachers "convey their own life orientations and expectations to children by creating total environments that reinforce values that give their own lives meaning," the students with whom we spoke were in the process of learning what their experiences mean for the way they will teach. The learning environments they create in the future will, like those of Lubeck's teachers, be a means of reaching ends. In Lubeck's study,

> The Head Start teachers work closely together and reinforce collective values; the preschool teachers work alone with children much of the time and encourage values of individualism and self-expression.

What students will do as teachers remains to be seen, but teacher educators can participate as students sort out what that will be and can learn from students at the same time.

Lisa Delpit (1995) cautions that the dilemma is not in the debate, in this case, over the value of play in early childhood education

> but rather in communicating across cultures and in addressing the more fundamental issue of power, of whose voice gets to be heard in determining what is best for poor children and children of color. (p. 46)

As she goes on to say, the responsibility to initiate communication by careful listening belongs to the one with greater power—in this case, the teacher educator.

The teacher educators and teacher supervisors, such as child-care center directors, who can listen openly and flexibly to students' and teachers' thinking about play can help students and teachers clarify and integrate their thinking about play. Beyond that possibility, those teacher educators and supervisors may also arrive at more complex and nuanced ways of thinking about play themselves.

Note

My colleague, Georgenne G. Weisenfeld, and I conducted this research together thanks to a PSC-CUNY grant (No. 655770-34). I am grateful for our work together collecting and analyzing the data and for her comments on several drafts of this chapter.

References

Ariel, S. (2002). *Children's imaginative play: A visit to wonderland.* Westport, CT: Praeger.

BMCC Factbook (2003–2004). *City University of New York.* Retrieved on August 16, 2006, from http://www.bmcc.cuny.edu/publications/factbook/current.pdf.

Cochran-Smith, M. (2004). *Walking the road: Race, diversity, and social justice in teacher education.* New York: Teachers College Press.

Cook-Sather, A. (2002). Authorizing students' perspectives: Toward trust, dialogue, and change in education. *Educational Researcher, 31*(4), 3–14.

Cooper, C. R. (1999). Multiple selves, multiple worlds: Cultural perspectives on individuality and connectedness in adolescent development. In A. S. Masten (Ed.), *Cultural processes in child development: Vol. 29, Minnesota symposia on child psychology* (pp. 25–57). Mahwah, NJ: Lawrence Erlbaum.

Delpit, L. (1995). *Teaching other people's children: Cultural conflict in the classroom.* New York: New Press.

Dyson, A. H., & Genishi, C. (2005). *On the case: Approaches to language and literacy research.* New York: Teachers College Press.

Kieff, J. E., & Caspergue, R. M. (2000). *Playful teaching and learning: Integrating play into preschool and primary classrooms.* Boston: Allyn & Bacon.

Klein, M. D., & Chen, D. (2001). *Working with children from diverse backgrounds.* Albany, NY: Delmar.

Laden, B. V. (1999). Celebratory socialization of culturally diverse students through academic programs and support services. In K. M. Shaw, J. R. Valadez, & R. A. Rhoads (Eds.), *Community colleges as cultural texts: Qualitative explorations of organizational and student culture* (pp. 173–194). Albany: State University of New York Press.

Lancy, D. F. (2002). Cultural constraints on children's play. In J. L. Roopnarine (Ed.), *Conceptual, social-cognitive, and contextual issues in the fields of play* (pp. 53–62). Westport, CT: Ablex.

Lubeck, S. (1985). *Sandbox society: Early education in black and white America.* Philadelphia: Falmer Press.

Manke, M. P. (1997). *Classroom power relations: Understanding student-teacher interaction.* Mahwah, NJ: Lawrence Erlbaum.

Rhedding-Jones, J. (2003). Questioning play and work, early childhood, and pedagogy. In D. E. Lytle (Ed.), *Play and educational theory and practice* (pp. 243–254). Westport, CT: Praeger.

Roopnarine, J. L., & Johnson, J. E. (2001). Play and diverse cultures: Implications for early childhood education. *Early Education and Care, and Reconceptualizing Play, 11,* 295–319.

Schultz, K. (2003). *Listening: A framework for teaching across difference.* New York: Teachers College Press.

Seidman, I. (1998). *Interviewing as qualitative research: A guide for researchers in education and the social sciences* (2nd ed.). New York: Teachers College Press.

15

Envisioning and Supporting the Play of Preschoolers
What the Frame Does to the Picture

REBEKAH FASSLER AND DOROTHY LEVIN

As an early childhood teacher educator, I (Rebekah Fassler) encounter many graduate students in search of a research-based rationale for inclusion of play in their curriculum to present to parents of the preschoolers they teach. Dorothy Levin, the coauthor of this chapter, was one such student. She became a teacher of preschoolers of African American heritage with special needs in the December before her last semester in the graduate program. For her master's project in my course the following spring, Levin decided to design an investigation of her own classroom to pursue a rationale for play.

Policy and Its Impact on Play

Levin and many other students are responding to the impact of contemporary policy decisions on early childhood settings—policy decisions that challenge early childhood professionals to make explicit the benefits of play. Current mandates for school policy in many states and nationally are pushing play to the edges of early childhood curricula. Under the impetus of such federal initiatives as Early Reading First (No Child Left Behind Act of 2001, 2002), mandates for delivery of very specific academic knowledge through whole-group, direct teaching strategies have seeped down to the preschool level.

The transformation of kindergartens and preschools brought on by the emphasis on academics has penetrated the public consciousness, as evidenced by special feature stories in magazines such as *Newsweek* (Tyre, 2006) and *People* (Fields-Meyer, Duffy, & Kramer, 2005). *Newsweek* (Tyre, 2006) had as its lead feature at the beginning of the 2006–2007 school year an article describing how parents are showing increasing concern over their children's difficulty and often failure to negotiate successfully preschool and kindergarten environments in which academic curricula and testing regimens predominate.

The impetus for academic preschools assumes a future-directed orientation in which the preschool experience is evaluated not in terms of how it matches children's current developmental needs but as an anteroom, a preparatory experience for first grade. The rationale is to level the playing field by providing intense academic preparation for all preschoolers so they will be "ready" for first grade. The word *players*, then, has nothing to do with children generating their own play scenarios with friends in the moment but takes on the very adult meaning of *competitive players* in an ongoing selection process in the future for the best grades in the best schools and ultimately for the best jobs.

In this current atmosphere, the rationale for including play in center-based preschool environments cannot be taken for granted or remain implicit; play as a legitimate school activity has to compete with other more academic curricular demands that were not previously applied so pervasively to preschool education. It comes down to how much time there will be to devote to children's play, given other curricular demands. The answer too often is: not enough time for rich, meaningful play experiences to develop.

Dorothy Levin and Her Search

This chapter is about Levin's search for a rationale for her preschoolers' play in the classroom. When the story began, Levin, a European American, was in the last semester of her early childhood master's program as a career changer. She had returned to school after raising a family and had a young grandchild of her own. She had already been in four other classes with me as the professor. During those classes, she embraced field experiences with great enthusiasm at an urban day-care center that served a local community of African American families representing a range of educational and socioeconomic levels. There she developed her observing and recording skills, and also documented a mini-inquiry project with kindergarten children, using the Project Approach (Katz & Chard, 2000). The delight with which she described the center where she did her field experiences and ultimately obtained a job communicated itself to other students in her courses. Consequently, several asked to pursue field experiences in that same center.

Pivotal to Levin's search for a rationale was her envisioning of the children's play and its significance for their development. We first present an example of collaborative pretend play as the basis for discussing a skills-focused rationale for play in the preschool curriculum. We then discuss a second type of rationale for play in the preschool curriculum—one that is more focused on the importance of children's expression of personal meanings. With these as a foundation for further thought, Levin's research project is described from its inception, during which a skills-focused approach dominated her vision of her preschoolers' play, to a turning point in her thinking, when children's intentions became more salient. Levin's rethinking of her research data led her to see new possibilities in the children's play behaviors and to devise ways to support their individual accomplishments. Finally, in reflections after her research was completed and she had graduated from the program, we consider how Levin's options for supporting the children's play might have been different if she had framed their play with the approach of play as children's expression of personal meanings.

Play Skills Embedded in Collaborative Pretend Play

Here is an example of the kind of collaborative pretend play Levin hoped to see, along with definitions of the specific skills exemplified in the episode—skills that Levin read about as significant for children's future academic success:

> Nora and Carlos are busy playing "dog and owner" in the kitchen center of a local kindergarten. Carlos is on all fours, barking like a dog, while Nora chases him with a green plastic pot in her hand, calling "Here doggie, doggie." Carlos turns and looks at Nora with excitement. Nora asks, "Do you want some soda?" Carlos turns away, and Nora says, "What's the matter doggie, you sick? I know, I cook you some soup." She goes to the stove, pulls out a soup can from the cabinet underneath and says to herself, "I will cook my dog some vegetable soup." As she is stirring the soup, Carlos crawls over to her, starts to bark, and places one "paw" on the stovetop. Nora stops him by saying "Doggie, be nice; you may burn yourself." Carlos looks at Nora and runs under a chair to sleep. Nora walks over to the chair, bends down, and pats Carlos on the head. "You stay in your house and sleep." She then walks back to the stove, turns the knob and says, "Now all done, doggie will get better." Carlos crawls over like a dog, and pretends to jump up on Nora, who says, "Doggie, stop playing. Go outside, while I cook your soup." Carlos stands up and turns to Nora and says, "I am big now. I am not a dog." Nora still pretends he is a dog and says, "Go outside." Carlos sits at the table and says, "No, I am a person. I am not a dog anymore." Nora brings him his "food" at the table, and the two begin to "eat," sitting side by side. (Dinaro, 2000)

In this 5-minute play scenario, Nora and Carlos are engaged in spontaneous collaborative role-play that seems to flow effortlessly. Yet specific skills and knowledge underlie their interactions. As the scene unfolds, each player reveals and incorporates knowledge of spoken English and of a "script" or "underlying cognitive framework for an experience" (Lederer, 2002, p. 234) from real life. Script knowledge specifies the people, objects, activities, settings, and dialogue appropriate to a given context. Carlos acts on the knowledge that dogs move on all fours, bark rather than talk, sleep under things, are willing to be petted, and sometimes play by jumping on their owners. Nora plays a nurturing but busy adult, who defines what her pet needs, decides where and when her pet may be encouraged to play, and expects to have to protect her pet from danger. Although they are guided by the lifelike scripts to some extent, they have the power to bend reality as they wish, serving soda and soup to dogs, and improvising and sustaining their own particular coherent narrative.

Their play highlights several cognitive skills defined in a Piagetian framework (Piaget, 1962). Each of the children integrates many separate schemas into his or her play. For instance, Nora integrates a sequence of pretend cooking actions into the play. Both children decontextualize the chair and recontextualize it as a "dog house." They both also show an ability to decenter, to consider each other's point of view. Carlos soon realizes that as a dog, he will be subject to the whims of his pet owner, which apparently don't include taking him up on his rough-and-tumble play invitations. Nora, on her part, realizes that Carlos will not continue to play with her if he is consigned to a dog's life.

Both also exhibit the skill of metacommunication as they stage manage the progress of the scene. Metacommunication is defined as "language used to jointly create and negotiate pretend play definitions according to the 'rules of the game'" (Lederer, 2002, p. 234), sometimes from within the play frame, as when Nora addresses orders to her dog, and by stepping momentarily out of the play frame, as when Carlos announces he is no longer in the dog role.

The children's desire to collaborate is something an observer might just take for granted but for the fact that we see them negotiate Carlos's role change and notice how Nora becomes willing to accommodate him so as not to lose a play partner. They both know that if they can't negotiate their differences, pretend play will break down. In Lederer's framework, they are cognizant of the rules of pretend play—that pretense and collaboration must be maintained either by acceptance or negotiation of transformations (such as from dog to person) proposed by their play partners.

Rationales for Play in the Curriculum: Rebekah Fassler's Overview

The above focus on play skills characterizes one of two stances towards articulating a rationale for play in the preschool curriculum that stand out in my mind. The first stance raises generic skills-related questions. What are the cognitive, emotional, and social skills that define play at its best? What do these skills have in common with processes necessary for learning to read and write? In what ways is engagement in such play predictive of later academic success? The second stance looks at pretend play not primarily as a set of generic skills but as children's preferred medium for intensely personal, individual, and socially communicated expressions of how they make sense of their world (Paley, 2004).

The Skills-Focused Approach

Pellegrini and Galda (1993), in their review of research on the relation of play to later learning, present evidence to support that the oral language used in children's symbolic play "is characterized by the narrative structures that typify many school-based literacy events" (p. 168). They also make the point that children's skillful engagement in transformation of objects to represent other objects in symbolic play may be predictive of writing because from a Vygotskian perspective, preschoolers first experience writing/drawing as directly representing objects rather than words (see, e.g., Dyson, 1990). Pellegrini and Galda (1993) cite their own and other longitudinal studies to support the notion that children's "ability to 'go meta,'" that is, to use language to talk about language, is predictive of later reading ability. Some have extrapolated from this that children's metacommunication in collaborative pretend play, when they momentarily talk *about* their play in negotiating its terms, prepares children to talk about language itself. The Lederer (2002) article, which Levin adopted as a mainstay of her literature review, is an exemplar of this approach applied to children with language delays. The approach will be discussed in more detail in relation to Levin's research.

The Play-as-Expression-of-Personal-Meanings Approach

Paley (2004) represents the second approach, highlighting play as an expression of personal meanings, in her statement: "The more complex the thought, the greater is the child's need to view its meaning through play and find the characters and situations that bring ideas to life" (p. 57). Paley's books (1984, 1986, 1988, 1990, 2004) are replete with examples of how children capture ideas and reveal understandings in their play. Moreover, through her strategy of having children dictate their stories and then act them out with classmates, she is committed to the importance of helping to make the images and logic of the children's play fantasies visible to their peers so that they create a wider community of empathy and understanding in the classroom. If Nora and Carlos's collaborative play were looked at through this lens, their ongoing adaptation of their roles from both inside and outside the play frame would seem fueled by a desire to maintain an ongoing connection—to be a part of each other's story—through at least a partially shared vision of a pretend world.

Whereas the skills-focused approach borrows from cognitive science in talking much about children learning "scripts for play" from real-life experience (e.g., how a dog or pet owner might behave), the play-as-personal-expression approach borrows more from a psychoanalytic view of play, stressing the capacity to bend reality (e.g., how Nora finds a way to define the dog and pet owner play so that she may play the busy but nurturing adult). Paley (2004) describes it this way: "The whole point of this play seems to be the invention of stories about what could possibly happen" (p. 61). The examples of children's fantasy play in Paley's books are also usually characterized by a fluency of children's language in expressing their ideas in play.

> In dramatic play, language becomes more vivid and spontaneous, enabling young children to connect, with greater fluency and curiosity, the words and phrases they know to new ideas. (Paley, 2004, p. 73)

Dorothy Levin's Research Question

When Levin submitted her research question, she included an explicit statement of her desire to find a rationale for including play in her curriculum. Both the question and her accompanying note to me explaining its purpose reflected a "future" orientation.

> What types of actions, e.g., behaviors, scripts, role playing, conversations occur in the Dramatic Play area when young children are able to develop their play spontaneously; and, how might these actions influence future learning? (Levin's Research Question—Draft 4, third week of Spring Semester, 2005)

> My purpose in wanting to study this area was first piqued in your "Play" class when I learned that there are many people who do not think that play is an important learning component of the child's growth. I wondered how I might be able to answer the questions of parents who would question why the children aren't doing "dittos" or something similar. With better insight into how play supports, fosters and you might say even "launches" *future* [italics added] learning, I will be able to provide parents with guidance. … Additionally, I will gain a better understanding myself so that I can also create "room to play."

At the time, my response to Levin's question and statement addressed this future orientation only in terms of the manageability of her question for a one-semester mini-research project, not as a philosophical or policy issue. I suggested that Levin focus on

> interactions in dramatic play as a variety of kinds of learning going on right now. … You yourself are not going to be able to show the actual influence on future learning in this research project.

For the purposes of her research, links between play and future learning would remain more of "a theoretical question" that she would discuss in her literature review. I did not reflect at that time on how acceptance of this future orientation might privilege articles featuring a skills-focused orientation while ignoring play as personal expression of intentions. Some articles that Levin herself found for her literature review (Bergen, 2002; Jones, 2003; Musthafa, 2001), and an additional reference (Lederer, 2002) that I recommended, predominantly reflected the same future orientation and emphasis on play skills.

Lederer's Skills-Based Approach to Play

The Lederer (2002) article became a centerpiece of Levin's literature review. Levin and I both felt that it had special relevance to her field investigation because it featured play as a recommended "treatment" for young children diagnosed as needing language intervention. All 11 preschoolers in Levin's class had been referred to the program through school district Community Special Education teams. All were receiving pullout services for speech and language once or twice a week, and most of the children were characterized as having some mild cognitive delays and some weak communicative skills. A few were also receiving counseling services and/or occupational therapy. All except one had been in this center-based program for 18 months.

Lederer, a speech pathologist, set out to provide a rationale and a method for "integrating collaborative pretend play goals into a general language intervention" (2002, p. 247) program. Lederer's explanation of the rationale falls into the generic skills-related stance described earlier in this chapter. She advanced the argument that children who have specific language impairment in the preschool years often go on to experience difficulty in the future. Therefore, intervention should address not only the specific impairment in the short term but should also provide a foundation for later language-based social and academic skill development. She then argued, citing Pellegrini and Galda (1993), that development of specific skills needed for collaborative pretend play provided several links to preschoolers' later academic and social success. Lederer (2002) defined three skills necessary for collaborative pretend play as "shared script knowledge, metacommunication skills, and knowledge of the rules" (p. 234) of pretend play—all of which were exemplified in Nora and Carlos's play scenario discussed previously. Lederer suggested observation protocols for evaluating children's skill levels in these areas and also ways of supporting the development of missing skills.

Applying the Rationales for Play to Children with Special Needs

Lederer and others who support "play-training" (Goldstein, Wickstrom, Hoyson, Jamieson, & Odom, 1988; Smilansky, 1968) see play through the prism of skills. The thrust of the approach is to intervene in the children's play. If only the children with special needs developed the necessary skills, they would engage in the collaborative pretend play that is predictive of later school success. The focus is on fostering greater familiarity with the details of scripts from real life that will give the child with special needs a common vision to be played out with other children. The play training does not highlight the question of what the children themselves individually think about, imagine, or wish for.

In contrast, what the children think, imagine, wish for, and intend is central to Paley's approach to their play. The thrust of her approach is to find ways to understand and connect the fantasy play of the child with special needs to that of other children. Her discussions of children with special needs (Paley, 1990, 2004) usually feature one child whose behavior is very different from that of typically developing classmates. She illustrates how she uses "storying" to forge connections between the very individual imaginings of the "different" child and the rest of the community of children. In doing so, she carefully observes and "narratizes" the play behaviors, intentions, and interests of the different child so that his or her story may be linked to those of others. For example, Paley (2004) carefully observes Simon, labeled autistic, as he periodically stops circulating the room to manipulate animals on a tray. When all the children have finished acting out the stories they dictated to Paley, Simon approaches the tape-bound area of the stage with his tray, and Paley expands the oral text "Walk, walk, walk" that he recites to his animals. The next day, Simon brings his tray over while stories are being enacted, and all the children join in reciting his text as he "walks" each animal over the hill. This exemplifies Paley's use of fantasy play as a way of helping children with special needs connect to others through their own individual visions.

Where Do Dorothy Levin's Preschoolers Fit In? Levin's Research Project

These two contrasting ways of envisioning and supporting children with special needs in relation to play provided the context for rethinking the conduct, results, and implications of Levin's research project. During the research project, Levin used her understanding of the skills-focused framework to structure her observations and her initial data analysis. However, a turning point in her research project led her to look at what her children were doing from another perspective. It was this shift that especially drew my attention and led to questions that lingered long after the research course was over. How might selection of the skills-focused approach have predisposed Levin to see some possibilities in her children's play and not others? What was the turning point in her research and how did it change Levin's perspective? In the next sections of this chapter, these questions will be addressed through a description and discussion of Levin's mini-project.

Dorothy Levin as Student and Teacher

In the December preceding her last semester in graduate school, Levin was enrolled in the research course and was offered a job as a head teacher at the center where she had been observing. Her full-day prekindergarten program serving children with special needs was designed for a student-teacher ratio of 12:1:2 (12 children, one teacher, one assistant teacher, and one paraprofessional). Levin also began to take additional special education courses at that time, with a plan to apply for an additional certification in early childhood special education.

Through her assignments in my previous classes, I had become familiar with some of Levin's qualities in relation to young children. She had an innate respect for young children and conveyed to them that she valued what they might have to contribute to a setting. The bulk of observation assignments in the course on observation were running records and anecdotal records. In her record of child observations, she was careful to write down direct quotes of children's language. During her integrated curriculum project, she would take pictures of individual children and mount them carefully with their quotes and this would be displayed in her classroom.

After she finished my research course and graduated from the program, I visited her preschool classroom and found that she took a playful but persistent approach in interacting with individual children and encouraging them to participate actively and verbally in classroom activities. She exuded an optimistic view of and excitement about young children's potential for growth and development. In her research question, Levin referred to "children," not to "children with special needs." It has always been my impression that this reflected Levin's natural inclination to see them as individuals with potential, not designated collectively by their clinically defined "deficits." Nonetheless, they were assigned to her class based on what they could not do.

Designing Her Research

Levin proceeded to read up on the skills embedded in children's play that were considered of value for their future academic learning (Bergen, 2002; Pellegrini & Galda, 1993; Jones, 2003; Musthafa, 2001). Taking her cue from the Lederer (2002) article, she focused particularly on skills that revolved around children's engagement in collaborative pretend play. Levin's research plan was to conduct several observations of two or three children during free-choice time in the dramatic play or block area over a 4-week period. Levin felt that if she could document that the children's engagement in collaborative pretend play involved the skills she had read about, this would help her to defend her decision to keep play as an important part of her curriculum. During the semester, she periodically submitted and received feedback on a research design, a literature review, a mini-field investigation with data collection and data analysis, and ultimately, a cohesive research paper on her chosen topic.

Dorothy Levin in Search of Collaborative Pretend Play

Levin liked the rather linear plan she had adopted, but the line from Levin's plan to its implementation was, while always interesting, neither straight nor predictable. Armed with concepts from her readings, Levin felt prepared to observe her preschoolers at play. The nine boys and two girls ranged in age from 4.0 to 5.1 when the research began, and she collected data on eight of them—seven boys and one girl. She planned to use a combination of field notes and audiotaping for her data collection. As it turned out, she used audiotape during the first four of six observations. Observations 1, 2, and 4 centered on miniature environments with action figures: a schoolhouse, a farm, and a space station. Observation 3 took place in the dramatic play center, which had a range of dress-up clothes representing many community workers, but was mainly set up as a kitchen. For observations 5 and 6, which took place in the block area, Levin relied solely on field notes.

Ordinarily, in the day-to-day functioning of the classroom, Levin did not assign children to the different centers but rather allowed them to select the centers of their choice. She deviated from that practice for this research, initially selecting two or three children who were functioning on a higher level verbally than the others, with the assumption that she would see them engage spontaneously in collaborative pretend play. However, she found that putting the selected children together to play did not result in their engaging in collaborative pretend play. She wrote in her field journal:

"Oh my!" I thought after my first observation on 2/18. It was very different to be the teacher/observer from my former role as a "participating observer." Sally told me she didn't want to play in the Kitchen; then she didn't want to play with Kenyatta. When I assigned Sally and Kenyatta to play in the School House Center, I thought they would know how to interact. I was so taken aback when they did not engage in collaborative play!

Levin noted that they only "played parallel." (Levin was using Parten's [1932] categorization of "parallel play" as a situation in which a child may play near other children and even with the same materials, but doesn't try to influence or modify the activity of children near him.) Thinking that perhaps this was because Sally had difficulty engaging in consistently appropriate behavior with her peers, as indicated in her Individualized Education Plan (IEP), Levin paired Kenyatta with another peer, Christian, for the second observation.

For this observation, Levin offered Kenyatta and Christian the miniature schoolhouse when they both indicated no interest in playing in the kitchen center. In reviewing Levin's notes, it was not surprising to me that, like Sally and Kenyatta in the first observation, Kenyatta and Christian spent much of their time exploring the different parts of the schoolhouse, which was a new toy in the classroom. Kenyatta then left the area after the first 10 minutes of play.

Levin reintroduced Sally for her third observation, and made clear how in this case, too, the pairing of Sally with a play partner did not emerge naturally. Here is how she described the persuasion she had to use to convince Sally (aged 5.2) and Karl (aged 4.10) to play together in the kitchen area.

At first Sally said she didn't want to play in the Kitchen; then she said she wanted to play alone. I explained to her that I was doing a special activity today and I wanted to see two children playing. I also recalled for her that 2 weeks ago she and Karl dressed up as the Mom and Dad during Center Time. Her eyes brightened as she recalled that time. I told her that she and Karl could use whatever they wanted from the Kitchen Center and that I wanted to watch as they played and that I was going to write a story about their play. They both agreed.

Levin volunteered to share the data from this third observation in the research class for one of our discussions about analyzing qualitative data.

While research students were still conducting observations, they would volunteer to share in class brief sections of typed-up field notes and their first attempts at analysis. This often resulted in group brainstorming and feedback to the student researcher from me and the other class members. Since Levin identified the group brainstorming around this observation as the major turning point in her research, it will be discussed in detail here.

Interpreting Sally and Karl's Play in the Research Class

For the presentation in research class, Levin had organized the record of Sally and Karl's play as a transcript with the two players as the actors. In her first tentative attempts to code her notes, Levin decided to see if she could categorize parts of her field notes by the elements of her research question and apply those elements as codes in a top-down fashion. The coding categories from her question were: Behaviors [B]—behaviors the child displays that may demonstrate ability to understand the play setting; Scripts [S]—talking or using props consistent with the play script; Role-playing [R]; Props [P]—use of props consistent with the perceived script/setting; and Conversations [C]—with play partner, doll, other object, or teacher. She added a separate code, Teacher [T], for any interaction between student and teacher. As is shown in the transcript below, the coding categories were applied to individual actors' turns, and there was no attempt at that point to use the coding to make explicit how children's individual turns related to the whole play event, or to relate acts/utterances of one child to those of the other. This lack of explicit connection between individual turns in the coding was reflected in Levin's comment while distributing copies of the data sample for group brainstorming. She stated that the children were only playing parallel, and how that was worrisome to her.

Levin's focus seemed to be on specific skills related to enacting play scripts and taking on roles. In my view, this seemed a very mechanical way to look at the data. I suggested another way to consider the material, because my own view of play was less mechanical and more personal. To my mind, the children's play was not about performance of a collection of skills but about the enactment of children's intentions. I suggested that the class look at what each child said and did in the larger framework of the whole play time event described. I also suggested that we not be boxed in by the terms parallel or collaborative play but that we look at each child's speech and actions in the context of the other child's speech and actions: Do the play actions in any way seem to reflect each child's intentions? Is there any evidence that the children are aware of and responding to each other's play? This was a less top-down and more inductive way of analyzing the data because it incorporated an awareness of the importance of the children's perspectives. With all that in mind, the class started to examine the coded transcript:

1 *Karl:*   Immediately goes over to the refrigerator and takes out the container of vegetables. [P]

2 *Sally:*   Goes to the chest that contains the dress-up clothes. [P]

3 *Karl:*   Walks over to the clothes chest when he sees Sally dressing. He takes out a jacket and tie and tries on two hats before he selects one. He then goes back to the vegetable container, which is on the floor in front of the refrigerator. [P]

4 *Sally:*   Is sitting on the floor putting on a dress. She looks over at Karl and says, "No food, only the dress up." She continues dressing, picks out a black pocket book and a small green frog and says (to no one specifically), "This is the baby." [P, C, R]

5 *Sally:*   "Baby," as she is putting the spoon to the baby's mouth. [S]

6 *Karl:*   Is still taking items out of the refrigerator and the stove. [S]

7 *Sally:*   Puts the baby on the floor and walks over to where Karl is sitting on the floor. "NO," she shouts, "no food, only dress up." [S, C]

8 *Karl:*   Looks up at her and continues placing the vegetables, one at a time, onto the rug. "It's a picnic, it's a picnic," as he lays many vegetable pieces onto the rug. [P]

9 *Sally:*   "I don't know where the picnic is?" [S, R, C]

10 *Karl:*   Continues putting the vegetables onto the rug, saying, "It is a picnic." [C, S, P]

11 *Sally:*   Retrieves the frog and places it next to her. She is now sitting next to Karl and she is also taking the vegetables and placing them on the rug. "What is that?" (pointing to a cucumber). Karl does not respond.

12 *Karl:*   Has finished removing all the vegetables and has also placed some cups and plates onto the rug. He says, "God is great, God is good. Let us thank him for our lunch." (This is our lunch prayer.) [S, C]

13 *Sally:*   Does not participate in prayer with him, but sits and moves the vegetables and plates to different locations on the rug. [C, S, P]

During the brainstorming, from the moment we stopped focusing on what the children were not doing—full-blown collaborative dramatic play—and began paying more attention to what they actually *were* doing, the children's voices and actions took central stage. Although most of the graduate students were in the childhood and adolescent programs, not in early childhood, everyone got swept up in an emerging vision of Sally and Karl as powerful *intentional* beings. All agreed that in Turns 1 through 7, Sally and Karl were displaying separate intentions. Sally was focusing on dress-up and on a nurturing role with the frog-as-baby. Karl made an initial choice of food handling. All agreed that both Sally and Karl showed signs of awareness of each other's activities—Karl by momentarily starting to dress up, and Sally by twice trying to ban food handling from the play agenda (Turns 4 & 7).

Class members suggested that Karl's allusion to a picnic was an announcement of the script that he had in mind for his play. They also commented that despite Sally's initial attempts to keep the focus on dress-up, not food, she was aware of Karl's picnic scenario, and her actions were influenced by it. This was particularly evidenced by her asking "I don't know where the picnic is?" and then her moving herself and her "baby" to sit down next to Karl on the rug. She then began to busy herself with food and utensils.

The group also agreed that although Sally joined Karl on the rug at the "picnic," she continued to be rather bossy. Common elements in the continuation of Levin's transcript (not displayed here) show that Sally engaged in a repeated pattern of trying to impose her will on Karl within the picnic scenario. Sometimes she showed this by issuing a challenge. For example, when she had set up plates and cups on the rug, she told Karl, "You're not going to take the cups." At another point, she tried to impose her will by physically placing a cap on his head. After three such attempts, he finally acquiesced and put on a baseball cap. When he dumped the eating utensils on the rug, she grabbed them and insisted, "One at a time!" Karl responded with an objection, "But how we gonna eat?!"

Class members pointed out Sally's role enactment of the nurturing mother with her frog baby off and on during the play event. They also commented on Karl's remaining focused almost throughout on his original interest in the food and kitchen utensils.

A Turning Point for Dorothy Levin: Reanalyzing the Children's Play

Looking at the transcript more inductively—with a focus on noticing what the children were intending in their play—was an eye-opener for Levin. She commented in her paper,

> The turning point for me was when my observation notes were discussed in class. I was able to step back and re-look at my field notes based on my classmates' comments. I saw many skills that the children were exhibiting that I hadn't seen before because I was so obsessed with the fact that they were not involved in collaborative play. ... I now re-reviewed my field notes with a different view of what the children were doing and saying.

In taking a fresh look at her data, Levin was also motivated to look more closely at some of her literature review articles to see if there were concepts that were a better fit for her children's developmental levels. She decided that there were examples in her data of children using the three Piagetian skills she had read about that didn't depend on collaborative pretend play: decontextualization, decentration, and integration. In addition, the brainstorming session involving Levin's observation of Sally and Karl led to taking a second look at her observations involving other children.

In her reanalysis, Levin took note of Sally's ability to decontextualize and recontextualize the toy frog as her "baby" to be gently rocked and patiently fed. One of the skills Levin noticed Karl exhibiting was his ability to integrate many actions into the sequence of his picnic play script despite Sally's frequent attempts to control his actions. Levin wrote in her paper that despite Sally's efforts to redirect his picnic play, "Karl persevered, placing condiments, utensils, plates onto the rug, and saying the prayer before eating."

In a postgraduation interview, Levin put Karl's behavior during this observation into the broader context of the progress he had made since December. She told me that Karl had been "kind of like a wallflower, almost afraid in certain situations." He was becoming more verbal at circle time, during read alouds, and at the table. He was becoming "his own person." He was just beginning to be comfortable expressing himself.

Levin also put Sally's bossy behavior in a broader context. Sally was receiving counseling twice a week for 30-minute sessions for her socialization and aggressive behavior. Earlier in the year, she would often get into physical fights.

> At the time of current observations, her aggressiveness has decreased substantially, although she does not share well and requires prompts to respond appropriately in social situations.

Rethinking after the Research Project

Levin ended her research paper with a statement of some of the implications for her future support of children's play in her classroom. Levin wrote that as a result of her mini-study, she felt that she knew better how to intervene to support her children's play. She cited Musthafa (2001) to introduce ideas for support. Previously she had taken literally the adage "Let everything come from the children." Any involvement in the children's play would make it her play, not their play. Now she felt that she could participate as a "demonstration," do a "think-aloud," or model something to help children expand their own play. Her main example was to help them expand their play scripts by modeling a role and by providing real-life experiences that would give them wider shared-script knowledge. This was very much in the spirit of the Lederer article.

A second idea Levin presented for support of play was that of fostering "engagement" (Musthafa, 2001), based on the assumption that children become engaged in their play when they are doing things they like and want to do. Engagement could be supported by providing children with choices. The focus on what children like and want to do seems more in harmony with Paley's views. This idea was not expanded in Levin's mini-project but has become more salient in postproject reflection.

In the period of postproject reflection, it has become clearer to me that the skills-focused approach represented not only a contrasting theoretical framework to the personal-meaning-focused approach to play but actually a contrasting "discourse." I use the term "discourse" here to mean a

> socially accepted association among ways of using language, of thinking, and of acting that can be used to identify oneself as a member of a socially meaningful group or "social network." (Gee, 1991, p. 3)

Any discourse highlights or privileges certain concepts, viewpoints, and values and tends to marginalize other viewpoints and values. Let us consider the case of Sally. What if instead of looking at her through the lens of the clinical language of the IEP, we were to focus on what intrigued her and what she liked to do? What implications might that have for support of her as a "player"?

Discourses That Mask or Reveal Interests

Just what were Sally's interests, and how would we know what they were from clinical language that does not focus on her unique perspective? In Levin's paper, she described her preschoolers in the language of IEPs, a part of a discourse routinely associated with students with special needs and with play as an "intervention." Terms and phrases such as *delays in cognition, communication, and socialization skills,* and *difficulty adhering to limit setting* were used to describe Sally and her classmates. These terms do provide important information about her limitations and about her progress in benefiting from special services. However, this language of deficits and behavior difficulties doesn't convey anything about what Sally likes to do and about how she envisions herself.

During our collaboration on this chapter, I asked Levin to provide a nonclinical recollection of Sally. It opened up different avenues for thinking about how to support her play:

> Sally is the "princess" of our class! At least, this is how she carries herself. She is always fussing with her hair and showing off her new hairclips, looking in the mirror. In her school bag, she brings her "makeup" which consists of real lip gloss and "make believe" cosmetic items that little girls play with, and various Cinderella or other princess books and figures. Her drawings often have representation of princesses or family members with herself in the middle. She is able to tell a story from her pictures and has a rich imagination using her "princess" experiences! Of all my students, Sally was the most likely to share a story with a classmate, teacher or visitor. Sally loved being center-stage all day long, if you let her. Most of her stories followed her "princess" experiences. Outdoors, Sally played on the "climbing apparatus" using it as her princess castle, which really is consistent with her sense of "princess-ship."

In this description, Levin adopts language more in tune with Paley's discourse of personal meanings and intentions. Having read this description of Sally, I can't help but wonder how she as a storyteller would respond to having her stories written down by a teacher to be acted out within the group. In Paley's use of a storytelling method, the child whose story it is gets to pick who acts it out and how it's acted out. That kind of control and the experience of being legitimately "on stage" might be very appealing to Sally. It is a context for fantasy play where it might become easy to add other people to her stories and perhaps make room for them in her play. Such a venue might provide a way to have her story connect to other children, where she could legitimately be in control, just as other children would have their own turn.

The discourse associated with IEPs and specific special needs labels resonates far beyond any individual classroom, as it is aligned with powerful decisions in a hierarchical system for providing services that structure children's options from afar. In the next section, I consider how decisions for providing services structure access to play partners, thereby affecting Levin's options for supporting Sally's play.

Barriers to Accessing Play Partners Whose Ideas Might Intrigue Sally

"Re-reviewing"—as Levin put it—Sally's actions in the kitchen area with Karl, it seems to me quite plausible that Sally relinquished her position on "no food, only dress-up" because she was genuinely intrigued with the idea of playing "picnic." Yet her prime way of initiating interaction with Karl was to boss him around, to try to limit his access to materials, and to set the parameters for how the picnic would be enacted. Karl, for his part, was not actively seeking her collaboration but spent his time trying to maintain his play theme.

The fact that Sally was one of the oldest children in a class where all were somewhat language-delayed made it rather unlikely that she would have an opportunity to interact with peers who easily expressed play ideas and actively sought her collaboration. Might she be more often intrigued if exposed to the play of those who were more fluent and fluid in developing play ideas in interesting ways and who modeled pleasure in active attempts to collaborate? At one point, Sally was reported by Levin to have assigned roles to different peers in the class in terms of how they should dress up, and they enjoyed her leadership. She brought more richness of ideas to their play. In her classroom of children with special needs, Sally had little access to children—and especially girls—who expressed a desire to collaborate and whose richly expressed play interests struck a common chord with her own and looked intriguing and pleasurable. Might access to such play partners, available in more inclusive classrooms, perhaps trump her need to dominate, at least at some times, and tempt her to be more collaborative in play?

Drawing on Multiple Discourses to Support Play and the Expression of Intentions

One of the strengths that Levin brings to her teaching is her intuitive faith that her students with special needs have the potential to develop and learn. But how such faith leads a teacher in efforts to support learning and development depends very much on the types of discourses selected deliberately or intuitively to guide practice.

As can be seen from the example of Sally, different ways of envisioning children's play and different discourses used to describe and think about children's play have real implications for the kinds of teaching practice enacted to support children's developing capacities. If teachers develop a meta-awareness of the language, values, and practices that flow from a discourse of skills-based play interventions and, alternately, from a discourse of play as personal intention and connection, these need not function as competing discourses in which adoption of one narrows the options for support of play that the other would suggest.

Trying to apply a future-oriented skills-focused rationale for play to her own classroom practice, Levin framed her observation of her preschoolers with a set of idealized play skills that were seen as predictors for later academic success. But as Levin began to rethink her data analysis, she realized that a focus on idealized skills led too easily to a deficit mind-set, highlighting predominantly what her preschoolers could not do. She also concluded, citing Casby (1997), that mild language and cognitive delays could make it more difficult for her preschoolers to use verbal fluency to make their intentions visible in their play. Yet that did not necessarily mean that they did not have intentions and that they were not imagining play themes.

Framing her analysis more in terms of the children's own intentions, Levin felt empowered to support individual children in relation to play skills they were already beginning to exhibit. Acknowledging the discourse of play-as-expression-of-personal-meanings also made room for Levin to consider play skills not as ends in themselves but as tools for children to make sense of their world. A skills-focused discourse had made it harder to recognize and value the children's attempts to find their own voices for exploring actual and possible worlds of events and people. Levin wrote in a postresearch reflection that she did see her preschoolers, such as Sally and Karl, trying to sustain and develop their own play scripts as expression of their views of themselves and their world.

Looking to the Future

Levin's engagement in recollection of what was unique about each preschooler constituted what Carini (2000) has termed "attending to children with care." The goal of such recollections of children is "to be more sensitively attuned to who they are and are becoming, so that, recognizing them as persons, we can assist and support their learning better" (p. 57). This deliberate recognition of children as persons is often missing from classrooms of preschoolers with special needs, where a skills-based focus has long been the dominant discourse. With the advent of such initiatives as Early Reading First, involving prescriptive mandates for specific academic preschool curriculum and long time periods of direct teaching, a skills-based focus could become the dominant discourse in virtually all preschool classrooms.

Such a discourse of skills-based interventions may lead one too easily to forget that skills included in a curriculum are not ends unto themselves but a means for students to develop a capacity to learn about and interpret the world and to relate to one another. For example, in the language of learning standards, literacy skills are expressed in terms of purposes beyond mechanics: Students will learn to read, write, listen, and speak "for information and understanding," "for literary response as expression," for "critical analysis and evaluation," and "for social interaction" (University of the State of New York, 1996). The discourse of personal meanings, as exemplified in Paley's writings, frames children's play skills with intentions of sense making and personal connection that are congruent with these purposes of more academic literacy learning.

A skills-focused approach exclusively applied in preschools would present a much narrower range of opportunities to support children's development by leaving play beyond the frame altogether, thus marginalizing a medium through which young children are already beginning to make sense of the world and their place in it. As Paley (2004) has expressed it, such programs leave no room for wondering who the children are as unique individuals, but instead decide quickly what should be done to fix them. We have discussed how the dominance of an exclusively skills-focused discourse already threatens the pursuit of social equity in settings for children with special needs. The extension of this discourse and its policies to all early childhood settings puts us in danger of framing our vision of the majority of young children exclusively in terms of what they cannot do.

In such a climate, making explicit the implications of different rationales for including play in the preschool curriculum takes on added significance. Teachers who, like Levin, continue to explore the different discourses that either hide or reveal diverse ways for supporting the development of a broad range of children may make a much needed contribution to the pursuit of social equity in early childhood educational settings.

References

Bergen, D. (2002). The role of pretend play in children's cognitive development. *Early Childhood Research and Practice, 4*(1), 27–41.

Carini, P. (2000). A letter to parents and teachers on some ways of looking at and reflecting on children. In M. Himley and P. F. Carini (Eds.), *From another angle: Children's strengths and school standards* (pp. 56–64). New York: Teachers College Press.

Casby, M. W. (1997). Symbolic play of children with language impairment: A critical review. *Journal of Speech, Language, and Hearing Research, 40*(3), 468–479.

Dinaro, D. (2000). *A running record of dramatic play.* Unpublished manuscript, St. John's University.

Dyson, A. H. (1990). Research in review. Symbol makers, symbol weavers: How children link play, pictures, and print. *Young Children, 45*(2), 50–57.

Fields-Meyer, T., Duffy, T., & Kramer, L. (2005, December 5). Bounced from preschool. *People, 64*(23) 119–120.

Gee, J. P. (1991). What is literacy? In C. Mitchell & K. Weiler (Eds.), *Rewriting literacy: Culture and the discourse of the other* (pp. 3–11). Westport, CT: Bergin & Garvey.

Goldstein, H., Wickstrom, S., Hoyson, M., Jamieson, B., & Odom, S. L. (1988). Effects of sociodramatic script training on social and communicative interaction. *Education and Treatment of Children, 11*(2), 97–117.

Jones, E. (2003). Playing to get smart. *Young Children, 58*(3), 32–36.

Katz, L. G., & Chard, S. C. (2000). *Engaging children's minds: The project approach* (2nd ed.). Stamford, CT: Ablex.

Lederer, S. H. (2002). Collaborative pretend play: from theory to therapy. *Child Language Teaching and Therapy, 18*(3), 233–255.

Musthafa, B. (2001). *Sociodramatic play and literacy development: Instructional perspective.* (ERIC Document Reproduction Service No. ED462138)

No Child Left Behind Act of 2001 (Pub. L. 107–110), 115 Stat. 1425 (2002).

Paley, V. G. (1984). *Boys & girls: Superheroes in the doll corner.* Chicago: University of Chicago Press.

Paley, V. G. (1986). *Mollie is three: Growing up in school.* Chicago: University of Chicago Press.

Paley, V. G. (1988). *Bad guys don't have birthdays: Fantasy play at four.* Chicago: University of Chicago Press.

Paley, V. G. (1990). *The boy who would be a helicopter: The uses of storytelling in the classroom.* Cambridge, MA: Harvard University Press.

Paley, V. G. (2004). *A child's work: The importance of fantasy play.* Chicago: University of Chicago Press.

Parten, M. B. (1932). Social participation among pre-school children. *Journal of Abnormal and Social Psychology, 27,* 243–269.

Pellegrini, A. D., & Galda, L. (1993). Ten years after: A reexamination of symbolic play and literacy research. *Reading Research Quarterly, 28*(2), 163–175.

Piaget, J. (1962). *Play, dreams and imitation in childhood.* New York: Norton.

Smilansky. S. (1968). *The effects of sociodramatic play on disadvantaged preschool children.* New York: Wiley.

Tyre, P. (2006, September 11). The new first grade: Too much too soon? *Newsweek, 148* (11), 34–44.

University of the State of New York. (1996). *Learning standards for English Language Arts* (Rev. ed.). Albany: New York State Department of Education.

16

Going beyond Our Own Worlds
A First Step in Envisioning Equitable Practice

**SUSI LONG, CLAVIS ANDERSON, MELANIE
CLARK, AND BECKY MCCRAW**

I'm thinking about the first time you suggested that we go beyond the
school's walls to get to know children better. I thought, "Yeah, right!
How could that ever work? Why would we need to do that anyway?" I
think the real reason I reacted that way was that the idea put me in an
uncomfortable place—the unknown. Fear, plain and simple. Fear of the
unexplored, fear of finding the bigot inside of me that I tried so hard
to ignore and deny all these years—the part of me that says, "I'm okay
and if you are not like me then you're not okay." By embracing difference, it's like saying that there is no one way to be right or normal and
that's something a lot of people have never really thought about before.
Before this, I really thought I held no biases and that I was quite forward
thinking and open to celebrating diversity but, as I sat down to write my
assumptions about a child and his family, I realized that I might not be
as culturally sensitive as I believed myself to be.

Over a 3-year-period, the authors of this chapter were involved in a range of
experiences through which we moved outside our cultural comfort zones to
learn in new ways, and to view children, their families, and members of their
communities as our most important teachers. Inspired by Moll's (González,
Moll, & Amanti, 2005) work with educators who identified literacies and
funds of knowledge in homes often considered to be illiterate or lacking in
knowledge, and by research that honors language and literacies in homes
and communities (Haight, 2001; Heath, 1983; Taylor, 1988; Valdés, 1996), we
ventured into worlds beyond our own. Starting from the premise that *normal*
in schools is typically defined in white, middle-class, Christian, heterosexual,
English-speaking ways, our experiences allowed us to confront biases and
consider the effect of such narrow definitions on children who find themselves
outside as well as inside that norm. As coauthor Becky McCraw describes in
this chapter's opening quote, it was a difficult yet essential endeavor through
which we ultimately came to see that going beyond our own worlds is a first
step in reenvisioning equitable practice—rethinking through doing.

We are all teachers. Clavis Anderson is a regional literacy coach with the South Carolina Reading Initiative (Donnelly et al., 2004). She works with literacy coaches across the state supporting their work with classroom teachers. Melanie Clark and Becky McCraw are school-based literacy coaches who work with study groups of teachers after school and spend their days teaching and learning in classrooms. Clavis, Becky, and Melanie are a part of a cohort of coaches who come together in Columbia, South Carolina for 2 days each month to continue their own course work in language and literacy education. Their cohort recently just completed its fifth year of study. Susi is one of the university faculty members who facilitated their graduate work. The stories described here are drawn from experiences within and beyond those courses. Moving outside the familiarity of our own lives, we discussed professional literature that describes sociocultural perspectives and the marginalization of children and families in schools and society; shared personally significant music, artifacts, and family stories; and ultimately ventured into homes and communities. Although we separate these experiences to write about them, it is their interwoven nature that allows us to reflect deeply as we write. That is the message we hope to convey. We have come to believe that there is no one engagement, activity, or event that provides the answer to envisioning equitable practice. Learning to value difference and considering possible implications for classrooms requires ongoing opportunities for examining ourselves and the world around us.

In the process of our journey, we found that opportunities to read, experience, and reflect held potential for moving beyond narrow assumptions, but they also brought new complexities to learning about teaching. To better understand others, we had to reach deeper, sometimes painful understandings about ourselves. We didn't always walk away from our conversations and engagements with a song in our hearts and a skip in our steps. We engaged, disengaged, talked, stopped talking, experienced, contemplated, shared, worried, and wondered. Frustration and guilt emerged, tempers flared, friendships came into question. We sometimes wondered if our relationships with one another would ever be the same as we went to hard places and struggled to move beyond them. Over time, however, some fears began to dissolve, stereotypes began to fall away, and new appreciations for knowledge and ways of knowing in children's lives came to life. While we, in no way, intend to communicate that we moved consistently in a positive direction or that our journey is by any means complete, we learned and we continue to learn.

Why Share Our Stories?

The field of education has recognized for years the need to reach beyond rhetoric to reenvision practices that move us toward social justice (Ayers, Hunt, & Quinn, 1998; Edelsky, 1999). Over and over, we read about the importance of going beyond piñata versions of multiculturalism or a "foods and festivals" approach to understanding difference (Ladson-Billings, 1994,

p. 131). University researchers receive accolades for their work in the fields of critical theory, social justice, and culturally relevant pedagogy, but we still have a long way to go as we consider what this means day to day in classrooms. We wonder if one reason that there seems to be little change in schools is that the translation of complex understandings is frequently misinterpreted as seeking a *quick fix* without recognizing the investment in time, experience, and conversation that is necessary before change can happen. We believe that the construction of doable ideas requires careful rethinking of school structures to create opportunities for teachers to engage in long-term, in-depth learning experiences in homes and communities in conjunction with opportunities for supported reflection. We share our stories to communicate the importance of making time to consider how such experiences might become foundational in the daily lives of teachers.

We Are Inspired By ...

Fundamental to our knowledge base as we ventured into worlds beyond our own were understandings that language and literacy learning are meaning-making processes, that we learn skills and strategies in the context of semantically based experiences that are meaningful to the learner, and that we learn more when we feel valued for what we know (Clay, 1998; Moustafa, 1997; Smith, 2005). We embrace a sociocultural perspective grounded in the belief that we learn more when we have opportunities to interact purposefully with more experienced others (Vygotsky, 1978), moving in and out of the roles of novice and expert as we bring varied schema to each turn of the interaction (Rogoff, 1990; Wells, 1999). Building from these convictions, we explored the notion that diverse funds of knowledge exist in every home and community as mediated through interactions with more experienced others (González et al., 2005). We considered the networks of support in children's lives and the invisible teachers within those networks from whom public school educators might learn more about teaching and conditions that support learning (Gregory, Long, & Volk, 2004).

What We Did

Beginnings

Drawing from these ideas, we engaged in a series of in-class experiences that allowed us to get our feet wet—to begin thinking about the existence of knowledge in homes and communities that is rarely recognized in schools. These engagements provided relatively safe places from which we could risk looking at ourselves and others. We shared "Me Boxes" filled with artifacts to help us communicate stories that defined us as individuals. We listened to each other's Me Box stories and, from them, identified bodies of knowledge, networks of support, learning and teaching strategies, and conditions for learning that existed in our own homes and communities. We considered those funds in contrast to knowledge typically valued in schools. We charted literacy acts used to demonstrate expertise within each fund of knowledge and discussed ways that these insights might inform classroom instruction. We wrote from the heart using Georgia Heard's (1999) six-room poem structure to craft written images based on Me Box moments in our lives.

Music from our lives became another window into getting to know one another in new ways. Each class session opened with a piece of music introduced by a classmate who shared its significance in his or her life. Songs led us deeper into the complexities of each other's worlds. Through music, we learned about special relationships; personal moments of joy, sorrow, and inspiration; belief systems; and family histories. Stories about the history and significance of favorite family recipes and traditions provided one more entrée into one another's life experience. In another engagement, we brought photos of significant life moments and created a class book with accompanying stories. We wrote partner poems (James & Tolentino, 2004), juxtaposing similarities and differences among us. We used maps of the United States and the world to indicate places and events significant in our lives. We brought artifacts from our home communities to acquaint one another with bits of history and heritage. Each engagement gave us insights about classmates that had not been revealed simply by working and studying together. As one class member wrote, "I've known these women for two years, but there was so much I didn't know."

Venturing Further

We ventured further into exploring ourselves and others through engagements that sparked complex and sometimes very difficult conversations. The song "You've Got to Be Carefully Taught" from the Rogers and Hammerstein musical *South Pacific* initiated conversations about bias:

> You've got to be taught to be afraid
> Of people whose eyes are oddly made
> And people whose skin is a different shade
> You've got to be carefully taught.
> You've got to be taught before it's too late
> Before you are six or seven or eight …

Prompted by the lyrics, class members talked about ways that they had been "carefully taught" to have bias or to look negatively at individuals or groups of people. Some talked about ways they might have, intentionally and unintentionally, communicated prejudices to their own children. We read children's books such as *The Bracelet* (Uchida, 1996), *The Jacket* (Clements, 2002), *My Name Is Maria Isabel* (Ada, 1993), and *Sahara Special* (Codell, 2004), provoking discussions about ways that children, families, communities, and cultures can be marginalized, devalued, or erased. A member of the local Somali community came to share Muslim beliefs to help us better understand Somali Bantu children and families arriving from refugee camps in Kenya. We visited the local mosque where they worshipped.

We watched the video tape *Family across the Sea,* detailing the trip made by a delegation of South Carolina residents to the village in Sierra Leone from which their ancestors had been captured and enslaved. We spent 2 days at the Penn Center on St. Helena's Island, the site of the first school in the United States for freed slaves and also the best-preserved site of Gullah culture in the country. There, we heard members of the Sierra Leone delegation describe how the trip led to realizations that the Gullah spoken by their grandparents was a legitimate, structured language and not the "bad English" they had been led to believe it to be. We visited an exhibition about the *Brown versus Board of Education* decision marking the legal end of segregation; we read and talked about whether or not schools and society around us represented the spirit of that decision. We attended a performance by the Halleluiah Singers, a South Carolina group known for its connection to African and local Gullah heritage. We watched the videotape *A Class Divided,* the story of Jane Elliot's blue eyes–brown eyes exercise in understanding discrimination.

Tensions

These engagements engendered difficult and important conversations that started, stopped, and sometimes closed down all together. On some days, they led to real conflict, concern, and division with the group. Fine and Weis (2003) write that "as previously unheard voices sing, there is a subtle polarizing, a freezing of positions ... there is nothing automatic about creating a community of differences in this space" (p. 124). We found that to be painfully true. Clavis explained, "I was a little worried about where we would end up as a group. I was afraid that we would be left with a lot of anger, resentment, and unanswered questions and that the cohort would never be able to function as a unit." Becky added, "We were asked to look deeply at our own belief systems. It took us to really hard places and we were not happy about going there." Melanie wrote, "The different things we did took us to places that, honestly, we would not have gone if we were alone doing the same sort of inquiry; we often stay away from places that are hard and that make us uncomfortable."

Susi, as the cohort leader, felt consistently incompetent and unsure. The experiences seemed to build higher walls not bridges:

> Every day, I felt that I was failing the teachers I loved so much. For 2 years, our time together had been a source of much joy and laughter. Now there was tension and a deep underlying sadness. I had no idea how or if we would get to the other side of it.

Some cohort members wrote, quietly reminding Susi that venturing into these kinds of conversations could be nothing other than difficult but that the venture was necessary. Others wrote that they were distressed with the level of discomfort felt among their friends and colleagues. Our experiences echoed those described by Cochran-Smith (2004), who wrote of her conviction that "this is a slow and stumbling journey and that, along the way, difficult pain, self-exposure, and disappointments are inevitable" (p. 101). We were, indeed, stumbling.

We stumbled on. The most helpful conversations occurred as we walked away from engagements and considered them a day or a week or a month later in the company of anyone who would listen. Then something happened that had a profound effect on all of us. After nearly a year of these kinds of explorations, we lost a beloved member of our cohort of literacy coaches. Rose Mitchell was killed in a car accident on her way to one of our sessions. The depth of our grief is impossible to convey. Rose had an unassuming, centered way about her and a genuine caring for others. Anyone who met her knew this and never took it for granted. When she spoke, everyone stopped to listen. Quietly, almost imperceptibly, she had caused people to drop defensiveness, think more, go further. Many of us live now with Rose as an anchor for our thoughts and conversations. Clavis wrote,

> When we lost Rose, we lost a living model of what it is we often said we believed but did not practice. She *lived* outside her comfort zone. In fact, I don't think that there were many places in which she was uncomfortable for very long. Through our grieving together and trying to cope with the loss of such a wonderful person, I believe we started really examining what it was we loved so much about Rose and whether or not we had those traits somewhere within us.

Clavis continued,

> Time passed. We talked more and more and ventured into territory where we would not have gone before. We began listening to each other and valuing what we had to say. We began to push the conversation beyond the surface to the things that exposed our core beliefs, our fears, and yes, our prejudices. We talked, but even more importantly, we listened, with open hearts.

The group soon rotated to a new cohort leader, Heidi Mills, who created new and important places to continue the conversation, safe places to move forward. Becky explained,

> It had taken a lot of time, tears, and harsh words to work through these issues but it was truly metamorphic. The transformation was evident one day when racial issues were brought to light by events surrounding Hurricane Katrina. Tempers flared but, this time, the discussion continued. Someone made the point that we could not have heard each

other a year earlier and that, if we had not gone to those hard places initially and had opportunity for dialogue around difficult experiences, we would have continued to pretend to understand one another or avoided the conversation all together. I likened it to a difficult time in a marriage. We had fallen in love with one another again. Even though we might not always agree, we could now agree to disagree and to stop patronizing each other.

Going Beyond

Before, during, and after our months of difficult conversations, some of us took the opportunity to go beyond in-class engagements to get to know children at a deeper level. This resulted in, perhaps, the most powerful learning about what it means to listen to and honor knowledge in children's worlds.

Jabril: Clavis Writes   My first memory of Jabril was when we were sitting on the floor with other kids in a circle. Susi and I had volunteered at a summer camp for Somali Bantu children, refugees who had recently arrived in the United States. The purpose of the camp was to give the children a boost in English-language learning before they enrolled in American school that fall. As we sat on the floor, I traced my hand on a piece of paper and pointed to a bracelet bearing my name. "Clavis. I'm Clavis," I said. Susi pointed to herself, "Susi." We pointed to each of the children and they each said a name. Having heard their names being used earlier, I realized quickly that they were switching names in what seemed to be a great teasing game. When Jabril said that his name was Hassan, I looked at him and said, "Uh-uh! You're Jabril." He shook his head, "Hassan." We went back and forth in this way for a minute or two. Then he gave me a look that, interpreted through the lens of my own experience, seemed much like the I-dare-you-to-get-to-know-me stare I had seen from many a little boy over the years. I gave him my Buddy-I've-got-your-number look and he laughed the biggest, most joyful laugh. It was the beginning of what, for me, became an amazing relationship.

Later in the day, while some of the children were doing puzzles, building with blocks, and writing and reading with Susi, Jabril started singing. He sang, "Bye bye teacher. Teacher in the morrow. I go home to see my mother" and he sang other words that I didn't recognize. I asked him to sing the song again. This time, the other children began to sing with him. Susi joined us and we encouraged them to sing more songs. We could not understand many of the words (we later found out the songs were a mixture of Swahili, Somali, and English) but we immediately wondered if there was a way we could use their music to support our learning as well as theirs.

The next day, Jabril wanted to play with the battery-operated cars that were usually in the room but had been put away that day. He was screaming and pulling on my arm because he wanted a car. I was just about at my wit's end when I walked over to the old, upright piano sitting near the window and started to play the melody of the song he'd sung the day before. In midscream, he stopped. He walked over to me, looked at me, and said, "Again." I played the melody again and started singing the parts of the song I remembered. He joined in. Each time, as the song ended, he said, "Again." He ran into the other room, gathered up some of the other kids, ran back with them, and said to me, "Again." Susi and I went to the easel and started transcribing our approximations of the words they were singing. My 19-year-old son, Preston, who was volunteering with us that day, made a quick trip to the corner drugstore and came back with audio cassettes so that we could capture the sounds of their songs. After most of the lyrics were written on the easel, I helped Jabril run his fingers underneath the words as we sang. He picked up the left-right movement almost instantly. He understood that the marks on the easel were his song. He brought some of the older children to the easel and showed them the song, running his fingers underneath the words. I thought this was brilliant for a 5-year-old who, to my knowledge, had never even seen his own language in print.

The next day, as Jabril and I sat together, singing and talking, he looked at me intently as he spoke to the Somali interpreter who was visiting that day. The interpreter translated, "He says that you are like a mother." I smiled, opened my arms, and Jabril fell into them. I was amazed that in just a few days, we had begun the journey across language and cultural barriers just by embracing what already exists in the heart and the mind and the experiences of one child.

Jabril: Susi Long Writes   A few months later, Jabril began school. That fall, I was teaching a group of undergraduate education majors. I wanted them to learn about the importance of valuing multiple languages within a school context so I taught their literacy course on site at an elementary school attended by children from many different language backgrounds—Korean, Spanish, Mandarin, French, and Somali/Swahili. I also asked to work at this school because Jabril and the other Somali Bantu children would be there. Every Monday, for 90 minutes, each undergraduate in my class worked with two children, one a native English speaker and the other, a native speaker of another language. Jabril was one of those children. One day, as the university students and the children were spread out around the room working together, I stopped to listen as Jabril worked with his undergraduate partner. Remembering his song from summer camp, I asked him to sing it and he did. I began to write what I heard on a large dry erase board again using the best approximations of the Somali/Swahili sounds that my English schema would allow. As I wrote each line, I tried to sing it back to Jabril. He corrected me as I stumbled over sounds. When we finished, Jabril picked up the dry erase board and carried it around the room engaging other children and undergraduates in singing with him, running his hand under the words as they sang. In a setting where he had few opportunities to demonstrate expertise, Jabril became an expert. At the same time, the worlds of those around him were broadened as they celebrated his words and music by joining in his song.

How easy it would have been to have missed what Jabril knows, can do, and values if we had not gone beyond what was accepted as "the norm" in school to learn more. How easily he might have been labeled as "at risk" because he came to school speaking very little English. In fact, a Somali Bantu peer who sang with us that day received "Needs improvement" under "auditory discrimination" on his report card that grading period. Without knowing how he used language in his home and community worlds, the teacher had little on which to base her judgment about his ability to discriminate sounds. Listening to and learning from them as they sang in their own language, however, it was clear that he and Jabril were competent and knowledgeable and definitely able to discriminate auditorally. And we had only tipped the iceberg of what we might know about them as we sought to value their worlds and broaden our own.

Thomas: Melanie Clark Writes   Thomas was a 7-year-old twin, a quiet, shy child who struggled with his own identity. Throughout his second-grade year, I could see glimmers of hope and progress, but as soon as he would take one step forward, he would take two steps back. We had many opportunities to bond and I felt that there was a great amount of trust built between the two of us. Thomas seemed to know that I cared and that I was willing to go the extra mile to help him. His Reading Recovery teacher made note of his low self-esteem and little self-confidence. Thomas constantly referred to his twin brother as the smarter one.

I began this study wanting to help Thomas maintain his reading and writing skills without going backwards on such a consistent basis. I wanted him to feel good about himself as a reader and a writer and to acknowledge that he knew a lot about many different things. I wanted to use his own experiences to help him feel successful. I wanted to access his schema to help him make gains. It was evident that Thomas needed to know that he was valued as a knowledgeable human being.

As I worked with Thomas in a small group, I worried because he was not responding in ways that I hoped he would. He attempted to participate, but when other students spoke up, he became quiet and did not even attempt to finish his sentence. He would read, but he would not discuss the story. Then I noticed something that ultimately became very important. Thomas's facial expression and his attitude changed when I asked him something specifically related to his family's chicken farm. His family raised chickens and he was truly a chicken expert. He knew, in great detail and sophistication, about the work it takes to farm chickens. That's when I knew I had to change my approach.

I began focusing on what Thomas knew rather than what he didn't know. To find out more about what he knew, I had to talk to him more. I began to make more time for real conversation—to be someone who would really listen to him. At first, having one-to-one conversations with Thomas was difficult. Even after a year of being with me, he would still shrug his shoulders and say, "I don't know nothin' to say." Talking about animals, chickens in particular, however, made all the difference. Thomas always wanted to talk about animals that he knew about from books, television, or his farm. One day, an amazing incident brought Thomas's expertise into the open. The assistant principal at another elementary school had a question about baby chicks. The literacy coach at her school had heard about Thomas's expertise from me, and so the principal phoned our school and asked to speak to Thomas. He was able to tell her all that she needed to know about chicks. That one small, very sincere act of interest in Thomas's knowledge made an immediate difference. Thomas hung up the phone, turned to me and said, "I didn't know that I could be a nonfiction book!"

From that point, I realized that, if a lesson or assignment could be connected to his family or a personal experience, Thomas worked much harder and performed much better. He persevered if he had prior knowledge about a subject. In the classroom and in one-to-one situations, Thomas often gave up if he felt that he had nothing to contribute. If he felt honestly valued for his knowledge, he shone.

As Thomas revealed his knowledge to me, I began telling the other children how much I was learning from him. I truly learned more from him than I had ever learned from a book, and I thought this was important for the other children to know. The year before, Thomas rarely spoke or offered information, but knowing that he was genuinely viewed as an expert, he began sharing often with his classmates and others. The students had all kinds of questions. Thomas knew the answers to most and when he didn't, he remembered to ask his dad and return the next day with the answer. The other students began coming to him when they were writing about animals. In one instance, a child was reading a zoo book and he came to a part about an embryo. When he saw the picture of an egg, he went straight to Thomas and asked about the word "embryo." Thomas was the much weaker reader but, with his knowledge about chickens and eggs, he knew the word and explained it to his classmate. This had an effect on the whole classroom. The children began looking for books, not just for Thomas, but for other experts in the room. We also used this opportunity to let his parents know how much he was contributing to the class. His parents were as excited as Thomas and could not get over the changes that were occurring.

Thomas's views about himself as a writer also changed considerably. He began following through with prewriting ideas that he discussed with peers and with me. He sought ideas for writing from a variety of sources. He realized that he could use what he knew to teach others. Thomas's writing began to make sense and became more consistent and detailed. His knowledge and voice were heard as never before.

As I was completing my study of Thomas, his mother came by my office. She wanted to make sure we had pictures of Thomas and his chickens and to thank me for taking him to McDonald's. With her eyes sparkling like stars and a smile as wide as a river, she said, "Since Thomas has been working with you he is a different person. He has more self-confidence than he has ever had. Thank you so much for helping him. I truly appreciate it. He loves working with you."

One person *can* make a difference in a child's life, if he or she is willing to invest time to go beyond limited views of the norm in schools. Children and parents recognize when you care enough to get to really know them and learn from them. I could easily have been Thomas's teacher forever and not found that pathway to learning for him. It truly took looking beyond school knowledge to find the connection that gave Thomas credibility for himself, his peers, his teachers, and his family.

Jonathon: Becky McCraw Writes Much like the majority of the teachers in my school, I viewed my job as a calling and a mission. Having been reared in the United Methodist church, I have learned throughout my life that we are called by God into service in His name. I saw my work as having a spiritual purpose and felt that what I chose to teach, the lessons of life on which I chose to focus, could have a great impact on my students. Then, through experiences in our cohort of literacy coaches and through the study of one child, I began to question my own mission.

My school is located in a small community in the shadow of a large textile mill that was, at one time, one of the major industries in the area. The mill is being torn down and the crumbling bricks stand as a stark reminder of the economic hardships that many people in the area face due to its closing. The town has a long history of racism and racial tension. It is divided by the proverbial railroad track. The school population is 69 percent African American and most of the teachers, like me, are white. I think that, without questioning it and often without even realizing it, we believed that our mission was to "enculturate" children to our own worlds. But when I began to look closely at myself, my colleagues, and the worlds around me, I was shocked at the realization that we merely gave lip service to issues of diversity. I wondered, How much is family culture truly being valued in our school? Do we really honor diversity? Little did I know that a third-grade boy named Jonathon would teach me more in answer to that question than I could ever have envisioned.

I first met Jonathon as a kindergarten student. He spent most of the first week of school crying because he missed his mother and grandmother. He seemed eager to learn, but it was clear that he did not see himself as a reader or writer. He would say, "I can't read." He prefaced any comment with a loud acknowledgment of the person to whom he was speaking, which often led to reprimands at school. His teachers perceived him to be hyperactive and lacking in self-control. Jonathon's parents did not always participate in school functions, so they were perceived as not interested in his school life. In my capacity, first as one of Jonathon's kindergarten teachers and then as the school's literacy coach, I followed him through 3 years of his literacy education. Through formal and informal assessments, I came to know a lot about him as a reader and a writer, but I didn't know a lot about him as a person. That is where my learning really began. I wanted to know more about Jonathon and that led me beyond the walls of the school to Jonathon's family and church life. What happened was that, in learning about Jonathon, I learned even more about myself.

Before venturing into Jonathon's home and community worlds, I began to think through my own preconceived notions about him. In doing so, I found my integrity called into question. I really thought that I held no biases and that I was quite forward thinking and open to celebrating diversity. As I sat down to write my assumptions about Jonathon, I began listing things I thought I knew about him. Shockingly, I realized that I assumed that, because he was black, he lived with his mother in the projects, had no regular routines in his life, his father might or might not be a part of his life, his family lacked literacy skills and were poorly educated, and he did not have anyone to read to him or help him with his homework.

I learned the meaning of the phrase "eating crow" after one 20-minute interview with Jonathon. We sat at a table in the large, empty cafeteria of my school. His words will stay with me forever. In that brief interview, almost all my assumptions were dispelled. I discovered that he lives with both parents in a two-bedroom home two blocks from our school. He is read to regularly, his father and mother sing a lot at home, his favorite thing to do is to watch TV in his parents' room "piled up in their bed." He likes the blues but "not the kind old people like and you're not supposed to sing on Sunday." Both of his parents work full-time at day-shift jobs and are very active in their churches. Church is very important to Jonathon. He sings in the children's choir and participates in plays at his grandmother's church. When I asked him why I did not know all of this before, he said, "You never asked me." He was right; I had known him for 3 years but I had not taken the time to really get to know this child.

When I called to make plans to meet with Jonathon's family, his mother told me that she had choir practice the next day at 3:00. I asked if I could come along. I was nervous about asking but she seemed pleased, so the next day, Jonathon and his mother took me to their church. As choir practice began, Jonathon and I sat side-by-side in one of the pews watching his mother and the other members of the choir. He thumbed through a hymnal and asked about my favorite songs. He said he liked the one called "God So Loved the World" and proceeded to recite John 3:16 verbatim: "For God so loved the world that

He gave His only begotten son, that whosoever believeth in Him should not perish, but have everlasting life." He spoke these lines with remarkable fluency. I asked how he learned them and he said that he had always known the words. This was the same child who had trouble learning 10 spelling words in school. As the choir sang, Jonathon listened patiently and did not display one sign of the hyperactivity reported by his teachers at school. He eventually stretched out on the wooden pew and fell asleep as his mother sang the words "I will go in Jesus' name."

I returned the following Saturday to work in the church's soup kitchen. Jonathon's mother volunteers there every weekend, serving food and delivering to shut-ins. I sat and talked with an elderly woman who shared advice on how to teach and rear children in "the way they should go." She quoted scripture "Train a child up in the way he should go, and when he is old, he will not depart from it" (Proverbs 22:6). She talked about the breakdown of the American family. After the food was prepared, all the volunteers gathered in the kitchen for prayer. I joined the circle of outstretched hands. Jonathon's hand slipped into mine and we all joined to bless the food and thank God for those who came to help. It was a powerful moment, and in it, I realized how glad I was to be there. What a lesson Jonathon's mother teaches her son each week! I began to think about stark contrasts between how she seems to feel in this setting and how she might feel at our school where she could be perceived as a parent who just isn't interested enough to get involved—this woman who gives her time every single Saturday to others.

The next day, I went to Sunday school and church with Jonathon, his father, and his aunts. Throughout the morning worship, the children sat quietly. At a designated point in the service, they left for Children's Church. The teacher asked the children to answer questions about the Bible and relate personal experiences. They were expected to know who wrote the Book of Romans, and they recited a verse from memory. As I sat there, it occurred to me that, even as a devoted member of my own church, I didn't know who wrote the Book of Romans.

In Jonathon's church, I found a congregation dedicated to the spiritual growth and upbringing of their youth as well as an environment rich in literacy. The lessons the students studied and the choral reading in which they took part had high levels of vocabulary, and all children were expected to join in the reading. The church newsletter was primarily devoted to celebrating the accomplishments of the children. Children sat in a place of true importance—the deacons and trustees to the left of the minister and the children to the right. I wondered if Jonathon ever feels as celebrated in school as he does in his church.

Perhaps my greatest learning from this experience is the need for teachers to look carefully at ourselves as we learn about others. So quickly, we make statements like "Those parents don't care about their kids" or "They won't read to them." Through this experience, I had to look at my own biases—the ones

I didn't think that I had. I was very fond of Jonathon, how could I have bias? But I was wrong about so many things. This leads me to believe that there is a lot of assuming going on in classrooms and that those assumptions can be the blinders that keep us from seeing what is really there.

The world is much bigger for me these days. Jonathon helped my world grow. I had known him from kindergarten through third grade. I knew what level he was reading on, how many sight words he knew, how phonemically aware he was, and how well he could work through words as he was writing, but I only knew a part of him. I could have followed him through fifth grade and not known what I know now.

Lessons Learned

Lessons learned through these experiences were many. We learned that getting to know children, their families, and communities in new ways allows us to uncover funds of knowledge and networks of support so that we can honor and build from what children know. We came to see that, if we genuinely value literacy learning as a meaning-making process, we have to find out what constitutes *meaningful* in the lives of children. If we believe that learners grow when valued for existing knowledge, then we must uncover, validate, and utilize knowledge from home and community worlds. We also discovered that recognition of previously ignored or devalued funds of knowledge can have an important impact on children representing the existing norm. Making home knowledge visible means broadening "worldviews for children from privileged cultures who receive messages sent about the superiority of their language and culture" (Gregory et al., 2004, p. 17).

Although we value classroom practices that encourage children to share, read, and write about family and community experiences, we learned that these structures are just a beginning. There is much we cannot know if we remain within the school walls. But it's not enough just to venture out. The deepest learning occurs when we shift our role from teacher-as-expert to teacher-as-learner. With that lens, we more easily recognize and overturn inaccurate and biased assumptions. Without venturing out and adopting a new lens, it seems more likely that we will only perpetuate the same surface nods to enacting equitable practice.

Finally, we learned that opportunities to examine prior assumptions can lead to emotionally charged conversations that are relatively easy to enter but difficult to move through and beyond. At some point, however, experiences that frustrate, sadden, and even anger can forever alter the way we view ourselves and others.

Teacher as Ethnographer

Envisioning equitable and inclusive practices begins with seeking the brilliance of others (Delpit, 2002) and making that brilliance visible, not just to support and honor those who are marginalized but to broaden the worldviews of every other child and his or her family—to deepen perspectives of what constitutes the norm in education and society. For this to happen, we must first believe that the brilliance exists. The only way to convince ourselves of that is to get to know children, their families, and their communities in new ways, through a new lens, positioning the teacher as learner, ethnographer.

We wonder how teaching and learning might be transformed if the notion of teacher-as-ethnographer became fundamental to teacher education programs and schools (Taylor, 1993). Ethnography by definition seeks to know how social action in one world makes sense from the point of view of another (Agar, 1996). Ethnographers are not just observers but participants in the culture in which they choose to be immersed. They see the task of seeking to understand others as a privilege. Ethnographers know that their interpretations are never accurate or complete and that they must engage insiders in helping them "figure out what is going on in their worlds" (Agar, 1996, p. 16).

Teachers as ethnographers make it their business to learn by asking, interacting, and engaging in events that define families' worlds. They place "listening at the center of teaching" (Schultz, 2003, p. 7). Teachers as ethnographers take an inquiry stance as they listen to children and families (Mills, O'Keefe, & Jennings, 2004; Schultz, 2003). They know that "listening requires proximity and intimacy" (p. 8), so they create school and classroom contexts that support proximity and intimacy.

Our challenge to administrators, teachers, and teacher educators is to make *knowing others* foundational to teaching and learning in schools. Seeking to understand beyond our own cultural comfort zones is, in itself, an equitable and inclusive practice. Create spaces for ongoing, supported conversation and engagement that help us recognize our own biases as we work to create a more inclusive definition of the norm. Agree to begin the school year focusing only on what children and families know and can do. Commit to going beyond classrooms to learn about ways of knowing, learning, and teaching in homes and communities. Don't assume that you can learn what you need to know by remaining within the school walls. This means much more than inviting Johnny's dad to come in to tell about how he builds engines (although that's a start). It is something very different from going into homes to teach parents how to read to their children or driving through neighborhoods to acquaint teachers with communities from behind the windows of a school bus. It's about spending time in homes and communities for the purpose of enlisting family and community members and children as teachers in *our* education.

Vivian Paley (2004) writes that, as educators, "We no longer wonder, 'Who are you?' but instead decide quickly, 'What can we do to fix you?'" (p. 47). Teachers as ethnographers do not settle for less than wanting to know children and families well. We create opportunities to go beyond their own worlds grounded in the belief that "difference does not diminish; it enlarges the sphere of human possibilities" (Sacks, 2002, p. 209). In the process, we have a better chance of creating equitable and inclusive practices for all children.

References

Ada, A. F. (1993). *My name is María Isabel.* New York: Atheneum.

Agar, M. (1996). *The professional stranger: An informal introduction to ethnography* (2nd ed.). San Diego, CA: Academic Press.

Ayers, W., Hunt, J. A., & Quinn, T. (1998). *Teaching for social justice.* New York: Teachers College Press.

Clay, M. (1998). *By different paths to common outcomes.* Portland, ME: Stenhouse.

Clements, S. (2002). *The jacket.* New York: Simon & Schuster.

Cochran-Smith, M. (2004). *Walking the road: Race, diversity, and social justice in teacher education.* New York: Teachers College Press.

Codell, E. (2004). *Sahara special.* New York: Scholastic.

Delpit, L. (2002). *The skin that we speak: Thoughts on language and culture in the classroom.* New York: New Press.

Donnelly, A., Morgan, D. N., DeFord, D., Files, J., Long, S., Mills, H., Stephens, D., & Styslinger, M. (2004). Transformative professional development: Negotiating knowledge with an inquiry stance. *Language Arts, 82*(5), 336–346.

Edelsky, C. (1999). *Making justice our project: Teachers working toward critical whole language practice.* Urbana, IL: National Council of Teachers of English.

Fine, M., & Weis, L. (2003). *Silenced voices and extraordinary conversations: Re-imagining schools.* New York: Teachers College Press.

Gonzalez, N. E., Moll, L.C., & Amanti, C. (Eds.). (2005). *Funds of knowledge: Theorizing practices in households and classrooms.* Mahwah, NJ: Erlbaum.

Gregory, E., Long, S., & Volk, D. (2004). *Many pathways to literacy: Children learning with siblings, grandparents, peers, and communities.* New York: RoutledgeFalmer.

Haight, W. (2001). *African-American children at church: A sociocultural perspective.* Cambridge: Cambridge University Press.

Heath, S. B. (1983). *Ways with words: Language, life, and work in communities and classrooms.* Cambridge: Cambridge University Press.

Heard, G. (1999). *Awakening the heart: Exploring poetry in elementary and middle school.* Portsmouth, NH: Heinemann.

James, S., & Tolentino, H. (2004). Brown doll, white doll: Partner poems help students talk back to stereotypes. *Rethinking Schools Online, 18*(4). Retrieved November 2005, from http://www.rethinkingschools.org/archive/18_04/d011184.shtml.

Ladson-Billings, G. (1994). *The dreamkeepers: Successful teachers of African American children.* San Francisco, CA: Jossey-Bass.

Mills, H., O'Keefe, T., & Jennings, L. (2004). *Looking closely and listening carefully: Learning literacy through inquiry.* Urbana, IL: National Council of Teachers of English.

Moustafa, M. (1997). *Beyond traditional phonics: Research discoveries and reading instruction.* Portsmouth, NH: Heinemann.

Paley, V. (2004). *A child's work: The importance of fantasy play.* Chicago: University of Chicago Press.

Rogoff, B. (1990). *Apprenticeship in thinking: Cognitive development in social context.* Oxford: Oxford University Press.

Sacks, J. (2002). *The dignity of difference: How to avoid the clash of civilizations.* London: Continuum.

Schultz, K. (2003). *Listening: A framework for teaching across differences.* New York: Teachers College Press.

Smith, F. (2005). *Reading without nonsense* (4th ed.). New York: Teachers College Press.

Taylor, D. (1988). *Growing up literate: Learning from inner-city fam*ilies. Portsmouth, NH: Heinemann.

Taylor, D. (1993). *From a child's point of view.* Portsmouth, NH: Heinemann.

Uchida, Y. (1996). *The bracelet.* New York: Putnam.

Valdés, G. (1996). *Con respeto: Bridging the distances between culturally diverse families and schools: An ethnographic portrait.* New York: Teachers College Press.

Vygotsky, L. S. (1978). *Mind in society: The development of higher psychological processes.* Cambridge, MA: Harvard University Press.

Wells, G. (1999). *Dialogic inquiry: Toward a sociocultural practice and theory of education.* Cambridge: Cambridge University Press.

Conclusion

Diversities across Early Childhood Settings

Contesting Identities and Transforming Curricula

CELIA GENISHI AND A. LIN GOODWIN

Where, after all, do universal human rights begin? In small places, close to home—so close and so small that they cannot be seen on any maps of the world. Unless these rights have meaning there, they have little meaning anywhere.

Eleanor Roosevelt

The authors of this volume have presented a range of ideas and actions related to diversities and social justice—what we could call "universal human rights"—nurtured in the close, small places of classrooms, centers, and schools. "Diversities" reflected a variety of educational settings and geographic locations. Nested within them were children and adults of varied race, age, ethnicity, ability, gender, or social class. Here we look back and seek commonalities and differences across the chapters, as we ask, "What are we rethinking? What are we doing to advocate for social justice? And what could we be doing differently?"

Our rethinking in this concluding chapter clusters around the intimately linked themes of curriculum and contested identities. These overarching themes are expansive enough to fold in multiple conceptions of other key topics like literacies and the nature of research. We do not conclude with a single definition of social justice, just as we don't offer tidy prescriptions for "best practice." Instead, we aim to offer chapter authors' multiple recommendations for thought and action that move us closer to ideals of social justice. Many authors grounded the need for rethinking curriculum within the current context of No Child Left Behind, which emphasizes the learning of skills, particularly in the area of literacy, narrowly defined as "reading." Others pointed out the gap in many educators' expectations for "at-risk" children, contrasted with children of middle-class background who are not perceived through this deficit lens or have not been labeled with a disability. We next review the authors' contributions according to the themes of curriculum and contested identities within the three sections of the book. The brevity of our comments is not meant to reduce their work to simple abstracts but to highlight possible links to these two themes and to encourage readers to revisit individual chapters for their rich details and challenging recommendations.

Curtain Up: Rethinking Identities of Children in Transformed Curricular Contexts

In the section on contesting identities, Anne Haas Dyson opens with the captivating metaphor of a theater curtain that conceals important aspects of child learners' identities. A similar curtain frames many of the chapters in this collection. In classrooms where definitions of curriculum are narrow and often limited to conventional skills, the curtain has to be pulled way back in order for children who are labeled "at risk" to step onto a stage that highlights children's other identities as able and imaginative persons. The first graders in Dyson's study, in particular Tionna, showed themselves to possess a wide symbolic repertoire, which underlay their identities as speakers of African American language and experts in popular music and some forms of "Standard" English so dominant in the official, teacher-directed curriculum. To help Tionna and her peers move forward as readers and writers, adults take children's knowledge of literacies and associated identities into account; or in Dyson's terms, when teachers provide space for an unofficial curriculum, children orchestrate complex symbolic systems into intricately produced, child-directed operas.

Looking behind a curtain is what Marjorie Siegel and Stephanie Lukas and Susan Stires and Celia Genishi also do in their respective chapters, as they urge a rethinking of child identities and curriculum. Siegel and Lukas addressed the challenges of enacting a mandated balanced literacy program. Lukas, an activist kindergarten teacher in a classroom that includes children of Latino, African American, and South Asian heritage, created "wiggle room" for her children with the aim of offering high-status curricular content, that is, science and technology. Kindergarteners Hector, Bianca, Jewel, and Terrance demonstrated their knowledge of literacies as they orchestrated symbol systems across the settings of reading and writing workshops and computer labs. Stires and Genishi also illustrated the rethinking of mandated curriculum in a first-grade classroom where the teacher made room for science. Alice, the focal child, demonstrated a response to the official curriculum and an unofficial one, in which she seemed to consider what her ethnic and linguistic identities were, or what some would call her hybridity. As a bilingual child of Chinese heritage, Alice also enabled the authors to contest the identity of "model minority" and to assert the need for strong child-teacher relationships.

Susan Recchia further highlighted the importance of caring relationships in an inclusive prekindergarten classroom that she studied. Kathy, a special education teacher, pushed back the curtain that used to separate typically developing children from those with special needs or disabilities. With a focus on Kathy and her students Joey, diagnosed with Pervasive Developmental Disorder, and Maria, a typically developing English-language learner, Recchia revealed the features of Kathy's curriculum. In contrast to the skills-oriented interventions that one might expect in special education settings, Kathy's "doing" highlighted social interactions through which children, regardless of labels and diagnoses, began to construct the identity of learner in a classroom community.

In quite a different context, Susan Grieshaber presented Nate, a child of Pacific Islander heritage, in a year 3 classroom in Australia (second grade in the United States). Nate had been identified as a child struggling with literacy and numeracy, within the conventional curricular definitions of print-based literacy and numbers. Without a close focus on his computer work, his skills and knowledge of computers and popular culture would have remained concealed, along with the status his expertise across literacies gained him among his peers.

Leslie Williams and Nadjwa Norton not only pushed back the curtain, but added texture and complexity by complicating definitions of child identity. Children's identities as sexual, spiritual, and "classed" beings challenged what is considered "acceptable" curriculum for those in the early childhood grades. Their work reminds us that children are fully in the world and display multiple "dimensions of diversity," dimensions that influence how they read the world, how they interact with others, and how they perceive themselves. "Doing" social justice means not only accepting the identities that children bring into the classroom but also using these diverse identities as lenses for curriculum designed to be inclusive and emancipatory.

All authors in this section demonstrate the inextricable link between our understandings and representations of child identities and the nature and reach of curricula. In classrooms and schools where significant numbers of children are labeled "at risk," individual teachers pull back the official curricular curtains so that children who would typically find themselves in the margins because of their socioeconomic, ethnic, racial, or linguistic diversities are supported to develop and perform a range of skills and knowledge. A consequence is transformed curricula, orchestrated by teachers and children resisting the constraints of labels and child-unfriendly policies.

Impact beyond Classrooms: Rethinking Policies and Programs

In the second section, authors push back curtains so as to afford us a view beyond normative definitions of "teacher" and the classroom as the primary stage where learning is enacted. By means of an after-school program, Althea Nixon and Kris Gutiérrez resisted state policy in California by reaching around the prohibition against bilingual (primarily Spanish-English) education in regular classrooms. The authors weave in the themes of contested identity and curriculum transformation, along with others that appeared in the first section, including the teaching of digital technologies and the importance of relationships, in this chapter between college undergraduates—and their playful creation, El Maga—and elementary school students.

Jennifer Adair and Joseph Tobin and Marci Sarsona, Sherlyn Goo, Alice Kawakami, and Kathryn Au took us from classrooms and centers to the families who participated in their programs. Whereas Nixon and Gutiérrez addressed the transformation of students' identity through experiencing new curricula and the status that digital tools confer, Adair and Tobin and Sarsona and her colleagues problematized the identities of adult experts. Adair and Tobin described an aspect of their multinational research in which parents who were immigrants discussed their views of preschool practices. The parents of Mexican heritage in this chapter expressed a preference for more academic instruction for their children and less practice that is grounded in progressive discourses, reminding researchers and educators that "developmental appropriateness" should not be a taken-for-granted standard and that parental views need not be an afterthought to rethinking curriculum.

Sarsona and colleagues described Keiki Steps, a program in which Native Hawaiian culture was center stage. Family members, including parents, grandparents, preschoolers, and their younger siblings, were involved in maintaining Hawaiian cultural values while preparing preschoolers for kindergarten. The rethinking of center-based care led to pushing back on the commodification of early care and education, which typically separated children from their family members at sites where the curriculum was not permeable to local values. In Keiki Steps, family members' identities might transform into teacher identities over time.

Whereas Sarsona and colleagues resisted the usual requirements of teacher preparation in rethinking curriculum for Native Hawaiians, Sharon Ryan and Carrie Lobman presented findings from a mixed-methods study that examined the current level of teacher knowledge about curriculum that is culturally responsive for increasingly diverse groups of young children in New Jersey. Ryan and Lobman thus pulled back the curtain of teacher certification to reveal that a large percentage of teachers in their study felt unprepared to teach children whose home language is not English or who have special needs. They suggested that part of the "doing" to address this gap in teacher preparation might include further rethinking through consideration of postmodern theories that can disrupt taken-for-granted notions of knowledge worth having and how children learn and develop. They also shine the light on teacher educators who cannot teach what they themselves do not know.

The authors of these four chapters demonstrate how wide the stage is when we refer to early childhood policies and programs. In general, states in the United States have policies supportive of early childhood education, but the ways in which those policies are enacted or are applied to improve the well-being and learning of young children vary locally, even as legislation like No

Child Left Behind requires standardization that attempts to obscure the size of the increasingly diverse stage.

Focus on Adults: Rethinking Teacher Education and Professional Development

There is little distance between Ryan and Lobman's work and that of the authors in the third section. In this section, however, we shift from policies and programs for children to particular approaches or particular adults as they become teachers or rethink themselves as teachers. As a whole, the authors have presented a complicated aspect of curriculum while holding their identities up to scrutiny, with the common hope of improving their own teaching practices.

Beatrice Fennimore challenged all of us to rethink our identities while we rethink the power of everyday language. She pulled back the curtain that concealed conceptualizations of children who are economically poor as "at risk" and thus unable to benefit from whatever curricula are offered them. The curriculum that we educators need to create for ourselves is one of language advocacy. This living curriculum cannot be purchased and requires continual listening and participation—a willingness to speak social justice into existence by literally interrupting those whose language demeans child learners and their families.

Looking to teacher educators to interrupt and disrupt deficit discourses, A. Lin Goodwin and Michèle Genor described the use of autobiography in a preservice teacher education program to engender self-reflection and conscientization of deficit or unidimensional views of learners. The students' written texts provided data during their student teaching year that allowed them, along with their instructors, to see and question their implicit beliefs about children, schools, and teaching. Using autobiographical analysis, their instructors disturbed the curtain to reveal how students' cultural knowledge influenced their perceptions of learners, their curricular goals and intentions, and their own identity as teachers. Drawing back the curtain on preservice students' views of children as framed by their own experiences enabled these neophyte teachers to rethink their assumptions about children, teaching, and learning as a first step to "redoing."

Students' cultural knowledge is an important aspect of Rachel Theilheimer's chapter as well. While asking her students, enrolled in a community college early childhood teacher education program, to articulate their ideas about children's play and learning, she was rethinking and "doing" by means of research. Unlike students in many 4-year or graduate-level teacher education programs, Justine and Fiona, the focal students in Theilheimer's study, were women of color. Thus their ideas about play at times reflected the marginalization and oppression that they had experienced in and out of school, as well as points of agreement or conflict with instructors' progressive stance on play.

Rebekah Fassler and Dorothy Levin examined issues similar to those that emerged in Theilheimer's study but from a different perspective. Also within the context of a teacher education program, the two rethought possible rationales for play at a time when play itself is simply pushed behind a curtain in many schools. The question of whether play is a child-driven activity that leads to important learning (the progressive stance) or should be skills-oriented and structured by teachers (an interventionist stance) was considered in the context of Levin's prekindergarten classroom for children with special needs. Reading this chapter alongside Theilheimer's pushes back theoretical and practical curtains to highlight how practitioners' stances on particular topics grow out of complex experiences grounded in social class, ethnicity, race, ideology, and course content.

In the final chapter of this section, Susi Long, Clavis Anderson, Melanie Clark, and Becky McCraw described how rethinking and doing for them meant understanding their own experiences as a first step in reenvisioning equitable practices for children and families. Over a period of 3 years, they wove together threads that are prominent in the other studies presented in this section: the need to push back curtains that reveal who they were in terms of such aspects of identity as social class, religion, ethnicity, race, gender, and so on, as well as the curtains they pushed back to examine how the curricula they created made space (or didn't) for the diverse identities of students, whether children or adults. Long and her colleagues concluded that they needed to go well beyond school boundaries to open those curtains—and well beyond their personal comfort zones.

The authors in this section underscore the critical role teacher identity plays in early childhood curriculum: who we are and the beliefs we hold dear can serve to limit or expand educational opportunities for young children. In essence, then, we cannot redo if we do not also rethink, and much of this rethinking begins with teachers looking at themselves, so they can look anew at children.

In bringing this book to a close, we know that there is no end to the complex work represented here. Our chapters are invitations to keep pushing back so many curtains that need to be opened, even as we push ourselves beyond personal comfort zones. In these days of constricted, child-unfriendly curricula, there is a clear disconnect between what enables all children to learn and what is mandated in many schools. Our response to this disconnect is a clear message common to our chapters: children are only at risk of failing in school when curricula leave no room for their multiple interests and identities; and teachers are the ones who, alongside their children/students, can push back curtains to create the "wiggle room" (Siegel & Lukas, this volume) and "tactical space" (Gatto, cited by Grieshaber, this volume) to enlarge the stage where curricula and children's experiences within them are transformed. And it is on all our close, small classroom stages where universal human rights—social justice—can begin.

Contributors

Jennifer Adair is an educational anthropologist. She conducts ethnographic research with immigrant families in the United States and is interested in how teachers and families can work together to improve educational and racial equity. Currently, she is working with preservice teachers to use anthropological and sociological theory to look at their own teaching practices and their role in the U.S. education system. She is a doctoral student at Arizona State University.

Clavis B. Anderson is a regional literacy coach and professional development provider for the South Carolina Reading Initiative. Formerly a teacher in grades 2 through 5, she now supports school-based literacy coaches throughout South Carolina and is a part-time instructor of graduate students in language and literacy education at the University of South Carolina focusing on issues of cultural and linguistic diversity.

Kathryn Au, Chief Executive Officer of SchoolRise LLC, was the first person to hold an endowed chair in education at the University of Hawai'i. A member of the Reading Hall of Fame, Au has been elected president of the National Reading Conference and of the International Reading Association. Her research interests are school change and the literacy achievement of students of diverse backgrounds. She is a founder, with Sherlyn Goo and Alice Kawakami, of the Institute for Native Pacific Education and Culture (INPEACE), an achievement recognized with the 2005 Native Hawaiian Education Award.

Ranita Cheruvu is a former early childhood and elementary teacher. Currently, she is a doctoral student in the Department of Curriculum and Teaching at Teachers College. Her interests surround multicultural education, peace education, and preservice teacher education. She is interested in research that focuses on the development of dispositions toward social justice and multiculturalism in relation to teachers' selfhood and its application to preservice teacher education.

Melanie Clark is a literacy coach in South Carolina. She formerly taught kindergarten, first, second, fourth, and sixth grades. Following her love of literacy, she now coaches teachers and works with students in kindergarten through third grade and teaches off-campus graduate courses in literacy education for Converse College in South Carolina. She is very interested in researching the lasting impact of ongoing professional development in comparison with 1-day workshops, week-long classes, and seminars.

Anne Haas Dyson is a former teacher of young children and, currently, a professor of education at the University of Illinois at Urbana–Champaign. Previously, she was on the faculty of the University of Georgia, Michigan State University, and the University of California, Berkeley, where she was a recipient of the campus Distinguished Teaching Award. She studies the childhood cultures and literacy learning of young schoolchildren. Her publications include *Social Worlds of Children Learning to Write in an Urban Primary School,* which was awarded the National Council of Teachers of English's David Russell Award for Distinguished Research; *Writing Superheroes*; and *The Brothers and Sisters Learn to Write: Popular Literacies in Childhood and School Cultures.* She recently coauthored a book *On the Case,* on interpretive case study methods, with Celia Genishi.

Rebekah Fassler is associate professor of education at St. John's University, Queens, New York, where she coordinates the early childhood master's program. She received her Ed.D. from Teachers College, Columbia University. A teacher educator since 1979, she previously taught children in early childhood and music and movement programs. She currently teaches courses in play, social learning and early childhood environments, inquiry-based integrated curriculum, children's literature, observing and recording behavior, and qualitative research. Her research articles focus primarily on language and literacy for diverse populations and on teacher education. She is the author of *Room for Talk: Teaching and Learning in a Multilingual Kindergarten.*

Beatrice S. (BZ) Fennimore is a professor at Indiana University of Pennsylvania and an adjunct professor at Teachers College, Columbia University. She received her doctoral degree in curriculum and teaching from Teachers College, Columbia University. Dr. Fennimore's teaching and scholarship focuses on child advocacy, young children and social policy, multicultural education, public school equity, and teacher education for democratic and civic responsibility. Her publications include "Brown and the Failure of Civic Responsibility" in *Teachers College Record,* "Equity Is Not an Option in Public Education" in *Educational Leadership,* and *Talk Matters: Refocusing the Language of Public Schooling,* published by Teachers College Press.

Celia Genishi is a professor of education and chair of the Department of Curriculum and Teaching, Teachers College, Columbia University. A former secondary Spanish and preschool teacher, she teaches courses related to early childhood education and qualitative research methods. She is coauthor (with Millie Almy) of *Ways of Studying Children* and (with Anne Haas Dyson) of *On the Case: Approaches to Language and Literacy Research.* Her research interests include collaborative research with teachers, childhood bilingualism, and language use in classrooms. She is a recipient of the Advocate for Justice Award from the American Association of Colleges for Teacher Education.

Michèle Genor was most recently an assistant professor with the Preservice Program in Elementary Education, in the Department of Curriculum and Teaching at Teachers College, Columbia University. Her professional interests include the professional development of teachers, critical reflection, teacher inquiry groups, and performance ethnography.

Sherlyn Franklin Goo is one of the three cofounders of INPEACE, a non-profit educational services organization created in late 1994, where from then to 2004, she served as executive director. Goo is a native Hawaiian educator who served for 24 years as an administrator for Kamehameha Schools in the Early Education Division, the Elementary School, and the President's Office until 1995. Goo received her undergraduate degree from the University of California and her master's in educational administration from the University of Hawaii. A champion of community programs for native Hawaiians, Goo has been honored by the University of Hawaii, College of Education for her innovative partnerships; and by Council for Native Hawaiian Advancement as 2005 Educator of the Year.

A. Lin Goodwin is professor of education and Associate Dean of Teacher Education at Teachers College, Columbia University. Her research focuses on the connections between teachers' identities and learning and their multicultural understandings and curriculum enactments, and on the educational experiences of Asian American teachers and students. Key publications include "The Case of One Child: Making the Shift from Personal Knowledge to Professionally Informed Practice" (*Teaching Education*); "Multicultural Stories: Preservice Teachers' Conceptions of and Responses to Issues of Diversity" (*Urban Education*); and "Growing up Asian in America." She is the editor of several books, including *Assessment for Equity and Inclusion: Embracing All Our Children.*

Susan Grieshaber works at the School of Early Childhood, Queensland University of Technology, Brisbane, Australia. Her research interests are framed by social justice interests and include early childhood curriculum and policy, families, gender, and information and communication technologies. Her most recent books include *Rethinking Parent and Child Conflict* (RoutledgeFalmer, 2004) and *Embracing Identities in Early Childhood Education: Diversity and Possibilities* (Grieshaber & Cannella, 2001, Teachers College Press).

Kris D. Gutiérrez is a professor of social research methodology in the Graduate School of Education and Information Studies, and director of the Center for the Study of Urban Literacies at the University of California, Los Angeles. Her research addresses the relationship between literacy, culture, and learning, focusing specifically on the processes by which people, informed by their own personal and sociocultural histories, negotiate meaning in culturally organized contexts. A prolific scholar, Dr. Gutiérrez' work appears in numerous journals including *Educational Researcher, Reading Research Quarterly, Harvard Educational Review, Linguistics and Education, Bilingual Research Journal, Urban Education,* and *Theory into Practice.* In 2004, she received the American Educational Research Association's Sylvia Scribner Award.

Alice J. Kawakami is a tenured Associate Professor of Education in the College of Education, University of Hawaii–Manoa and one of the founders of the Institute for Native Pacific Education and Culture (INPEACE). Her research focuses on indigenous perspectives in early childhood and elementary education, teacher education, curriculum development and evaluation. She has been a part-time remedial reading teacher at the urban Honolulu for the Hawaii Department of Education (HI DOE), a research-demonstration laboratory school teacher, specialist, teacher researcher, and coordinator of in-service training for the Kamehameha Early Education Program (KEEP). She served as Director of Research and Evaluation at the Pacific Regional Educational Laboratory.

Dorothy Levin currently teaches a combined second/third grade class of students with special needs at an urban public school. Previously, she taught prekindergarten children with special needs. She is certified in Early Childhood Education and Special Education. Levin is a change of career professional who came to the teaching profession after a career as a health care administrator. She has a master of science in early childhood education and a master of business administration, both from St. John's University in New York. She is a member of NAEYC and received the *Who's Who among America's Teachers* award in 2005.

Carrie Lobman is an assistant professor of education in the Department of Learning and Teaching at the Graduate School of Education, Rutgers University. She received her doctorate in curriculum and teaching from Teachers College, Columbia University. Her research interests include early childhood teacher education and the development of innovative, improvisational approaches to teaching and teacher education. Together with Sharon Ryan, she recently completed a 3-year study of the system of early childhood teacher preparation and professional development in New Jersey.

Susi Long is an associate professor in early childhood education and language and literacy at the University of South Carolina. Her work focuses on learning and teaching in multicultural and multilingual settings and the experiences of teachers as they work to implement innovative practices. Recent publications include a collection of studies that illuminates mediators of literacy across cultures, coedited with Eve Gregory and Dinah Volk, *Many Pathways to Literacy: Young Children Learning with Siblings, Grandparents, Peers and Communities;* and articles in *Young Children* (November, 2005), *Language Arts*

(May 2004), *Journal of Teacher Education* (May 2004), and *Primary Voices* (October 2001).

Stephanie Lukas has taught kindergarten in the New York City public schools since 1999, including 6 years at her current school. She has worked closely with Teachers College, Columbia University, through their Professional Development School Partnership, serving as cooperating teacher, clinical faculty member, and study group facilitator. An active researcher, Lukas has presented her action research at several national and local conferences. She is currently pursuing an Ed.D. in curriculum and teaching at Teachers College.

Becky McCraw is a literacy coach in a K–5 elementary school. She formerly taught third and fifth grades and now coaches teachers in reading instruction and teaches professional development courses in literacy instruction at Converse College, South Carolina. She is a doctoral candidate at the University of South Carolina in language and literacy. Her research interests include teacher change, how poverty impacts literacy development, and how oral language development influences early reading success.

Althea Scott Nixon is a Ph.D. candidate at the University of California, Los Angeles, Graduate School of Education and Information Studies. She researches children's and adolescents' use of communication technologies in play, with a focus on multimodal literacy learning and identity development.

Nadjwa E. L. Norton is an assistant professor in the Literacy Department at City College, City University of New York (CUNY). Her scholarship focuses on multiple literacies practices, spirituality, teacher education, equity-oriented multicultural education, and collaborative qualitative research designs. Committed to change, she engages in multicultural feminist critical frameworks as a way of influencing the systemic inequalities that make it difficult for all people to learn. In accordance with this vision, her work has included being a teacher, staff developer, curriculum developer, educational consultant, counselor, researcher, poet, and mentor. Although her primary expertise is in early childhood, she has been fortunate to have experiences in elementary, junior high, and high school, in public and private schools as well as alternative educational institutions.

Susan L. Recchia is an associate professor and coordinator of the program in early childhood special education at Teachers College, Columbia University. She serves as faculty codirector of the Rita Gold Early Childhood Center, an inclusive and culturally responsive center for early education, professional preparation, research, and outreach. Her research interests include the role of social and emotional experiences in early learning, issues in inclusive early care and education, and early childhood teacher development. Her recent publications include "Early Childhood Special Educators Reflect on Their

Preparation and Practice" and "At the Crossroads: Overcoming Concerns to Envision Possibilities for Toddlers in Inclusive Childcare."

Sharon Ryan is associate professor of early childhood education at Rutgers, the State University of New Jersey. Her research interests include early childhood curriculum and policy, early childhood teacher education, and the potential of critical theories for rethinking early childhood practices. Her most recent research has focused on the development of policy and practices that might lead to a more unified system of teacher preparation and professional development. She is also coauthor with Susan Grieshaber of the forthcoming book, *Practical Transformations and Transformational Practices: Globalization, Postmodernism, and Early Childhood Education.*

Marci W. Sarsona is executive director of the Institute for Native Pacific Education and Culture (INPEACE), a nonprofit educational services organization dedicated to improving the lives of Native Hawaiians. Sarsona was raised in the Hawaiian homestead community of Waimanalo, Oahu, where she continues to reside. She earned a bachelor's degree in elementary education from the University of Hawaii and a master's degree in business administration from Hawaii Pacific University. An innovator in the delivery of early childhood programs to Native Hawaiian communities, Sarsona was recognized by the *Pacific Business News* as one of Hawaii's most promising business leaders under the age of 40.

Marjorie Siegel is associate professor of education at Teachers College, Columbia University, where she teaches courses on literacy education in the Department of Curriculum and Teaching. Her research interests include literacies and technologies, content-area literacies, and multiliteracies. In 2003–2004, she spent a year in Stephanie Lukas's kindergarten classroom studying children's participation in a mandated balanced literacy curriculum. She is the coauthor, with Raffaella Borasi, of *Reading Counts: Rethinking the Role of Reading in Mathematics Classrooms* (Teachers College Press, 2000).

Susan Stires is a professor at Bank Street College of Education and a former lecturer at Teachers College, Columbia University. She has been a part-time staff developer for District 2 in New York City and a consultant in literacy acquisition and development. Formerly, she was an instructor in the New Hampshire Reading and Writing Program at the University of New Hampshire, and taught in the Education Department there as well. Her 30 years of elementary experience includes teaching at the first-, third-, and fifth-grade levels in rural and urban schools. She was a primary teacher at the Center for Teaching and Learning, a demonstration school in Edgecomb, Maine. She was also a learning disabilities specialist and a classroom teacher in Boothbay Harbor, Maine, and Boston, Massachusetts.

Rachel Theilheimer is professor of early childhood education and chair of the Department of Teacher Education at Borough of Manhattan Community College (BMCC), City University of New York (CUNY). She is a former child-care teacher and director and now teaches a range of early childhood education courses at BMCC. She received her Ed.D. from Teachers College (1995) and has also taught at New Mexico State University and Bank Street College of Education. She is the author and coauthor of articles about diverse perspectives on early childhood education, about children and sexuality, and about early childhood teacher education. She is also a member of the Visible Knowledge Project, which involves scholarship of teaching and learning research based on her work with early childhood students at BMCC/CUNY.

Joseph Tobin is a professor in the College of Education at Arizona State University. He formerly served as a professor at the University of Hawai'i at Manoa. His research interests include educational ethnography, Japanese culture and education, visual anthropology, early childhood education, and children and the media. His publications include *Preschool in Three Cultures* and others on early childhood education and classroom ethnography. He serves as a member of the National Research Council's Board on International Comparative Studies in Education.

Leslie R. Williams is a professor of early childhood education within the Department of Curriculum and Teaching at Teachers College. She works with both master's and doctoral students interested in the improvement of early childhood educational practice through focus on curriculum design, initial preparation of teachers, continuing professional development of early childhood center staff and school faculties, and collaborative teacher research. Over the past 20 years, she has developed multicultural courses and other experiences for students and faculty, leading toward infusion of a multicultural approach in practice, research, and theory building in her field. Additionally, she is a faculty codirector (with Susan Recchia) of the Rita Gold Early Childhood Center located at Teachers College, which serves young children from 6 weeks to 5 years of age and their families, with associated programs of research, professional preparation, and community outreach.

Index